MW00787459

Fragile Finitude

Fragile Finitude

A JEWISH HERMENEUTICAL THEOLOGY

Michael Fishbane

The University of Chicago Press   CHICAGO AND LONDON

The University of Chicago Press, Chicago 60637

The University of Chicago Press, Ltd., London

© 2021 by The University of Chicago

All rights reserved. No part of this book may be used or reproduced in any manner whatsoever without written permission, except in the case of brief quotations in critical articles and reviews. For more information, contact the University of Chicago Press, 1427 E. 60th St., Chicago, IL 60637.

Published 2021

Printed in the United States of America

30 29 28 27 26 25 24 23 22 21   1 2 3 4 5

ISBN-13: 978-0-226-76415-3 (cloth)

ISBN-13: 978-0-226-76429-0 (e-book)

DOI: https://doi.org/10.7208/chicago/9780226764290.001.0001

Library of Congress Cataloging-in-Publication Data

Names: Fishbane, Michael, 1943– author.

Title: Fragile finitude : a Jewish hermeneutical theology / Michael Fishbane.

Description: Chicago : University of Chicago Press, 2021. | Includes
  bibliographical references and index.

Identifiers: LCCN 2020041094 | ISBN 9780226764153 (cloth) |
  ISBN 9780226764290 (ebook)

Subjects: LCSH: Bible. Job—Criticism, interpretation, etc. | Hermeneutics—
  Religious aspects—Judaism.

Classification: LCC BS1415.52 .F565 2021 | DDC 296.3—dc23

LC record available at https://lccn.loc.gov/2020041094

♾ This paper meets the requirements of ANSI/NISO Z39.48-1992 (Permanence of Paper).

For Mona
שׁוֹשַׁנַּת הָעֲמָקִים
with lifelong love

Contents

Prologue

My subject is Jewish theology, and my concern is with its voice and modes of expression at this hour. What formulations address the challenges of contemporary thought and social experience, while retaining the principles and values of tradition? The conditions of understanding expand and contract continuously, and as one method waxes and another wanes our intellectual probity is confounded. How may one best engage the historical sources to invigorate our present religious situation? If responsible renewal starts with our spiritual inheritance, it must first be accessed and evaluated with critical honesty. And if we are bound by loyalty to tradition—we must also view it with modern eyes. Integrity is the core of theological responsibility.

In the ensuing work I shall take a personal stand on these issues, in the conviction that there is no abstract or universal position to which all may assent or concur. I nevertheless hope that my insights and formulations will resonate with those of others (both within Judaism and more broadly) who are similarly impacted by the challenges of modernity—but who are also, with eyes open, determined to live within the framework of traditional commitments. Taking both considerations into account, my primary intent is to formulate a theological stance for a modern Jewish interpretative community centered on core convictions and exemplary texts. The hermeneutics of life and canonical sources are thus the double matrix of this exposition: a hermeneutics influenced by contemporary theories regarding the construction and evaluation of meaning, as well as traditional exegetical methods. As such the present book continues the enterprise begun in *Sacred Attunement: A Jewish Theology* (2008), but goes further by offering a multilevel God-centered religious orientation and interpretation for our time—from the sources of Judaism. Insofar as we experience life at various levels, a living theology should similarly draw from multiple hermeneutical sources that mediate diverse spiritual dimensions. Jewish theology locates the foundation of this matrix in scripture and its traditional modes of interpretation.

Modernity presents us with many intellectual and spiritual challenges. Particularly notable is the issue of "self-evidence" and its related considerations. According to a number of converging discussions, spanning several disciplines, neither the self nor evidence is self-evident. Neither one can be taken for granted. The human subject as a self-contained or independent entity is compromised from within and without, and the notion of evidence as a self-standing or objective entity is also undermined. The subjective self is influenced by many external conditions, both known and unknown, so that our attempts to evaluate experience are fraught with diverse presumptions. Similar cautions complicate our interpretation of worldly data. As is commonly agreed, personal knowledge (acquired through entwinement with the issue considered) is a working assumption of scientists and humanists alike; hence embeddedness in the conditions of thought is a methodological factor to be weighed at all times. We can no more extricate ourselves from the hermeneutical process than we can jump out of our shadow. This requires us to acknowledge that truth is a function of both method and one's engagement in its use. Abstract or ideal categories that once dominated Western philosophical thought (whether based on concepts of regnant reason or its limits) are now replaced by the concrete and conditioned categories of symbolic thinking (which affirms that the social structures of reality are cultural constructs derived from lived perceptions and imagination). Touching and feeling and using the world are now deemed primary interpretative categories, with the result that the knower, the known, and the act of knowing dynamically converge during one's involvement with the world. Inevitably, these factors affect the forms of interpretation and their modes of explication. The so-called linguistic turn in contemporary thought underscores this hermeneutical reality, its proponents even contending that understanding the conditions of language is fundamental for understanding the very nature of human meaning and making sense. In short, we are hermeneutical creatures from start to finish, and language emerges from the most primary filters of perception. If the "old thinking" (from Plato to Hegel) took its stand nowhere in our concrete reality, since it employed transcendent and ideal concepts, the "new thinking" (as typified by William James, Henri Bergson, and Franz Rosenzweig) always speaks from within lived experience. Discourse and dialogue unfold in shared time, intersubjectively; and interpretative understanding is embedded in our concrete existence.

Given the thickness of embedded living, there is no pregiven certainty as to what standpoint should take precedence in a particular circumstance (for personal or social reasons), or the criteria that should condition our judgment. Topics interpenetrate and methods cross disciplinary lines. There is no foolproof way to circumvent this complication; hence one is constantly evaluating or interpreting the factors at hand, trying to determine the scale of significance relative to the given phenomena. The fallout for religious thought is inevitable. Moderns are challenged to reevaluate such theological topics as the nature and reality of God, in light of the cognitive limits of experience and knowing; or the authority of sacred texts and their traditions, in light of multiple and often competing methodological considerations (influenced by other religions or intellectual orientations). Significant differences also surface between traditional hermeneutical procedures and contemporary forms of interpretation; and the underlying fault-lines shift one's mental plates in fundamental ways—with crucial implications for religious convictions or commitments. At times, defensive and apologetic solutions emerge in response, and these affect the spiritual life that is lived and the topics of tradition privileged or considered. It has been argued that contemporary "fundamentalism" is not so much the literal understanding of a religious tradition as a dogmatic assertion of selected tenets. To transcend these considerations, I deem it vital to discern the consonances between our primary hermeneutical condition (as interpreters of texts and experience) and traditional values—which are similarly the product of hermeneutical factors. On this basis, their presumed dissonance will wane—not for apologetic reasons but because the cognitive truths of experience will be seen as inherent in the teachings of tradition itself. Explicating the alignments between the hermeneutics of lived experience and Jewish theology is a central concern of this book.

There are two other significant challenges: reductive scientism and technology. Both can diminish and trivialize the mysteries of existence—deeming the latter to be merely occasions not yet unexplained by more refined methods. Combined, these factors conspire to unhinge the human spirit and alienate it from its natural condition. By seeking control, we lose touch with primary sensibilities. A major poet formulated words for this situation. Responding to the spiritual crisis of his time, William Wordsworth lamented: "The world is too much with us; late and soon . . . laying waste our powers." In his view, the impact of technological achievements and an all-consuming busyness stifled one's sense of the world. Both the spiritual intimations of nature and one's innate proclivities for wonder were affected. Thus, he concluded: "Little we see in Nature that is ours; we have given our hearts away, a sordid boon!" The climactic cry "Great God!" resounds with despair.

Moderns have reaped this technological whirlwind—and stand speechless. What is there to say when, after centuries of scientific innovations, human purposes have been shunted aside by abstract or applied aims; or when new forms of fission and combustion have so ruined the environment that we are (literally) breathless? We are victims of our achievements, allowing our technical insights to skirt or repress guiding values. The ecological fallout is well known and threatens our children's future, while utilitarian greed burns the rainforest to ashes. This apart, decent hearts are devastated by a century of wars and ethnic tribalism, instigated by barbaric mentalities that have harnessed technology into agents of mass death. We cannot ignore the stain on human nature or the sabotage of nature itself. The moral effects shadow our spiritual lives and undermine optimism.

If other technology has made life easier, and provided options hitherto unknown, it has simultaneously infiltrated the human spirit in corrosive ways—impinging on our inner life with one cyber temptation after another. The explosion of information leaves us senseless and robotically at their mercy, as we "waste our powers" in trivial pursuits and newer hyperlinks. Like ancient idols, these technical devices have eyes that do not see or sensors that do not feel; and we are being formed in their image. For this "brave new age," scenes of suffering or beauty are occasions for impersonal pixels viewed on a screen—not events of human pathos. Turning inward, we fear emptiness and assuage loneliness through virtual realities; when we face outward, the cosmic expanses mock our search for secure meaning. The old exclamation "Great God!" rings hollow. Words fail or fall shallow; and if and when we use them, they often configure short-term solutions counted in bytes of information. Slowly, against our better intentions, we are ensnared in a dark web.

Is "theology" even possible in our time? Can a "God-informed existence" inspire wonder and purpose, and constrain technological hubris at its core? Where might we begin the reconstructive process, given the philosophical and cognitive challenges? Where can a contemporary hermeneutical approach find a foothold? Small hints suggest a beginning, for amid our routine experiences the vitality of life may suddenly break forth—stimulating a longing for ultimate truths and attention to events near at hand. We may be called up short by a solitary cry or the shudder of catastrophe, by visions of sublime beauty or acts of simple care. From these feelings we may suddenly perceive something "other" than the ordinary or commonplace. Without warning, we are addressed and claimed to the core. Can these caesural occasions reawaken the human spirit to a sense of radical transcendence—one that reaches beyond claims of cognitive dominion and inspires us to a humane hermeneutical position? Simply asking this question is crucial, and helps restore us to our natural being and the mysteries of existence.

The Spiritual Quest: Initial Perceptions

We search for basics, for some basis in experience to reorient our lives. It is close at hand: in the stream of life, pulsing everywhere, and the acts of knowledge that help us name reality. We feel the rhythms of existence within and without, and try to transform them into meaningful thoughts. The claims of experience and our attempts to understand constitute the core components of our human nature: two shoots implanted into the fiber of our being, like the primordial trees of life and knowledge planted in the Garden of Eden. Impelled by inner necessity, we seek life and respond to all the worldly elements that may help sustain this purpose—elements that are "desirous to the eye" (Genesis 3:6) and serve our basic needs. In primary circumstances, to stabilize or sustain life, physical needs and survival predominate. Alert to the life potential of things, we perceive the natural world as a kaleidoscope of intersecting phenomena, our minds being like some "revolving sword" (herev mithappehet) that apportions what we see and feel into diverse series of ever-changing elements (Genesis 3:24). Eventually, with the help of experience and tradition, we may sort and conceptualize the entities of existence that can serve our life in more intentional ways, and can structure our experience into patterns of stable and significant knowledge. We cling to these hermeneutic correlations between life experience and interpretation for the world-order they reveal. But we overreach when we presume their inherent, even a priori status—precisely because these cognitive links are only inventive necessities. In this way, we forget our fundamental hermeneutic nature, and doing so, think falsely about experience.

At some point the heart knows that the tree of life (vitality as such) contains the fruit of death, since a consequence of our reflection upon life is the transformative consciousness of temporality. This perception yields the fundamental insight needed to help regulate responses to daily experience and reclaim a responsible finitude. An ancient psalmist put it this way: "Teach us to count our days rightly, so that we may obtain a heart of wisdom" (Psalm 90:12). With this prayer, a fundamental theological stance is articulated—one that recognizes that it is within the conditions of daily life that we may discern the measures from which a thoughtful existence may develop. The speaker indicates that these determinations are not readily evident or subject to clear evaluation. Mere life just is. Without principles to guide our judgment, we would bounce between desires and limits, beset by the maelstroms of phenomenal reality. Hence the speaker supplicates divine assistance for cognitive discernment. Theology—a "God-informed existence"—begins here. It begins with taking the transcendent measures of our mortal, temporal life, and seeking a path for their implementation. Rooted in our natural limitations and the inherent mysteries of wisdom, the quest is founded on lack and humility. Theology begins with spiritual longing and the confession of need. We confront our finitude at last.

As remarked, we rely on inventive techniques to help transcend the limits of our human condition. Bound by the necessity to "work" the earth and "protect" it in a sustainable manner (Genesis 2:15), we strive to cultivate a mind of practical wisdom. The words used in this enterprise often mirror their utilitarian purposes. As a tool for survival, language responds to the natural rhythms of life, and formulates the tasks of existence. But language is more than a utilitarian instrument. It is also a symbolic form of fundamental spiritual significance, since we do more than name the visible world and interpret the provocations of existence. Cultural horizons exceed the practical through acts of the creative imagination and attempts to formulate meanings hidden from view. In this sense, human language is also an agent of spiritual insight and possibility, constructing narratives that inculcate these elements into the heart, to be transmitted to future generations. These formulations are subsequently preserved as a cherished heritage— reinforced by their repetition and ongoing explication. This achievement notwithstanding, the vaunted wisdom of this material may falter in the face of new experiences, revealing disturbing or puzzling gaps. Such perceptions rend the seeming inviolable texture of tradition that pervades our lives. Suddenly the very words that served to formulate the basic cognitions of life need hermeneutical revision or clarification.

The Hermeneutic Turn

What, then, is hermeneutics if not the fundamentally interpretative character of our human existence—the determination of sense and significance within the world and beyond? Hermeneutics processes the external, objective influences of things through the subjective channels of human thought and feeling. And more: it helps determine whether some topic serves spiritual or practical ends, or if some expression is meaningful or requires revision or reinterpretation. Such cognitive interventions (acts of engaged knowledge) rejoin the stream of life and its natural achievements. Both individuals and master teachers (those who have mastered this insight) take up this challenge by shaping the known and knowable into values of personal or social significance, or reinterpret established (canonical) traditions for new circumstances. Since hermeneutical engagements are cumulative and continuous, individuals must cultivate a heart of wisdom to help evaluate new ethical and spiritual concerns. When these formulations bear on ultimate matters—on Divinity and on issues of fundamental import—these expressions may be called "hermeneutical theology." It is a crucial component of the religious imagination overall, since it articulates life experience in transcendent terms and interprets prior traditions in creative ways. Accordingly, hermeneutical theology is a dynamic process: it is founded on God-informed revelations of the world-order and its mysteries, and mediated by disclosures of the human spirit through acts of discerning interpretation. This achievement impacts every aspect of a religious culture, and every person within it, at all times.

The Jewish hermeneutical imagination partakes of these multiple processes in its own way, grounded in the language of scripture. The words of this text, in their canonical formulations, constitute the primary frames of new meaning over the millennia. Narrative, law, and theological values are filtered through these linguistic prisms, as topics in their primary literary contexts and in response to the challenges of life. Interpreters are always "other" than the text, for each interpreter comes to it with dispositions of one kind or another—derived from scripture and its traditions, or from extratextual considerations. The result is the bounty of interpretations that provide the resources for new times. This is especially the case for theology. When there is no cognitive gap between the teachings of scripture or its traditions for later readers, they are routinely appropriated as the authoritative and living voices of instruction. But when cognitive dissonance is felt, older teachings are either relegated to historical theology or reinterpreted in new ways. Hermeneutical freedom fails when there is fear of new interpretations, or when an innovation is deemed a betrayal of some presumed "authentic" or unassailable tradition. In the process, one forgets that every topic of "historical theology" was once, originally, an innovative act of "constructive theology"—one that creatively engaged the older sources, so that they might speak again for new times.

The difficulty of creative appropriation is due to more than the inherent gravity of historical tradition. It is also affected by the difficulty of reinterpretation, when a cognitive or epistemic rupture has occurred in the wider intellectual environment (be this philosophical, scientific, or psychological), and there is no evident means to recast the meaning of the sources, saving the tradition and personal integrity at one and the same time. Jewish historical theology is replete with instances of transformative exegesis, creatively discerned and inventively justified in the sacred sources—giving new intellectual formats and formulations to the received tradition. Just this is the challenge and desideratum for our time. Accordingly, the task is not to show *how* Jewish theology "speaks to" our contemporary lives and condition (an apologetic approach), but to demonstrate *that* the truths of God-given life and experience are "revealed through" scripture and its traditions. The cognitive gap (between modernity and tradition) will then be overcome, and scripture (with its traditions) will again structure new life meanings and thought. In the process of reformulating our experiences of the world and its values (an essential aspect of hermeneutics) through the received languages of Judaism, the latter (both our general understanding and Jewish topics) will be reconstituted and revealed anew.

The hermeneutical stance of creative theological insights does not inherently undermine traditional values, or constitute a marginal phenomenon of tradition-making itself. To the contrary: this is its heart and soul. Dialogical engagements with the elements of life and culture are processes renewed over the millennia, and regulated by the communities involved. Life and tradition are in constant interaction, stimulating new insights in the one and the other. Creative exegesis allows these perceptions to be expressed through canonical sources, reinterpreted in accordance with the purposes of those who enact their practices and beliefs. As an earlier Hasidic master formulated this issue, scripture was not given as something final or "mute" (*golem*), but as (repeatedly) conducive to vocal "interpretation" (*peirush*) and "inventive understanding" (*hiddush*). Rightly performed hermeneutics gives the sacred text its reinvigorating voice. It is the spirit of the letter.

Reclaiming the Task

A vibrant hermeneutical theology also relies on confidence in the capacity of "tradition" to guide engagements with the ongoing conditions of life. This is a precondition of every authentic community of interpretation—and it is therefore the task of a contemporary Jewish hermeneutical theology to maintain that trust. How it does so is a measure of the spiritual vitality and will of interpreters and their community. Because these hermeneutical factors intersect, communities of interpretation will re-form continuously. Bearing this in mind, the present work will reverberate most directly with those whose proclivities resonate most closely with the theological approach developed in the ensuing discussions. In the process I shall draw from the entire history of Jewish scriptural interpretation, explicating its religious experiences and values, and reappropriating its concerns in a contemporary mode. Consonant with hermeneutics generally, the coherence of my interpretations is without an external or objective proof. Their value only proves itself through the lives of those affected by the meanings proposed. This is the experiential test. Any other is an abstraction.

The Present Spiritual Project

The purpose of the present enterprise is to cultivate a heart of wisdom. This means the cultivation of a God-centered awareness that connects the individual to the mysterious reality of existence. This mystery is not some "spiritual substance" hiding within the tangible forms of life, awaiting verbal explication. It is rather a "participatory awareness" of the fullness of what is happening, as it happens. Such a mode of attention is an attachment in active consciousness to the experiences that impose themselves upon one's lived being—each in their particular form. Guided by spiritual principles intuited from life or instituted by religious tradition, we may become responsive to the claims of existence that summon attention in all ordinary circumstances, or that open us unexpectedly to the bounty of life. This living awareness allows the divine mystery to be experienced as a direct, instructing immanence. In his poignant formulation of this matter (initially penned during his years in Theresienstadt), Leo Baeck stated that the forever Incomprehensible and Infinite One—that both surrounds us and supports us within the span of eternity—gives us the vitalities of existence at every moment. And thus: although we cannot know God directly, or as such, we may nevertheless experience a sense of the mystery that eternally surrounds God. Becoming conscious of this reality, and remaining steadfast to its claims, we may perceive portions of the natural laws of life, and strive to articulate them in accord with our spiritual concerns and moral purposes. For God gives life, ever and always; and through God's catalyzing life-force the attentive heart may intuit principles that can guide or protect the streams of life. This dynamic involvement is our challenging covenant with God. The two divine trees (the tree of life and the tree of knowledge), experience and interpretation, must be grasped together, as time and tradition inspire, and as they take shape in one's heart at every moment. Sensing this, one heeds the "life call" of God.

*

The poet's lament that "the world is too much with us" is now inverted and reveals a positive expression of all-bountiful plurality—each element of which is a sacred particular. To understand this complexity in the ebb and flow of existence, through the lens of texts, we shall follow a twofold path: the hermeneutical path of explication and reformulation. In the process, a new-old reconstruction of Jewish theology will emerge: one that will guide spiritual vision in the everyday and give new depth to religious thought and behavior.

That the world is perceptively "with us" is a primary given of our existential being; and that the world has a created divine origin is the primary given of both scripture and its theology. The interface between these two realities—between our lived lives and the explication of scriptural language—is a fundamental feature of Jewish hermeneutical theology. As it is said, "[The world is that] which God has created, *la'asot*" (Genesis 2:3)— "to do" and "to make" continuously—not only through species adaptation and their regeneration, but also through ongoing human interpretation and evaluation. Creative hermeneutics is thus a component of every formulation of our life in the world, and creative theology is a vital subset of it: a partnership between perceived reality and received tradition. We are their creative nexus.

* PART ONE *

Introduction

Seeking Spiritual Ground: Reengaging Theology

The spiritual challenge of a living theology requires a focused determination to live in the everyday with a threefold goal: to cultivate a mind devoted
to God's all-creative vitality in worldly reality, to transform all one's acts into
expressions of this focal awareness, and to speak with thoughtful intention
and purpose. Such theological living is an attempt to attune one's thoughts,
and deeds, and words to Divinity and divine manifestations at all times and
as truly as possible. Jewish theology takes up these goals in its own distinctive manner, by finding their source in scripture and tradition, and appro-
priating them through works of thoughtful personal performance. As an
ensemble, these topics typify the classic hermeneutical dimensions of Jewish theology, as reformulated over the generations. Phrases like "Know God
in all your ways" (Proverbs 3:6)—mindful thought, "My entire being shall
proclaim 'O Lord, who is like You?!'" (Psalm 35:10)—devoted action, and
"May the words of my mouth and the meditations of my heart be accept-
able to You, O Lord" (Psalm 19:15)—perfected speech, have been repeatedly
expanded as spiritual instructions in diverse genres and settings. They are
fundamental components of Jewish religious practice and thought.

Some commentators perceive a concise expression of these ideals in the
biblical exhortation that the divine instruction is not "beyond reach," but
near at hand: "in your mouth and in your heart to do it" (Deuteronomy
30:11–14). The medieval sage R. Baḥye ben Asher (thirteenth century, Spain)
observed that "three things are mentioned here: the mouth, the heart, and
the deed—since all the commandments are comprised of these three [essen-
tial] elements. There are commandments requiring speech, others requiring
the heart, and others requiring action." Speaking thus, R. Baḥye follows a
line of explication famously developed by Maimonides and other halakhic
codifiers. This threefold ideal is equally articulated in the mystical tradition,

where the emphasis is on the sanctification of existence and cultivation of one's spiritual life. Pertinent passages in the Book of Zohar were cited and explained to enforce this process. Particularly notable among these teachers and commentators was R. Elijah de Vidas (sixteenth century, Safed) and subsequent generations of Hasidic masters. Though difficult to achieve, it was believed that these ideals were "within reach"; hence exhortations for their realization were frequently made. According to many traditional Jewish practitioners, the legal (halakhic) and mystical ideals went hand in hand. The halakhic practices were deemed a codified means to center and order one's spiritual life—indeed, to give that life a worldly embodiment.

As heir of this tradition, contemporary theology will also wish to retrieve this triad, and give renewed focus to the integral themes of thought, deed, and word. The present situation, however, makes this difficult, for there is virtually no area of modern life that has not undergone a significant change in sensibility and thought, and these influence our behavior in multiple ways—at the prereflective level of daily experience, where the influences of modernity have a silent effect, and at the more reflective levels of conceptual analysis. To produce a reformulation of Jewish theology that may guide us toward these spiritual ends, we must first consider some of the factors that complicate our modern situation. Each can be specified on its own terms and in relation to the overall theological framework to be constituted in this book. Annotating these matters is therefore a necessary first step.

Preliminary Considerations: Prereflective Matters

As mortal creatures, we naturally confront challenges to our thoughts, words, and deeds. Already at the prereflective level, physical impulses and bodily needs precondition many responses and values, and compel us to seek solutions for our safety and sustenance. Thus concrete existential matters often take precedence over other considerations, affecting them substantially, despite all our best intentions. We are also easily thrown off course by unconscious drives or external events. Such is the way of the world. Its impingements require a reckoning; but whether we do so or not, they exact their toll in every case. In addition, many contemporary factors have ramped up these issues in disconcerting ways, beginning with our primary levels of experience. From morning to night, numerous technological stimuli assault our bodies, often in unfiltered ways, unnerving their normal homeostasis. Similarly, a great mass of information simultaneously floods our thought processes, leaving us at odds with ourselves, as we struggle to sort out topics of significance to inform and guide our actions. But like a roiling undertow, each topic offers new temptations in turn; and without stable principles to guide our judgment, we swirl in a sea of uncertainty or cynicism. Secular and traditional minds share this cultural predicament. To protect ourselves and achieve some temporary balance, many turn inward; but with this shift (personal or social), our ethical axis narrows and becomes self-centered. Autosatisfactions now rule the day— often measured by a thick cyber-catalog of "likes" and "un-likes." Theological discourse is a victim of this situation. Beset by constant stimuli, it too has lost touch with the life-rhythms of the natural world or human order. As a result, a sense of inner space has imploded against our will, and silence is under constant siege. Little wonder that contemporary theology has erected ideological or social barriers to filter the inrush of confusions, or (through a more inner process) has turned to meditative therapeutics to help recenter the dislocated spirit. Numbed by a battery of stimuli, social walls or interior isolation seems a good-enough strategy. But the cost is considerable.

The crisis of sensory overload weakens the ability to focus in a resolute way. We swing from one impulse to another, worse off, it seems, than the ancients who responded to "moment gods" when experiencing sudden manifestations of natural power. They at least had hope in the life benefits of these transient gods, and thus constructed rituals for their appeasement or solicitation. By contrast, we live in a barrage of invasive information, and are hardly comforted by ritual responses to each (momentary) ping from some cyber-device. These intrusions affect even the traditionally minded— disrupting ritual and spiritual practices that yield to these new autonomic responses. Distractions shade the uniqueness of life events or their felt mystery: "things" merely come and go. Futility, said the Preacher in Ecclesiastes, all is futility: we are provoked by whatever makes the most immediate or alluring visual appeal (*mar'eh einayim*); and are left without a clear spiritual direction (*mahalakh ruaḥ*), or the will to find one (Ecclesiastes 6:8). Moments occur or disappear in endless rhythms, seemingly disjointed and without wonder. The sun *also* rises and sets, coming and going without impact; and that is that.

Speech, too, is affected. Everyday discourse is routinized by cant-like formulas and media-sponsored memes. In the process, topics of concern and their speakers lose their distinctive voice. Platitudes rule the day and clog the airwaves with stereotypes, all the worse for wear. We talk past one another, avoiding the presence of living speech-partners. Genuine dialogue—one that speaks with the rhythms of living breath, and answers only after listening—is shunted aside; and the mysteries of language and voice lose their resonance, replaced by archives in cyberspace. No revelation speaks from such virtual, vapid truths; and the voice of being is stifled— both within and without. One becomes tone-deaf to any call or claim.

Reflective life and thought fare no better, having their own complications.

Considerations of Method and Analysis

The intellectual critiques of modernity have challenged or undermined the
certainty of our cognitive frameworks. In the process, traditional moor-
ings have been cut, and once authoritative teachings are suspect or have
a diminished effect. They all require reassessment, or revaluation, in light
of circumstances. Take the example of Benedict Spinoza, our intellectual
predecessor in several cultural areas. With critical and trenchant clarity,
he applied methodological considerations that have become increasingly
valid or convincing as one seeks to negotiate modernity with mental integrity. Consider the impact of his *Theological-Political Treatise* on traditional
Bible study, and the role of scripture as a coherent document by which one
might appropriate collective or valorized wisdom. For over two millennia the sacred scriptures constituted a foundational canon of knowledge,
read along with the innumerable interpretations that gave authority and
guidance to thought and action. But under the scrutiny of Spinoza's critical analysis, the threads of its verbal texture unraveled. Applying a scientific hermeneutic that examined sacred texts with the same principles used
to assess the nature of nature, Spinoza and legions of successors were no
longer able or willing to regard scripture as a harmonious order of sacred
truth. It was no longer a stable code or matrix of instructions. Suddenly its
literary contradictions and diversity were exposed, but not resolved by one
harmonistic strategy or another.

The traditional practice of intertextual readings that reconciled or
realigned contradictory or redundant expressions lost its methodological
privilege. Simultaneously, scripture lost its special status as an integrated
"teaching" for new spiritual edification, and was reduced to a mosaic of
elements of historical interest, at best: an ethnographic ensemble to be surveyed at the requisite, dispassionate distance. This new hermeneutic took
the meaning of texts at their face value, as their "plain sense" suggested, and
wholly without any allusive or allegorical depth to speak of. This opened
a cognitive rift between this literary corpus as a site of historical details (a
fund of cultural information to be evaluated piecemeal and subsequently
reconstructed into new narratives) and scripture as a foundational document for religious actions and belief. Scripture was no longer a "master narrative" to be treasured, with self-evident authority, but simply one "other"
textual terrain to be surveyed in this age of cultural explorations—a text like
other texts, to be read in a similar straightforward and ordinary manner.

Such was the driving force of early biblical criticism. Even those steeped in traditional commentaries had to devise exegetical methods to save the spiritual and literary coherence of scripture. The hermeneutical controversies that resulted were part of a struggle for a religious modernity that had to grapple with the pivotal role of reading in the reception and meanings of culture. Contemporary hermeneutic theory has further complicated these issues. Forcefully asserting that all exegetical acts are fundamentally affected by the horizon of one's cognitive situation, the vectors of scripture have been narrowed in the opposite direction as well—making all textual interpretation a function of individual perspectives or predilections. Questions of meaning and coherence were reduced to the view of the beholder, often subjectively or ideologically imposed. And insofar as each reader claimed independent authority, the social basis for the hermeneutical results was fragile. Whatever the value of any given interpretation, the difficulties for building a common spiritual life upon this exegetical foundation were evident. Scripture was no longer the basis for a valid, communal hermeneutic, but a sphere of culturally determined exegetical strategies. Even calling textual interpretations a "language game" offers little comfort, since the forms of life and meanings that language expresses are correlated to particular communities that agree (implicitly or otherwise) on the interpretations made for specific purposes or shared understanding. For religious communities, all this was either lost or severely fractured.

The crisis for the modern reader is a contested belief in textual meanings that can both assert a personal resonance and strive to build (or reinforce) a common ethical or spiritual vision. In an open society, subject to diverse mentalities, the forms of life reflected by texts often reflect the political perspective of their practitioners; and for this reason their implicit hermeneutical justifications are subject to the "critique of ideologies." For those who celebrate this social situation, hermeneutics is believed to serve a more liberated life by breaking the unconscious chains of exegetical presumptions. Indeed, the very deconstruction of such hidden ideologies is felt to have a near-prophetic agenda (a variation of political theology, in fact). As a result, the control of meaning was put under critical siege: no textual corpus retained a privileged status, and no textual community was immune to this social critique. One now reads to unread or to undermine latent determinants, not for cultural growth or social stability.

So we must wonder, Are we left without any canonical ground, without any textual basis for an integral theological enterprise? And if scripture may still retain a viable status, what kind of sense can it convey to sustain our theological-spiritual projects or guide our common language and deeds? Can it still provide a hermeneutical basis for religious thought without denying the plausibility of the modern critique? Or even more fundamentally, Can scripture be read with both a critical eye and spiritual purpose—the two together and in tandem—or must readers now chose one approach and ignore the other? This question has perturbed postmodern generations in search of both scriptural meaning and intellectual integrity, hoping to "save the text" as a spiritually coherent document and activate its content for contemporary purposes. At the present juncture, each side is enveloped within its own cognitive presuppositions. Those who champion the cultural contingency of interpretation frequently turn this into an ideology, whereas those who hold onto the special or inviolate authority of scripture construct self-serving exegetical procedures, or maroon themselves on epistemological islands of their own formation. These are two worldviews at apparent cross-purposes. But for those who feel the need for some alignment or conjunction between these two orientations, a reconsideration of the complex issues is required. The ensuing theological project shall take up this challenge, and attempt to reground Jewish thought in a new-old scriptural hermeneutic.

Another Complication

The difficulty in discerning a literary-hermeneutical foundation for modern religious culture intersects with another consideration: the methodological problem of correlating part and whole. Here too Spinoza provided a formulation of decisive significance. For if the issue of canonical texts highlights the methodological issue of language and interpretation, this topic focuses on a thinker's relationship to what is thought. Responding to a scientific query that solicited his advice, Spinoza said that if the particular parts of nature are all composed of intersecting units—so that wholes contain parts, and these parts are composed of multiple particulars—one's analytic standpoint must take this into account. Every assessment is qualified, for the viewer is inescapably part of the content being studied, and thereby integral to its meaning and coherence. It is now common to concede that an individual is not totally outside the conceptual frame being considered or measured. In short, there is no "view from above"; and, since Kant, there is also no absolute or unqualified metaphysical position that purports to encompass the totality of thought. We have lost our former transcendent vision: the sky has fallen to human proportions and projections. And here below, we must also confront the epistemological revolutions of the new physics, and come to terms with the fact that our analytic position influences what we see and construe. If we are co-constructors of meaning, from every standpoint we choose, how might we locate any sure ground for thought, or think about transcendence in a viable way? Without guidance, cultural hermeneutics often shrinks to cognitively limited or preferred perspectives charged with personal or social power; and the critique of hierarchy that ensues may also endanger the search for superior positions or values. Is the only choice between the anxieties of anomie and the assertions of personal perspective? Can subjectivity be a creative, cultural project, or is it the default position of private purposes?

The names Nietzsche and Freud have become code words for the powers of will and subjectivity that mark the absence of any solid hermeneutic ground. We are left disoriented from within and without. Appearances are rife with ambiguity, and our thoughts and assessments are beset with unconscious drives and deceitful displacements. Self-assurance is weakened and fallible and, in response, becomes reactively assertive. With authority and confidence under siege, the conflict of interpretations is often overcome by either false fideism or triumphalist constructions that rebuild confidence by the suppression of diversity. When these features are also bolstered by political power or technological industry, our repressed fears return as hate and fanaticism, which in our time have produced barbarisms of every kind. Hence it is not hermeneutics, as such, that must be overcome, but the fear of freedom and the lack of stable coordinates of value that might anchor the self as a responsible interpreter—attentive to the various claims of existence (human and natural) that call out on a daily basis. Traditions (and their interpretative engagement) provide a rich fund of possibilities, but these must be sorted and assessed for the values or principles that can meet the challenges of modernity and its crisis of responsibility. Theology stands at the headwaters of these challenges, for it situates the self within the vastness of cosmic mystery and worldly purpose—from the life-forms existent all around to the formulations we give to the forces (perceptible or otherwise) that shape our lives. So we ask, Can theology be reconstructed for a responsible freedom—to support a God-directed life of spiritual purpose and moral courage? Contemporary theology must confront its hermeneutical heritage and modern predicaments—simultaneously, directly, and with integrity.

Facing the Challenge

How can we move forward, given our inability to think beyond our cognitive limitations—hardly adequate for ordinary purposes and utterly inadequate to think of God in any sense? For if worldly thought cannot grasp objects in their totality, but is limited to specific standpoints, themselves of contested merit, what thought could conceive of God in whole or part?

Words can speak only from within their circle of linguistic sense, so how can we even imagine formulations of ultimate matters? Situated within the whole, we cannot think the whole; and bound to our subjective selves, objective ground slips away. Are we trapped, then, in a vortex of silence, without consolation; or can our fundamental ignorance be the spiritual breakthrough we pray for?

Theology must face these cognitive difficulties if it would again offer a new opening to God. It must narrow to the null-point of mortal thought in order to be cognizant of the unthinkable as such—of God and the infinite bounties of reality. Abstract formulations must give way to lived, concrete experience, and to verities validated by personal experience. We must confront conceptual uncertainties in order to move forward in truth, and we must think in and through our embodied particularity to see more clearly. The specifics of lived language offer a concrete opportunity. They arise at every turn and carry thought on the arc of its specific possibilities.

In such a situation, can scripture help? Can it help stimulate an existential orientation that may guide us to a new theological position, or must it remain mired in sectarian or modernist squabbles? Can scripture still help us create a new reconciliation of epistemology and theology, or has its time passed, so that we must find some new axis for thought and inspiration? These questions require responses if we would resolve our postmodern predicaments—both personal and cultural. It is therefore of prime importance that we again ask whether scripture still provides a foundation for a contemporary hermeneutical theology. Is there hope that it can support a new exegetical enterprise, attuned to our modern situation but rooted in the richness of Jewish tradition and its verbal particulars?

I propose to address these questions directly, through the resources of Jewish religious culture—initially by engaging a biblical text that finds new theological ground when dealing with the theme of human suffering and divine providence. That text is the book of Job—a bold treatise set against a universal background, in which a series of protagonists respond to the travail of Job from within the framework of their inherited beliefs. This restricts their contentions to what has been said or thought in the past, and sharpens the theological controversy. Speaking from within the parameters of their culture, the friends of Job look at his sufferings—his loss of family and possessions through an avalanche of disasters—and presume that this catastrophe is explicable on the basis of traditional ideas about retributive justice. On this model, Divinity requites sins and thereby offers an inducement for repentance. But although Job also experienced his travails from within a similar theology, the challenge of his interlocutors increasingly falls flat. He remains convinced of the punctiliousness of his past piety, and emotionally rejects the theological generalizations asserted. With increasing insistence, Job demands an answer to his specific situation. The deadlock of perspectives is dramatically evident at every turn. As readers we are also privy to a more ironic view of the matter, having been informed in the book's prologue that the entire travesty is a scheme concocted in heaven to see how Job might respond to undeserved suffering—and thus we follow the arguments with "a view from above" that neither side has. Paradoxically (and strategically for pedagogical purposes) only the reader is aware of these preliminary considerations, and knows that the theologies of the protagonists are both vacuous and ignorant. As the debate unfolds, Job holds fast to his presumptions of innocence and knowledge until the unexpected events at the conclusion—when God appears. Suddenly the conceptual lens widens to a divine dimension, and with it there is a new opening for theology and religious consciousness. This moment bears close scrutiny, as we likewise seek to reevaluate our theological lives and ground our thinking in personal experience. And since the cognitive turn for Job occurs at the null-point of his presumptions, I shall also use this textual feature as a cornerstone of the present theological enterprise. It is altogether remarkable that a book in the biblical canon offers this conceptual opportunity. Through the collapse of older ideologies, a new religious perspective is revealed to Job—inspiring those who think in his wake.

The Model of Job: In Search of Integrity

Faced with inconsolable loss and suffering, Job and his cherished convictions are tested at the core. His question becomes ours: Will our prevailing worldview blind us to what seems to stare us in the face, as a result of cognitive myopia or forced explanations? The spiritual challenge is crucial, and pits prior resolutions against present circumstances. Dissonance can prevail only so long. Bravely, one repeatedly tries to refurbish older positions until the adjustments between the events and their evaluation break down. Such was the case with Job, whose confrontation between past convictions and present reality is so powerfully presented by an unknown theologian of antiquity. Job's internal drama is evoked by a series of dialogues that bring his theology to a crashing heap. Pious liturgies give way to perplexity and despair. His struggle for a personal truth is intensified as the abstract answers miss the mark. Job ends at loggerheads with the friends. They came to comfort, but delivered hollow canards instead.

A stark juxtaposition marks the difference between Job and the others: his arguments of (confessional) self-justification vs. their rhetoric (propositional) of divine justification. Job refuses to qualify his pious actions in the past and the dire sufferings he has endured. In his view, there is no proportion between the two. He grants a theology of chastisement, but maintains his sense of an incongruent divine response. Hence he presumes a rift between God's powers and justice. He cannot fathom that his pain is merely a divine attempt to induce a state of piety that was (he contends) his status quo ante. To assume such an argument would force Job to deny his prior life or undermine his sense of self. Maintaining his integrity, he holds out for an explanation that would address his personal situation. Although the cultural categories of theological thought gave him both the terms and a frame of reference, Job maintains his subjective convictions despite the onslaught of the representatives of their common tradition.

A Theological Breakthrough

Job is caught in a dynamic of emptiness and fullness. Emotionally depleted by family losses, personal pain, and the vacuity of the debates, he is overwrought by his sense of justice and innocence. The forensic mode with his friends enforces his concern to buttress his subjective self and bridge the gap between inner and external reality. Repeatedly, we get a sense of how the traditional belief in retributive justice played out in Job's mind—since he often reformulates these arguments in the course of reaffirming his personal situation. Other readers have proposed that the book of Job is only a literary construct that personifies national factors. Accordingly, such commentators have perceived these debates as a stylized portrayal of the struggles with tradition that engaged some ancient Israelites after the destruction of the First Temple and exile (already the Talmud speculated that "Job" was a mere parable). Whatever the case, the poignancy of Job's arguments reflects attempts to challenge an unconvincing theology. Honesty was the seal of Job's life. Hence jousting with opinions would not suffice. A more catalytic response was needed.

God's address to Job from the whirlwind has this effect (Job 38–41). It challenges human knowledge with a series of impossible questions, none of which are answerable by mortals, and none posed for this purpose. Rather, the queries are designed to unhinge human pretensions to understand the cosmic order. Job's silent no (his not knowing the answers to any of God's unanswerable questions) is the only honest response he can muster. The querulous rhetoric pierces his mind and heart—leaving him at his wit's end. "Where were you," he is asked, when the earth was formed and the stars hung in the sky? Does he know the "way of light" or "the place of darkness"? Can he weigh the mist or enter the storehouse of snow? And what about those strange and imponderable creatures that are found throughout the natural world—like the ostrich that gives birth and stomps upon its eggs, or the vulture that circles above for predation and survival? Can one truly understand the power of horses, gulping air with a primal energy; or the ways the onager and stork care for their young? Could any person presume such knowledge (Job 38–39)? All human wisdom is inadequate before this panoply of existence—both in its fullness and its entwining of life and death. The ostrich ostriches: that is its nature; the vulture vultures rapaciously, swooping down in predatory arcs on creatures below; and lithesome hinds give birth in rocky crevasses to protect their progeny. All this must be brought to mind—for if human beings cannot understand this imponderable cavalcade of divine providence as a whole, the ability to marvel at its parts is sufficient to dislodge human-centered theologies of world-order and purpose. Challenged by the reality with which he is confronted, Job is humbled and his presumptions shattered. But from this null-point new openings appear: a new theological consciousness is in the offing. What was formerly concealed is now revealed to his broken (but newly attentive) heart.

Following the divine speeches, Job enunciates his spiritual transformation. He knew, he says, that God is "capable of all things" (*ki khol tukhal*); but now he also knows that he spoke intemperately of things vastly beyond knowing. Prior knowledge was a "hearing of the ear"—the received transmission of theological traditions; but now there is personal perception, a direct experience of divine wonders seen by the inner "eye." This realization induces self-judgment and deep regret: "Therefore I despise myself and repent (*niḥamti*)—being but dust and ashes (*'al 'afar va-'efer*)" (42:2–3, 5–6).

With this confession, Job pivots around two spiritual attitudes. The first accentuates the disposition of humility, whereby Job proclaims personal remorse for speaking with hubris about God. Having held a theology of retributive justice, Job tried to make sense of the dissonance between his religious past and the sufferings he endured. But now Job realizes that divine dominion is manifest in the mysterious gift of life as such; and that God's providence is evident everywhere in nature—in the teeming complexity of existence that is not oriented around human life or needs (is not one of the mysteries that there can be rain upon an uninhabited wasteland, when settled areas suffer drought?). Perceiving this, Job repents and states that he is a mortal being of elemental nature. Like Adam, Job too was "dust of the earth"; and likewise his soul was transformed when he could properly name this mundane reality. Awareness of the complexity of world-being is a precondition for a change of perspective. Earthbound, Job's mind now opens to the inestimable cosmos. His self-assurance is radically transformed, and he is forced to face the world and God in a new way. Confronted with an overwhelming spiritual apprehension (not a comprehension) of the ontological plenum, Job acquires a disposition of divine reverence and human limit.

The second reading of Job's confession turns his consciousness in a different direction. If the first interpretation follows a vertical axis, such that Job recognizes the hubris of his contentions and repents in humility, the second sits on a horizontal plane. Job is overwhelmed by the polymorphic nature of existence, with its multiple species all contesting to survive—and draws an ethical conclusion. He says that he regrets his prior assessment of the human condition, and is now filled with "sympathy" (*niḥamti*) for human beings "because" (*'al*) they (like he) are but "dust and ashes": mortal creatures who struggle for subsistence and to find purpose from birth to death. Construed thus, Job's confession is his response to the panoply of creation. It is a realization of the incalculable coexistence of life-forms, and inspires a moral disposition of co-responsibility—an attitude enacted by Job when God instructs him to intercede for his interlocutors and offer sacrifices on their behalf. The contrast with the initial scenes of the book is palpable. Job now graciously does for his critics what he formerly did for his family, not out of a sense of duty or fear of sin, but because of a new species-sympathy. He realizes that his neighbors are also mortal beings and concerned to make sense of their life—even with theological assertions at odds with his own. Like Job, they too walk the narrow ridge of life, and inherit hearsay to make sense of experience. But the fundamental difference between these others and Job is that they remain bound by the dicta of tradition, whereas he has come to acknowledge the impropriety of his former convictions. This difference is arguably the import of God's assertion that only Job spoke *nekhonah* (or "rightly") about God (42:7). In this second about-face, Job turns toward his fellow creatures from a new perspective: a sense of empathic humanity—a spiritual disposition of loving care. The entities of existence now appear to him in a fundamentally new way.

With his acknowledgment, Job asserts his theological insight. The moment marks a radical transformation. Death (of kin) and the desire for personal death give way to a transformed focus on life and gratuitous care for others. In fact, this new creature consciousness reciprocally catalyzes a new ontological ethics: a new way of living born of a new way of thinking. This realignment changes his life.

This shift in Job's religious consciousness points to a new theological and moral disposition: an orientation initiated by the depletion of prior presumptions and self-centeredness. God is the source of this transformed moral consciousness—not as a legislator but as the revealer of the created world for human assessment and ethical reflection. It remains for each individual to deduce the hermeneutical imperatives latent in creation, and to cull personal wisdom from the flow of existence. By doing so, Job models a way forward.

New Possibilities

The conclusion of the book of Job restores theology, and resets theology on the foundation of the natural world. The poverty of explanations valorized by tradition is exposed, and the ontological foundation of human life is disclosed anew. That foundation is "dust and ashes": physical mortality and the consciousness of this fact. For Job, these were the two factors that induced the disposition of humility and the sense of mortality that reconnect him with the plenum of worldly beings. If animals and birds necessarily hunt and prey, intertwined with other life-forms for their welfare and subsistence; and if other creatures subsist with vastly different ecological necessities—the same can be said of humans, in their various orders of need, love, and aggression. If there is a significant difference between these realms, it lies in the human recognition of the conditions of their existence *and* the capacity to alter their thoughts and actions accordingly. Sympathy and care can be part of the human endowment, if one draws that conclusion, and the same can be said for our sense of wonder and moral duty. The book of Job orients us toward these spiritual possibilities, and is thus a work of sacred instruction. It reveals a human standpoint of enduring value, within the divine cosmos; and this reveals, in its turn, a new way of acting or deportment within the ever-changing circumstances of life. Here is a basis for a heart of wisdom that may discern regulative principles from the vitalities of existence. Opening our heart to God and worldly transcendence invites a transformed consciousness of our mortal condition. Like all creatures, we are part of the infinite cosmos and the particularities of our finite habitat. Job's radically new religious vision is threaded with moral implications. The divine question that had so shaken Job—"Where were you when I established the earth?"—is now internalized, and he takes its terms reflexively: Where are you, here and now, before the tasks of the world? What are the spiritual and moral issues to be considered? The divine address comes from within and without.

Revelation is an opening of awareness: its impact is primary. Before God comes to mind, God comes to the heart and the fullness of experience. Revelation is the shock of presence. It speaks directly to the soul, and commands a committed attention to its claims—through an engaged hermeneutic understanding.

Regrounding Theology: The Book of Job and Beyond

In sum and substance, the book of Job provides a revaluation of theological discourse. Set within a universal framework, it makes no reference to the events of ancient Israelite history or its religious traditions, though it is full of allusions to biblical themes and theology; and just this verbal indirection gives it special heft within the scriptural canon. For millennia, commentators have refracted its content through their particular theological and hermeneutical lenses. I shall do likewise in the ensuing attempt to reformulate a Jewish theology for our time.

As noted, the final chapters of the book open a transcendent perspective on the natural world. The human eye and heart are bidden to take it all in, and realize that this profusion—ever regenerated and interacting—expresses God's sustenance and providence for existence. Perceiving this majestic arc of life, the self falls silent, cognizant that world-being does not turn on a human axis, and that there is an infinite number of intersecting centricities up and down the great chain of Being. With this realization, a numinous awareness seizes the soul. This overwhelming sensation is called the *mysterium tremendum* by Rudolf Otto—for it transfixes the human spirit in a state of radical awe. From this rupture of consciousness, an unsayable mystery transforms the heart.

Modern theology may draw certain conclusions. For his part, Job learned about the limits of human cognition and the possibilities of creature care. This is a fundamental reorientation and regrounding of value and of meaning. For those who would build on this Joban foundation, what is disclosed is something of the primordial twofold divine commandment: *love* and *limit*. These are two archetypal expressions of the world-order. Other expressions of these primary elements include desire and restraint, urge and inhibition, and *eros* and *thanatos*. Intersecting with all life at all times, these dynamics constitute the natural laws of God's world-creativity: both eternal and ongoing. Coming to terms with this intertwined reality, knowing it in both explicit and implicit ways, is a coming to terms with existence. We obey or disobey God's will at our peril.

Love is the primal surge of propagation for the sake of creativity or survival. The law of love expresses itself as protective care for its own kind most of all, and diverse species can never be too careful in this regard—given the potential dangers and complexities of survival. Nevertheless, erotic desire is a divine gift, for all its elemental nature. Who would deny the primary life-force of all creatures, or the drive to mate for breeding and social continuity? Love produces the successive generations of its kind, and instructs the young with strategies for sustenance. Love also seeks to protect life against threat or primal danger. Hence supererogatory acts are expressions of selfless devotion for one's kind. But if care may overstep its natural limits in times of danger, love can also inspire legal regulations for the sake of restraint and order. This happens again and again. It, too, is a divine gift; but how it is used depends on inherent species-wisdom or the instructions of tradition—whether mimetically enacted or verbally transmitted. In a word, love has its positive and negative actions—its modes of yes and no, and do and don't. These are also inculcated into the layers of memory or culture, which one obeys or disobeys at their peril or benefit. Love and *eros* thus have their limits, to be considered and weighed. They hold back ill-considered urges and desires.

The other divine commandment is *limit*; it too is a fundamental component of organismic existence—of life in its various forms. Nature circuits endlessly, with its cycles repeating and regenerating. But this is not the case for living beings, whose physical existence terminates with death. Whatever rejuvenation one might experience in the course of life, it is time-bound and snuffed out with mortality. As a result, the fear of extinction generates diverse strategies of survival, each according to its kind and mind. The diversity of world-being reveals an astonishing complexity of species and their means of dealing with aggression and scarcity. Look high or low: the vultures and reptiles in sky and sea, the wild ass and serpents of the ground, all have their distinctive forms—outfitted and evolved over time; and each body has its physical features and practical limits, balancing inner possibilities with external necessities. Still other limits are produced by conflicts between creatures over the available elements, by the availability of air and water, food and other resources. The natural command of God, in all these cases, is the species-specific law of physical survival: an imperative that may instigate the life-threatening breach of limits for food or propagation. In order to persist, life-forms must learn appropriate types of risk and restraint—of yes and no, and do and don't—or reap the consequences. Such matters are inculcated into brute species as instinct or mimicry, or ingrained into human creatures through ongoing instruction and tradition. The positive and negative commandments of all existence are measured by the ways creatures find accord with these primal laws of existence. As a creature scans the horizon, natural restrictions and boundaries condition the value of all things. Respect for difference can lead to fear and restraint, or take a gratuitous turn with recognition of the inherent fragilities of life. Cognition of these matters is vital and affects each species in its struggle for survival.

Within the multitudes of divine creativity, a "Joban eye" may perceive in the realities of desire and limitation regulative principles that command our respect for differences and induce an ethic of concern for other creatures. These principles are both primordial and evident in the vast totality of existence. When taken to heart, one may reclaim a vision of divine providence that provides a radical regrounding for ethics. For God's worldly providence, as envisioned here, is expressed through the laws of individuality and species propagation: the great differences of creatures all striving to survive and increase, given their native proclivities or acquired capacities. This may engender an ecological ethic, through recognition of the complex balance of animal and vegetal life; and a social ethic, through the realization of the fragile fact of existence—in all its diverse balances of limit and love. Since times primordial these "unwritten laws" of God (at the heart of existence) have been lived and taught in every group, according to their kind and nature: by ordinary people, who intuitively sensed God's natural law within existence; and by teachers and holy persons, who have attuned their souls to the core of being and perceived God's eternal word expressed through all life. These God-given laws (or regulative conditions) were subsequently reformulated by culture and taught as "oral and written traditions" for the sake of durable limit and love. But new life circumstances reveal God's regulations in new forms or with new demands. This requires new hermeneutical capacities to devise new arcs of limit and love over social culture and the life-world itself. Such ongoing adjustments are a recurrent dynamic.

Theological living begins in the thickness of the quotidian, with an intuition of creative existence and one's incorporation within this reality. The self is fundamentally constituted by the comprehensive life challenges of this realization, and by the actions required for subsistence and innovation. From its onset, theological living is inherently committed to hermeneutical awareness and responsibility. This orientation faces forward with resolve, repeatedly construing possibilities tied to spiritual purpose and cultural direction. The fragility of life imposes the spiritual imperative of care and consideration. Theology tries to keep both uppermost in mind—for the sake of a God-responsive existence shaped by value and thoughtfulness.

An Assessment: The Hermeneutical Prism of Scripture

Why have I taken my mark from the book of Job? I have done so for two critical reasons. The first is to establish the scriptural basis for a theological disposition that bears the weight of our cognitive condition while simultaneously inculcating an ethical imperative able to bear the weight of moral responsibility. The former (the theological focus) redirects human attention to the marvel of the universe—allowing us to perceive it in new ways, conducive to considered modes of worldly care (the ethical disposition). Without diminishing the concrete valences of one's location, the individual shifts from regarding life experiences as a series of distinct subject-object coordinates to a more holistic and relational mindset. Theological and ethical truths arise from these diverse synergies, as we shall see in subsequent chapters. We are part of the universe and must live the consequences. Culture is grounded in the created orders of existence.

The second reason for my turning to Job stems from my attempt to reformulate a Jewish hermeneutical theology. This project seeks to identify regulative principles of thought and action consonant with the teachings of Judaism and the challenges of our time. On this basis, spiritual dissonance from the regnant tradition may be converted into new reasons for religious and ethical behavior. The book of Job is a paradigmatic instance of this process. It opens our minds in unexpected ways. Beginning with this foundation, we shall attempt to construct a new hermeneutical theology of Judaism—one that will try to recover new coherences in scripture without evading the challenges of contemporary life experience. On the way forward, we shall wend our way through the thick archive of Jewish scriptural expression. This is our hermeneutical circle and its open-ended hope.

With these considerations in mind, I turn to the structure and focus of the present project—one that correlates levels of our lived life with levels of Jewish scriptural and related interpretations.

A New-Old Theological Model—Four Levels of Life and Thought

As creatures in the world we live simultaneously at different levels. At the primary level, we are natural beings who are part of an omnipresent and impinging world. This sphere solicits our attention and response, if we are attuned to it; unless, by dint of routine or disregard, we become tone-deaf to the voice of things. It is to this panoply of entities that we must give heed— for "everything is a voice," Victor Hugo said; and "everything, infinitely, says something to someone." The multiple oscillations of experience may become new evocations for our attentive regard or rejection, insofar as they solicit desire or caution limit. These occasions signify types of existential value that become the basis for the general and specific norms of God-given reality—life expressions of the primordial divine providence of limit and love. As cultural creatures, at the second level of living, we may formulate these matters into types of *nomos* and narrative—frames of culture with authoritative significance. *Nomos* refers to the norms (oral and written) that motivate or protect collective life; and "narrative" denotes the accounts (both oral and written) that link one to a chain of cultural-historical memory, with projected expectation and hope. At this social-communal level we join our personal needs and individual identities to the group, using collective pronouns to express this (notably, the shift from "I" to "we"). The maintenance of order and common purpose now has an external, public reference.

The balances between the first and second levels require regulation and adjustment, for these are often in tension, and neither cancels the other. In fact, the tensions between the first (individual) and second (social) levels may be variously creative and instructive. Precisely how our universal and shared humanity (or personal proclivities) correlates with group values must be regularly reassessed and given attention. Such reflective evaluations also pertain to the relationships between the second level and the succeeding one, since this third level focuses on how an individual—a participant in the norms and narratives of the group—may interpret them in distinctive ways, for spiritual enhancement or refinement of moral character. In this way, the tradition has both a collective and a personal dimension that are dynamically correlated. But there is more. Beyond selfhood and the social unit we also belong to an infinite universe, and may attempt to expand our awareness to include a cosmic consciousness. At this fourth level, the most comprehensive of all, religious seekers strive to integrate the other strata (and their anthropocentric concerns) into a more supervening state of awareness. Consciousness of being part of this all-embracing whole influences one's spiritual and moral awareness at the other three levels. The theological and ethical challenge is the integration of these four levels.

The New-Old Model Hermeneutically Applied

These four levels of general experience and consciousness correlate with the four types of traditional Jewish scriptural interpretation, characterized in rabbinic parlance as *PaRDeS*—this being a medieval acronym for *peshat*, *remez*, *derash*, and *sod*. The first type, *peshat*, refers to the "plain sense" (or contextual, lexical level of textual meaning) of scripture; indeed, its canonical frame is the Hebrew Bible. The second type, *derash*, refers to the "exegetical sense" (or the legal and theological levels of rabbinic interpretation), and its vast literary corpora include the varieties of classical rabbinic Bible commentaries. The third type, known as *remez*, refers to the "allegorical sense" (or the philosophical and spiritual-ethical levels found in scripture), and its range of sources embraces a broad variety of theoretical and practical interpretations. Finally, the fourth type, *sod*, refers to the esoteric or "mystical sense" (or the supernal signs and symbols encoded within scripture), which includes a large spiritual and theosophical literature. Over the millennia, these hermeneutical levels produced a great diversity of scriptural meanings. They explicate the formulations and facts of biblical historical memory or religious expression (*peshat*); examine and elaborate the details of law and theology for their social value and significance in rabbinic culture (*derash*); reinterpret the words and figures of scripture with an eye to the allegorical tropes that encode philosophical or ethical ideals (*remez*); and plumb the language of scripture to reveal the literary traces of a mystical superstructure that conceals the most ultimate reality of Divinity, in its primordial and continuous unfolding throughout the cosmos—and beyond (*sod*).

Different commentators have preferred one exegetical type or another, establishing diverse hierarchies of meaning and value in accord with their specific proclivities. Taken together, these four levels of interpretation helped formulate a ladder of religious or spiritual development, with each successive level absorbing the truths of its predecessors into a dynamic synergy. In the following discussions, this hermeneutical spectrum will be appropriated and processed through a spectrum of scriptural texts— selected to exemplify these diverse exegetical and theological layers. The larger goal is to construct a theological epistemology: an inquiry into the multiple meanings of experience perceived through the fourfold prism of traditional Jewish textual interpretation. The texts drawn upon have themselves often been perceived through this hermeneutical prism. Hence, the contemporary challenge is to retain their integrity and authenticity while allowing them to speak in direct and instructive ways to our situation. In the process, the older sources will find a modern voice and mediate a contemporary theological ontology—scripturally based.

My approach to the *PaRDeS* model will use it as a template for theological reflection—stratified into four distinct levels, but interactive and integral at its core. I intend to understand the first mode (*peshat*) as a hermeneutic domain that gives expression to our primary sense of living in the natural and social world: the level of ordinary and religious experience, where the phenomena of existence solicit our attention and require some response. Reading scripture at this level will consider examples from this literary sphere and then, through them, formulate a theological construction of our lived experience. In this way, it will provide textual models for alertness to the events and decisions of daily life. The second mode (*derash*) will reengage the multimillennial range of rabbinic traditions and their interpretations of scripture and the world, whether for personal and social celebration or ritual sanctifications of its God-given reality. Though the primary world of experience remains the basis of this second, reinterpreted domain of rabbinic culture, through its hermeneutical forms worldly experiences are processed and enacted differently. Occurrences of nature or happenings in time (biblical or rabbinic history), as well as religious experiences (whether personal or social in nature), are not mere worldly or human occasions, but events to be experienced in terms of their Jewish values and theological significance. Reading scripture at this level appropriates these events in terms of contemporary theological consciousness and its concerns. The central role of language in classical rabbinic thought will offer many exemplars for use in a revitalized hermeneutical discourse—in particular the relationships between revelation, language, and law. Taking up the third mode (*remez*), we shall strive to follow traditional models in order to inculcate paths of personal development. In this setting, the individual remains a Jewish cultural being, infused by the values of the rabbinic tradition. But now the personal meanings and appropriations of the tradition are stressed, in accord with individual proclivities or character. As in the other levels, the biblical sources will be reinterpreted through rabbinic sources to exemplify these concerns. Finally, the fourth hermeneutical mode (*sod*) will attempt to awaken religious consciousness to an ultimate awareness: the absolute dimension of God, and immensities unthinkable and ineffable as such. This theological level involves a total reorientation of one's worldly, located being—presenting it within the all-encompassing reality of divine Being and creativity. As with the previous cases, scripture will be read in hermeneutical terms—but now, by adducing examples from Jewish mystical sources, we shall hope to reformulate their interpretations in language conducive to contemporary understanding. In new-old ways, scripture may thereby again provide a vehicle for profound theological insights and redirected consciousness.

How these four hermeneutical levels will interface depends on the perceived theological goal—and the particular interpreter. Diverse modes of life require distinct responses; hence certain levels will be privileged in certain circumstances. Nevertheless, the overall goal is to increase awareness of their dynamic interplay, so that no level is reified or cut off from the others. Being aware that we live at multiple spiritual and cognitive levels requires a theology that is multivalent in form and content. This will not fragment the four types of hermeneutical activity or deprive them of coherence. Just the opposite: it is my conviction that these several levels may reinstill awareness of the diversity of life experience and the plurality of ways to engage it. And although there may be a cultural hierarchy in play, if we think of these levels as modes of awareness we may appreciate their dynamic intersection. Thus performance of rabbinic practices within a community may be enriched by awareness of how these actions respond to the givens of nature, how they may assume personal significance, and how they may also participate in expanded spheres of consciousness. The ideal is a hermeneutic pluralism with multiple possibilities in play. As an ensemble, the conceptual and structural diversity of *PaRDeS* gives expression to the variety of human and theological experience, and to the interpreter's role in the process.

The challenge of a contemporary Jewish hermeneutical theology lies before us. God is the omnipresent source of meanings; our human interpretations provide the means for their ongoing expression. This is the core of a creative hermeneutics with God at the center.

Interlude One

Living theology begins with lived experience and its verbal expression. This is its twofold ground: it is ever new because life circumstances change and require hermeneutical adjustments; and ever old because we are repeatedly affected by life experiences and instructed by teachings from earlier generations. Theology is thus comprised of the intersection of life and knowledge, events and their reformulation—both past and present.

Experience is primary. We belong to the world first and always through the medium of our senses. The continuous impact of worldly stimuli on our minds and bodies is the primary "reality" of our lives. We are totally encompassed by this reality even as we feel and process its impact from within. These sensations break into consciousness as tactile valences of heat and cold, light and dark, and wet and dry. Frustrations and satisfactions also have their effect. From within the crevice of awareness things pass over and through our bodies, leaving traces of what "has been" for us to make sense of. Such preverbal experiences are not nameable as such, but nevertheless convey our initial sense of difference and degree, and condition such primary temporal sensations as "this-now" or "not-yet." Perceptible distinctions of limit and longing gradually emerge as our responses become more deliberate or intentional. At first, negative limits are conveyed by a vocal cry—the primordial expression of needs or solicitation; and positive realities by a coo—the incipient expression of somatic gratitude or relief. Eventually these sensations are annotated as patterns of expectation, and encoded into the neural fibers of our being. When some lack causes distress—physical or emotional—the anxieties of absence can be overwhelming. These ruptures or inconsistencies are as primary to our lived reality as are sustenance and continuity. With them the face of care (the expressions of love) is withdrawn, and the pathos of longing (the sense of limit) is felt with unnerving force. We are embedded in *that which* "is" and "shall be" our whole life long.

However felt or experienced, the ways of this "reality" comprise the daily touchstone of self-awareness. It is "actuality" *as such*—wholly independent of how we construe or "make sense" of its impact. To lose touch with this realm (through disregard or habit) is to lose touch with the primary conditions or factors that affect our lives. Who could dismiss the elemental sensations of color and sound, pleasure and desire, or hunger and its satisfactions? They solicit our attention in many ways—each one evoking a distinct concern and value *for us*. Instinctively or with reflection we seek to determine what "ought" to be in any given situation, and act appropriately in response. With instruction and memory we may become more calculating and deliberate, and then what "ought" to be (physical or ethical) assumes a more authoritative character. All this becomes the basis for trusted or anticipated knowledge. What seems achievable ("this-now") ingrains a sense of the possible, whereas what is deferred or potential ("not-yet") inculcates the quality of hope. We swing repeatedly between these poles, striving to keep the dread of anxiety (the fear of "not-ever") at bay. But this primary emotion repeatedly breaks through, because the particulars of life don't necessarily suit our personal needs. Self-centered, constitutively localized in body and mind, we come up short and settle on what seems suitable or available to our specific concerns. We thereby hope to close the gap for particular or practical purposes. But the primordial qualities of "reality" invariably exceed our cognitive grasp, and remain ultimately mysterious and ineffable. An imponderable remainder hovers over our cognitive constructions, evoking the premonition of existence as an impersonal, often terrifying unknown. This cognizance is a primary impulse of theology. Inherently incommensurate with our minds, the eternal upsurge of existence is overwhelming—and fundamentally nameless.

But we do name it and give it expressions through the agencies of language, hoping thereby to frame the strata of life in human terms or harness them to our needs or will. By conjoining and dividing sounds, and modifying breath, we enunciate specific tonal patterns to mark certain aspects of the evident world—verbal delineations that (through agreement and convention) give us a primary purchase on reality. For all their limits as products of our natural being, words are daily miracles, creating the knowable and discernible realms of life from our primordial need to know and survive. Without language humans would not have a world to speak of, or any thinkable fragment of existence. Language expresses our desire for order and orientation. But inevitably and necessarily, we respond to the suffusing reality of existence from within its sensate conditions, siphoning off "life meanings" from the sea of sounds and impact of feelings. We can never transcend ourselves. Despite all our verbal artifacts, the inherent reality of things is beyond reach—inconceivable by our minds. By transforming this vital mystery into problems to be solved we exploit our practical rationality, but thereby reduce the mysteries of existence to the measure of our human limits and purposes. Entranced by the effect of words, we spin linguistic webs around existence and regard ourselves as a center point. In the process, "things" are domesticated into forms that reflect our nature; and when we deploy or exchange words as "real" objects, we are duped by our achievements. Whatever *is* "as it is" becomes merely something that is "for us"—not more.

Caught in the confluence of experience and expression, we need words—but must respect their limits. Some words may echo the sounds of things and so seem resonant with that reality. But not for long: the cacophony of existence exceeds these correlations. Sooner or later we become conscious that the words we use are not the thing itself, but only "like" it; and that verbal likenesses represent the world through conventional attributions and terms. This is a transformative insight, for with it the fundamental gap between language and its referent becomes shatteringly concrete. We must live with this core realization, and create meanings within this consciousness. It therefore behooves us to become aware of our limited claims on reality, lest we slip into false presumptions about our creative abilities. This is a danger particularly with respect to those eminent artifacts we call poetry. Though far more intentional and deliberate than ordinary speech, poetry can produce misprisions as well, when it appears to convey privileged accounts of reality, rather than imaginative projections of it. Metaphysical poems are a special instance of this temptation, when they so evocatively name aspects of the sensate reality of life (as Wallace Stevens so often declaimed) with word patterns that pierce our heart through oracular modes of depiction. In doing so, they seem to bespeak the ineffable; and then we often sense that something of the "nature of things" has been disclosed. Transformed by these representations, one must resist their aesthetic enchantment. Even if poetry is an exalted predication of the experience of reality, it nevertheless remains a predication, a mimetic construct set between experience and our expressive soul.

Theology is of a different order. Whereas poetry purports to give expression to reality through the medium of the creative imagination, theology seeks to bear witness to its manifestations as they address our mind and heart. Rather than offering verbal artifacts that try to reimagine reality in words, theology tries to annotate the evocations of reality *itself* as it imposes its conditions through a human filter. Hence, these evocations are often deemed the worldly conduits of something radically transcendent. Because of their numinous quality, recipients of such occasions may believe that a divine revelation is involved. More than just being "heightened feelings" or "sublime sentiments," these moments inspire the conviction that something wholly "other" than impersonal reality has become personally present—and that the divine force of creativity has become a life-imperative to be heeded. Persons may answer yes or no to these demands, but some response is required. According to some accounts of them, individuals who acknowledge such experiences perceive these invocations to be at the edge of cognition, where normal calibrations have been overwhelmed. These sensations convey the belief that one's mental limits have somehow been exceeded. And even if the ultimate mysteries of reality are not thereby revealed, the evocations are deemed a tipping point of consciousness: stimuli of theological sensibilities and new acts of personal commitment.

These experiences betoken the sense that aspects of divine transcendence have become immanent, inducing a response that redirects one's life. In subsequent testimonies, these transformative events are acknowledged, along with the recontextualization (mental or physical) of one's life. Persons may even call the addressing presence "God," speak its "Name," or even characterize the event with the help of a cultural tradition. The ensuing Divine Name indicates the theological character of the experience, along with the reciprocal conviction that one has been personally named and addressed. Hence many accounts of such events report that the particular individual was called "by name," and simultaneously informed of the Name of the addressing divine presence. Such naming gives a seal of verity to the occasions that so fundamentally transform selfhood. But whether named or not, these manifestations of a divine presence exceed nomenclature; and for that reason the impulse to articulate these Divine Names borders on the blasphemous. This concern notwithstanding, subsequent articulations of these experiences are often expressed with a numinous aura, and attempt to convey their values for themselves and others. Understanding this point is crucial for appreciating the role that such testimonies play in a cultural canon. They are not written as literary artifacts—dry and remote—but as spiritual memoirs that seek to preserve personal instances of instruction for our theological edification. Heeding these accounts in Hebrew scripture is therefore crucial for cultivating a contemporary theology of *peshat*. More than words to be "read" with the eyes, these narratives must be "experienced" in the heart, for they are preserved as paradigmatic events of the spirit. It is from these stylistic settings that they continue to speak across the generations.

Scriptural Testimonies

Scriptural texts record pivotal moments in the lives of major ancestors. In a multitude of ways these persons responded to a sudden solicitation for a significant action—moments when divine reality was manifest to them as a divine voice or living presence, calling them to a life-changing decision. Collated from a traditional fund of reports, literary accounts of these events have been gathered in scripture because of their spiritual value for the nation: evidence of human acts of obedience (Abraham and Moses) or of God's beneficent providence (continuity of the ancestral blessing, and fulfillment of the promise of divine deliverance from Egypt). As reformulated there, these narratives were transmitted to influence the religious consciousness of subsequent generations. There are still other cases in scripture of both moral and legal instruction, designed to cultivate worldly wisdom and specify exemplary behaviors for certain situations. Just as the behaviors of the ancestors instill theological values (obedience and the readiness to serve), these hortatory and legal exempla convey religious norms as well (control of desires and protection of life). As Jews, we belong to scripture as the foundational template of "instruction" in our lifelong engagement with ultimate reality. It is thus necessary to study these canonical depictions of theological living and to appropriate them in accordance with scriptural values, tradition, and our modern sensibilities. In this way these testimonies may instruct our natural condition, and give life a theological vector and voice.

From First- to Second-Order Appropriations

To study scripture for the sake of a *peshat* theology is not merely to focus on the plain (or contextual) sense of an episode. Such readings will convey only the historical and religious information of the text, not its theological impact or challenge to one's life. To appreciate the latter one must go beyond the literary artifice to the personal experiences given verbal expression. In phenomenological terms, one must bracket the external or purported historical realism of the event, after having clarified its literary depiction and language, and strive to understand its theological intention and spiritual structure—in these instances, human lives lived in response to divine solicitations, experienced as a direct, personal "voice." These responses are not of one type, nor are the consequences similar. They are arguably preserved in scripture for that very reason. By studying these narrative archetypes, and meditating on their theological intentions, later readers may cultivate (or acquire) new spiritual dispositions. Precisely this is one of the primary concerns of the theology of *peshat* to be explored below. Thickly embedded in reality, we are not always able to ascertain such divine solicitations or know how best to evaluate their claim and import. Determining how the "divine voice" may be validly perceived through existence is a challenge for even the most spiritually attuned. Study of scripture focused on the phenomenology of experience that informs it can prove instructive (and cautionary). We are then challenged to translate these accounts into modern terms and categories; and then the language of scriptural instruction may be perceived anew—for its revelatory voice and life-directing values.

*

For us as bearers of scriptural tradition, the goal is to reengage written scripture so that its content becomes theologically actualized in lived life, albeit not in a literal way. The aim is not to appropriate the content of scripture as pieces of information but, through hermeneutical reflection, to be appropriated *by* the text, so that it may inform our lives. Stimulated by this dialectic, scripture may be personalized as a vital spiritual heritage, and provide models for how to live and act with theological conviction. We are the mediators of this transformative condition.

PART TWO

Peshat

Beginning with the World

As discussed in the introduction, Job's confession, *'al ken em'as ve-niḥamti
'al 'afar va-eifer* (Job 42:6), renews theological consciousness in a decisive
way. According to the two interpretations of *niḥamti* given there, the human
ego (Job's "I") is conjoined to the earth ("dust and ashes") through a twofold
pronouncement of self-reproof and sympathy: I "regret" (he avers) my prior
theological assertions, being mortal and uninformed; and I have "compassion" (he adds) for all who share this human condition. Job's remarks specify the conjunction of mind and body in a new spiritual disposition. His
mind responds to the overwhelming phenomena of life from the position
of a creature; and this induces his new sense of participatory involvement
in existence—not because of any legal obligation, but because of his transformed sense of finitude. For Job, both a cosmic and a creature consciousness interpenetrate. This is a catalytic event, the foundation of an ontological ethics.

Our Bodily Nature

We may also come to such a realization though reflection on our creaturely existence. As natural beings, we experience the world through a
multitude of sensations that condition our awareness. We feel the play of
light, the shock of sound, and numerous cognitive qualities. They constitute
our primary realities. We are constantly filled and formed by the impression of "what matters." Equally basic is the pressure of physical needs—
experienced initially as prethematic sensations requiring immediate resolution. Accordingly, the pressure of physicality is a formative condition,
and it elicits a broad spectrum of somatic and emotional vulnerabilities. We
respond to these occasions as concrete qualities and quantities, not abstract

entities. Indeed, these features are the elemental particulars that stimulate daily awareness and regulate our consciousness. We think because we feel, and are inclined toward thought through verbal accounts of these physical sensations. Subjectivity is a radical factor of human nature. It conditions our "plain sense" of life from moment to moment.

Our initial cognition of these matters is mostly a fleeting sense of the impulses involved. Nevertheless, some sensibilities stand out. These include the "yes-no" or "stop-and-go" imperatives we perceive in the natural world, whether by trial and error or by modeling and parental guidance. Such instructions constitute our basic guidelines for sustenance and survival. Through their aid we try to decode the signals that will help regulate behavior. Primary sensibilities are construed through a deep grammar of intuited perceptions and lived syntax, and all these are transformed or encoded according to our innate capacity. Slowly, we get a sense of the import of things, filling in gaps though experience. Perception and the lived world conjoin. We come to trust these impressions as a primary ground of meaning. Our existence depends on it.

In the face of prethematic experiences, language constructs verbal symbols that serve our needs. These terms specify imperatives that indicate significant "approach-avoidance" and "benefit-danger" conditions. Over time, these signifiers are sifted and integrated through personal experience or group traditions, and produce life norms of positive action or restraint. The result is a *hermeneutical fund* for the group. We inculcate such matters from earliest childhood; and on their basis we position ourselves in physical and social space, adjusting to circumstances as they arise. Over all, concerns for physical or emotional benefits or protections proceed with a relatively smooth automaticity—as long as the needs can be met or the options for corrective action are available. But if and when difficulties arise, of whatever kind, they elicit needs for immediate resolution. The world is then not simply "there," as something to be "lived" with fixed behaviors or settled interpretations. Its primary contingencies rise to the surface and require a deliberated assessment or decision. The now-ruptured fugue state of life— the automaticity of habit and presumption—may then generate a new state of awareness, what we shall deem one's *hermeneutical self-constitution*. This is the percipient awareness that our life experiences are constituted by acts of interpretation and determination. Since the disruptions vary—ranging from realistic dangers to ambiguous situations, or from enticing solicitations to less definite concerns—our assessment of their value requires new acts of judgment. In the process, we become conscious of our creative role in the decoding of experience. "Hermeneutics" thus refers to the active, interpretative formulation of the *primary* conditions that influence our "sense of being." It begins with attention to each "this" and "that," and extends to all the evaluations and determinations that establish our place in the various realms of life. Caesuras—ruptures in nature and experience—reveal the fragility of existence; their creative overcoming is the work of hermeneutics.

Hermeneutical Insight and Its Implications

The processes just described include another component: the realization that worldly experiences are humanized through language. Meaning is not pregiven a priori or part of the nature of things, but is constructed by tradition and culture. This hermeneutic insight is transformative at both an intellectual and an ethical level: intellectually, since we become aware that our world perceptions have a subjective particularity—transforming the universal world environment (*Umwelt*) into a life-world (*Lebenswelt*) with humanly construed meanings; and ethically, since we also become aware that our cultural constructs give events their moral import—transforming the "merely-so" of mere existence into a sphere of human values. The principles that help to regulate our orientations in the world (orientations of sense and sensibility) integrate experience and expression in creative, human ways. Our interpretations express moral intention and purpose, and evoke a valence of responsibility. Hermeneutical consciousness is the germ of moral freedom.

With the intensification of awareness one becomes conscious of the "miracle of presence." Certain events so pervade our field of attention that we cannot grasp them as mere objects of thought. We rather feel surrounded by their all-embracing reality. Such occasions induce a sense of total givenness: an unbidden bestowal of existence, a gratuitous happening (*ḥesed*) of transcendent import. These moments influence our sense of being recipients of worldly realities, not their maker. One's formative "animal faith" (the conviction that the world is stable and reliable; that we are bathed in light and feeling) is affected by this consciousness. Put in Joban terms, we become aware of our human nature in a God-given universe. Or stated in dialogical terms, we become a "you" when repeatedly addressed by the elements of the world, and summoned to determine their meaning or significance. These factors impact our self-constitution in the most fundamental ways. Awakened from the fugue state of habitual feelings, the self becomes an intentional agent. God's worldly gifts open our mouth in response—long before "God" is a named reality of experience.

Suddenly we become aware of the "miracle of language"—our cognizance of making sense with words. It is the core of a hermeneutical perception of reality. Nothing just is, but varies with their attributions and names.

Our localized and spatial situations of near and far, like our various personal relationships, all evoke linguistic responses that reorient us to new conditions. With some nouns we name the world, with others we characterize it; and with verbs we describe or prescribe actions. Attentive to the omnipresent voices of reality, we are also summoned to "be silent and listen" to the phenomena all around, and challenged to attend to their different modes of expressions. Hearing deeper, we may even sense in the evocations of existence—the voiced and unvoiced creation—a primordial vitality that impels all entities toward their "natural destiny" (be it their endurance, perseverance, or propagation). This is the call of life that speaks in and through reality—the myriads of communications and movements that are the worldly expression of these primary impulses. Speaking through the depths, these life-formulations are generated by the primordial sparks of creation. Acceding to a transformative intuition, this infinite bounty of existence may be theologically conceptualized as God's all-creative "word." We resonate with this life-surge because we, too, participate in its reality. This "divine word" vitalizes our creaturely world from day to day, and is the stimulus that informs all human meanings. Put differently, God's speech is the activation of life, at all times and in all ways. It is the omnipresent revelation of reality, which we make humanly knowable through language. Meaning is born from this primal mystery. God's "word" becomes human speech, and, therewith, a new creation is formed. As creatures, we see "things" because we hear the "word."

God's "word" is not like human words, which filter existence through our limited sociolinguistic constructions. It is rather world-*creativity as such*, and constitutes the *inherent vitality of all things*—above and below the thresholds of human consciousness. It apportions the spirit of life to all creatures, inducing their adaptation to the challenges of existence. The panoply of world-being is a multivalent divine discourse, a "speaking" that does not refer to any signified thing, but is *the complex fullness of all signifiers*. Hence the bounty of life is more than a worldly expression of God's creative infinitude. It is a universal manifestation of divine generosity (*Ḥesed*): a heavenly beneficence generating the life expressions of all being. Humankind is but one modality of this omnipresent effectuality, though manifestly capable of blocking or extending the flow of life. Because of this capacity—mediated by positive intelligence or corrosive perversity—we can decisively affect the vast ecologies of existence. It is therefore incumbent upon the human species to gauge its world responsibilities and enhance the intertwinements of all existence on this planet. Human *ḥesed* must model the *Ḥesed* of God as best it can. A flourishing "capacity for generosity" is the godly heart of wisdom for which we yearn, the foundation of a theological life and ethics. With *ḥesed* we may open the heart of our companions and restore them to life and love. Verbal disclosure (and all silent communication) is built upon this primary grammar of shared existence.

The significance we give to things often corresponds to the external signs they evoke. We are endlessly embedded in semiotic loops of possible meaning, and try to decode their apparent cues for our benefit or purpose. This epistemic challenge cannot be minimized, and we must monitor the tendency to project our "human nature" on the "nature of things." This said, we readily perceive that most life-forms manifest something like willful or purposeful actions, and display something akin to deliberate or reactive decisions. These inherent manifestations are evident up and down the chain of existence. And for that reason, some scientists describe this capacity for dynamic responsiveness as the bio- or zoö-semiosis of world-beings— referring thereby to the ways life-forms strive for creative adaptations to the complexities of their environment. This all-embracing process is the primary providence of God's "word"—giving and sustaining life everywhere and for all kinds. To interpret the world in all its forms is therefore to parse the creative "divine word" with the limited resources of our linguistic and epistemic competence.

This transformation of the world from a natural manifestation into a spiritual expression is the germ of hermeneutical theology. The *primal source and truth of all communication come from God*; but *its meanings and significations are* only "God-like"—*interpretations construed through human understanding.* Divine revelation (the manifestations of existence) is thus an attestation of God's creative bounty. Human interpretation, manifest through language, is its ongoing witness and creative core—bound to social and historical tradition, but not limited to it. These correlations between divine expressions and human interpretations are the generative font of a *peshat* theology.

Reality: Manifest and Hidden

Gillui ve-khisui ba-lashon: God's creative word is the "revelation" bestowed into world-being by Divinity. But its full sense remains "concealed"—despite the world-revealing acts of human language. In the normal course of things, our words are essential instruments for human significance and survival. This is their primary value. And yet, inspired by occasions of breakthrough consciousness, words also strive to express the vectors of transcendence that may disclose spiritual directions and instruction. Formulated in awe, and transmitted with care, these accounts are found in religious recitations and sacred scripture. They serve as beacons for the spiritual initiation of others.

Markers of the divine mystery, they are an essential theological resource. We see further by their light. But insights into the mysteries remain limited and opaque, since the constructed character of verbal formulations conditions our vision. The simultaneity of the "revealed and concealed in language" (*gillui ve-khisui ba-lashon*) is at the core of consciousness. It is a primary prism in which our spiritual destiny is refracted.

Words face us, revealing their presence and apparent sense: both the word of God, through world-being, and the words of cognitive reformulation—in daily discourse and in scripture. They shine bright, manifestly, through the known or presumed, providing a purchase on mystery; and so we value them and hold them in mind, with our best understanding and ongoing interpretations. But our words are also turned toward the ineffable, to its mysteries and hidden meanings; to its possibilities, only imagined by our hermeneutic artifice and tradition. Boldly we strive to formulate wisdom from the infinite unknown of Divinity, before which we are humbled into silence. An unfathomable depth is the primordial ground of all the cognitive constructs that come to human awareness. A responsive theological consciousness must keep this in mind. God's revelation of world-being, impersonal in its primordial nature, only becomes a human event when any of its particulars confront consciousness and evoke a response: a living assent whose meaning is constrained by human capacities and the conditions of interpretation.

An Attestation in Scripture—Hermeneutically Construed

For the hermeneutically attuned, for whom scripture is a foundational text and source of instruction, various formulations can confirm and direct the preceding theological intuitions. Thus in a certain sense, scripture can provide proof texts for the truths of experience. Or as we shall explore below, the hermeneutics of life and of scripture can be mutually reinforcing.

The revelations of God throughout world-being are not the historical "Torah of Sinai," but an "Infinite Torah"—primordial and cosmic—known through all human interpretations of its experienced or perceived features. For human consciousness, this divine reality is foundational: it is the constitutive realm of all existence. As scripture states, the earth upon which we live "was *tohu* and *bohu*" (Genesis 1:2); it *was* once (and may ever be) an infinite congery of "inchoate" and "unformed" elements, whenever it appears to us without shape or sense. But then, with a sudden insight, our intuitive spirit may generate meanings from this vast realm of possibilities. What the theological mind perceives here is that an all-inspiriting divine word enunciates a sense-inducing and all-effectuating "let there be" (*yehi*) throughout existence—a creative evocation and promise of possibility—

that brings the primary elements to human consciousness (Genesis 1:4, 6, 14). Suddenly, what seemed "inchoate" and "unformed" (*tohu-bohu*) induces "wonder" and "astonishment" (or *tohe* and *bohe*). And then, with this radical evocation, the mind is awakened to its epistemic potency and affirms *bo-hu*—there is "something here" (literally, "in it"); and with this intuition formulates cognitive structures of one kind or another. These hermeneutical events stimulate and express the basis of cognitive experience. Accordingly, to perceive the inchoate (seemingly indeterminate) swirl of matter "as this" or "as that" (that is, to intuit something uncertain as a distinct epistemic entity) is a hermeneutical act and veritable transformation of mere existence.

For the sake of human comprehension, God's word, expressed throughout existence, must be repeatedly parsed and clarified. God's ways (of expression) are manifestly not our ways (of understanding): for what ineffably vibrates in the divine depths is "wholly other" than any or all mortal pronouncements. Hence one must be mindful of the hermeneutical dialectic between *tohu* (the "all-inchoate potential" of world entities) and *tohe* (the "sudden sense of wonder"), between *bohu* (the "ineffable intermixture of things") and *bo-hu* (the perception of an "inherent or actual meaning"). The meanings construed thus turn on a hermeneutical axis, ever concordant with our creative capacities, and constitute our world-effecting will, renewed each day. As the prophet intoned, "[God] did not create [the world] for *tohu*, but formed it to be inhabited" (Isaiah 45:18), as a human reality, through exegetical enactments or achievements. Cognitively correlated with the primordial divine creativity, human interpreters are cocreators of earthly sense and significance. We give meaning to the God-given spectrum of worldly possibility, but God's creativity is the meaning that makes human meaning possible—however contingent or elusive this may be. The scriptural word *yehi* betokens the promise of possibilities: that creativity lies at the heart of existence; that what "is" is not all that can or might be. The numinous is not only a feature of the ineffable and intractable. It impacts the effable as well, through the wonders of making sense. God's ever-new proclamation of *yehi* (a key word of the creation narrative) silently prophesies this eventuality. We must learn to hear it for the potentialities inherent in creation—waiting to be fulfilled through our hermeneutical engagement.

A Philosophical Reflection

The initiation of perception and the birth of insight are not yet objects of consciousness. They hover between the naught-"not-yet" and the aught-"ought" of whatever comes to mind. Precisely here is the catalyst of creativity. It participates in every generative act of thought, but is stultified by every closure of the human spirit. The core of this revelatory moment is the opening to wonder. As an incipient experience, cognition naturally tries to name it. But this impulse must be resisted. For the sake of the God-given mystery of existence, all that may properly abide in consciousness is the initial sense that this opening of awareness expresses the sacred mystery of whatever "shall be" (or come to mind) in our human world. Simultaneously, a sense of futurity is born in this primary moment of happening—when the human sense of possibility (the spirit of "shall be") becomes part of the divine "Shall Be" coursing through life. Inevitably, human acts of naming and specification are after the fact (of experience), and mark the realities we project forward in time, as participants in the swirling flow of existence. There *was bohu*; but now there *is* (or shall be) something more: an inhabited, hermeneutical reality! The creative word cleaves the inchoate into articulate shape—the shapes of human significance and meaning.

Hermeneutical Discernment

The recurrent conjunction between the primordial structures of existence and our hermeneutical percepts reflects our attempts to interpret the all-creative voice of God—expressed in and through all the entities of world-being. But where in this primordial realm may we humans find regulative guidance? Are we completely at the mercy of happenstance or intuition, without any certain measures to guide us here in this "our interpreted world"? Who or what stays our hand as we construct meanings or name the shapes of existence?

In the light of our hermeneutical freedom we must hope to discern the nature of things and ascertain reality as best we can. As positioned beings, we can hardly stand at all places at the same time. We repeatedly shift our stance and accumulate experience. To go to "the things themselves" is not to perceive the full spectrum of things at one glance; we must rather rely on experiences and memories that are stored in mind. These help "round out" the limits of perception. Grounded in the natural world, we are involved in a lifelong process of conditioned understanding, as we move repeatedly from the known to the unknown, from part to whole. But even when we rely on conventional or acculturated percepts, we yearn to perceive something of the deeper actuality of things—something of their inherent truth—to guide our vision and judgment. Artists like Cézanne have formulated this longing. Attentive to the deeper alignment or lineation of things, he once said: "I would like to paint space and time so that they become forms of color sensibility. . . . Nature isn't at the surface; it's in depth [*profondeur*]. Colors . . . rise up out of the earth's roots: they're its life." Klee, through his singular vision, turned nature's shapes into the semiotic architecture and deep structure of our phenomenal world. By virtue of his art, we are inspired to experience anew—and in new forms—the bounty of reality. Seeing surface and depth may guide our hand and help regulate our lives through a more penetrating worldly wisdom.

These painters return us to the mystery of line and light, and the colors and contours so often concealed from our everyday mind. Their achievements remind us of our hermeneutical responsibilities: to heed the primary shapes of the life-forms we encounter, and to call them to mind. What, then, guides our hand? It is both God's ever-present revelation of the world—in all its spectacular and imposing vitality; and human hermeneutical freedom—ever representing new perceptions of existence through dispositions and acts. Longing for meaning, we are participants in the creation, but limited by the finite refractions of our human spirit. Two factors may guide our way: God's all-creative forms and our creatively constructed content.

Put theoretically, we never escape the hermeneutical circle of possibilities, requiring ongoing determinations for our life. God's gift of existence must be lived to be discerned—a hermeneutical evaluation of parts and wholes. Bound to a covenant with divine creation, the yes and no of events reveal their truth and demands to the attentive heart. These, in turn, are refined by tradition and reformulated for the sake of social life and higher spiritual purposes.

Toward a Hermeneutical Peshat-Consciousness: First Considerations

Hermeneutical theology seeks to receive the world—as infinite evocations of "divine speech"—with an attuned awareness. It attends to all the mute or physically expressive elements of existence, and transforms them into literary figures. Several notable formulations occur in scripture. Of paradigmatic significance is the creation narrative in Genesis 1, which may be deemed a primary account of our hermeneutical situation—wherein we repeatedly receive the stimuli of existence (God's Infinite Torah) and reformulate them into meaningful and taxonomic expressions. Through names or verbal adjectives we designate and classify experiences. Evocatively, the world is given new reality, daily. In this way, Genesis 1 articulates the ever-new rebirth of the world through language. It presents a liturgy of the divine word that constitutes the world in all its bounty. Concealing the speaking voice throughout, this old narrative formulates the world and existence as wrought from formative divine enunciations (repeatedly annotated as

"good"). Creation is thus portrayed as a set series of divine evocations—
whereby word and its designated being are dynamically correlated with
one another, and not mere approximations or representations of the actual
nature of things. This verbal conjunction accords with a primary human
sensibility (we speak and things happen), and reinforces the theological
sense that the God-given world expresses God-given creative intentions,
whose character can be named and specified.

Other scriptural theologies formulate this "word-voice" in quite different terms—by focusing on our experience of its creative reality or power.
Among these cases Psalm 29 is especially striking, since its contents are
structured around a sevenfold declaration of the "voice of the Lord" (or *qol
Y-H-W-H*). For the psalmist, these references to the divine "voice" depict
some of the potencies of Divinity effectuating worldly existence. The *qol* of
the Lord is both a shattering resonance that resounds upon "the waters" and
"primordial deep," as a thunderous clap, and a primordial *koah*—"power"
and "potential," or *hadar*—the "glory" or "aura" that qualifies all beings.
In addition, God's *qol* is depicted as the force that "shatters the cedars"
with "flashes" of "fire" and roils the "desert" in "travail," "causing calves to
birth." As a multivalent mode, the divine "voice" induces both natural terror
and the numinous sense of "divine glory." It is an awesome force in every
sense: neither a voice domesticated for human use nor a word imparted
for instruction. The *qol Y-H-W-H* just is. As a theological event, it is the
natural-phenomenal impression of a supernal reality breaking into human
consciousness. Hence the *qol* requires spiritual "strength" (*'oz*) to sustain its
transcendent impact, without trying to give it human meaning. Formulated
as a paean of power, Psalm 29 may awaken the theological sensibility of its
readers or reciters, and reorient them to the overwhelming divine voice of
creation. In this way, the psalm opens the heart to the manifestations of God
throughout the natural order: manifestations experienced by the religious
imagination and formulated through the poetics of language. As a theological construct, it brings something of the Infinite Torah to conscious form
and expression. The psalm enunciates a theology of experience wherein the
voice of God impacts and redirects our sensibilities. Something opens our
mouth and we speak.

Another biblical theologian tried to articulate the spiritual character of
this voice, and by doing so invoked a new hermeneutic principle. Com-
menting on the thunder and storm that swirled around the prophet Elijah
(in 1 Kings 19), a voice states (in something like a narrative voice-over) that
the Lord was not "in" any of these natural phenomena. Rather, "after" these
natural powers expressed their numinous force, a *qol demamah daqah*, "a
qol of resonant silence," was perceived: and just this vibration is said to truly

attest to the reality of the divine "voice" just experienced. This paradoxical formulation gives the experience an ex post facto theological explication. For according to this account, the divine voice is not hearable as such within the natural phenomena, but leaves the trace of an ineffable mystery, a spiritual echo of the awesome experience. We are thus not relieved of our fundamental hermeneutic situation, but are forced to realize that even primary religious experiences require interpretation, secondary reconstruction of the traces they induce. The physical storm is a "natural" event that reveals to an attuned consciousness some hints of the sublimity of God. The formulation of a "resonant silence" pushes theological consciousness to the borders of the effable, where the transcendence of God's actuality "touches but does not touch" human cognitive sensibility. God's voice generates, but does not constitute, worldly phenomena. We can attest to this truth (as does Elijah) only from within our conditioned human endowment. We witness it through the limits of human experience, but not more. Expressive nature conceals a divine mystery for the attuned spirit. We must hear with a heightened supernatural sensibility. The linguistic expressions that produce new spiritual meanings are fonts of theological hermeneutics. Holy texts collect and canonize them for later generations. They are cultural testimonies of a sacred event.

Living with hermeneutic "after-effects" requires the courage of steadfastness. There is a danger of misguided interpretations whenever we try to explain events through the lens of personal proclivity and self-interest. If we align our experience with prior mental ratios, the shapes of the divine voice will be become figures of our mortal minds, images of the human desire to know or determine the unknowable. And then we have lost doubly; we have lost the living God and betrayed our spiritual freedom.

Can we hope for more? Can we learn from some concrete biblical cases? Hermeneutical theology is marked by hearing and doing—by lived responses to the divine evocations of existence *before* they are fully comprehended. Cultural memory has collected exemplary scriptural instances for spiritual edification—canonical types filtered through the generations. These may help guide our way. They do not reveal the depths of nature, but rather the call of destiny to which the self must respond. In scripture, this summons is sensed as the voice of God. It is the call to decision and the demand of choice; it is a revelation requiring response. "Behold, I have placed before you this day blessing and curse; the blessing if you hear the commandments of *Y-H-W-H*, your God" (Deuteronomy 11:26–27). Said R. Yitzḥak Meir of Gur, the blessing is the ability to hear the call of the divine voice each day: to behold what is near at hand, and to decide rightly.

Further Considerations: Learning from Spiritual Exemplars

Scripture is a cultural resource that provides multiple paradigms of human responses to the divine "Torah-before-Sinai." Unique in their particularity, these cases are not so much instances to be imitated—given the events and individuals involved—as models for spiritual or edifying instruction. As written, they present specific typologies for how principal ancestors perceived and responded to God's summons. The occasions run the phenomenological gamut: from a directing voice sensed at a key juncture in one's personal life to an attunement to a sudden social event, from the pathos of a heart-wrenching decision to occasions involving the capacity to perceive a mysterious moment and its challenges. These are situational components of the *peshat* theology of scripture. A contemporary *peshat* theology must access these cases and appropriate them in a different hermeneutical way: by noting the theological event at hand (between the God-given reality and the self), and intuiting correlative axial moments in one's life. Doing so, one must "bracket off" the specific historical occasion or event and analyze its spiritual structure and dynamics. The capacity to stand firm and connect oneself to the manifestations and demands of life—the occasions of God's all-effecting word—is a component of a contemporary theology of *peshat*. Attentive to such scriptural examples, we may be instructed in the demands of lived decision and commitment. Such a hermeneutical reception requires a new translation and appropriation of the terms and structures involved. Each reader must establish the valid parameters for their own time and place; and then the significance of the text may become personal.

The theological challenge is to become worthy of scripture through a robust (hermeneutical) engagement with its various exempla of spiritual living. Heeding them one may develop a new theological orientation: that human life is potentially present to the living voice of God, this being the call or command of the moment. The task, therefore, is to become "vigorous in strength . . . to heed the sound (*qol*) of God's word" (Psalm 103:20)—however it occurs. By reading the scriptural record closely, attuned to its dynamics and language, our ancestors may instruct us and point a new-old way into life.

The Summons of the Moment—and Acts of Spiritual Resolve

Avraham Aveinu (our ancestor Abraham) is the first personality to consider. He repeatedly demonstrates, through the events of daily life, how one may respond to claims made upon one's eyes, ears, and mind—and how to live, determinately, with the challenges. In the narrative cycles depicting these events, the theme-word *ra'ah* (to see) recurs with instructive emphasis. Of the seven episodes where this verb predominates, three are considered below. The first is a diptych of sorts—conjoining the death of Abraham's father (Genesis 11:32) to a new turn in his life. Inevitably, a genealogical rupture marks a caesura in one's psyche. In Abraham's case, this caesura conditions the possibility of a new spiritual direction. Suddenly a divine voice addresses him with the challenge, directing him to transcend the older, established traditions of family, culture, and homeland—and realize a new personal and religious destiny. Betwixt and between, Abraham finds himself in a liminal zone: between the tried and true, inculcated since his birth, and the as-yet-unknown manifested here as a promise. The challenge is pivotal, requiring discernment and decision. Nothing could have prepared him for this axial moment. God says: "Go from your land and your heritage and your ancestral home to the land that I shall show you (*are'eka*)" (Genesis 12:1). If these words orient Abraham toward a new future, they are without any certain direction. Their realization is embedded in a general and indeterminate promise. Futurity holds itself open, in anticipation of a promised event still to come. The promise entails risk and ongoing resolve.

The center of Abraham's consciousness is expectation and deferment. To realize his personal destiny, he must suspend the familiar past and trust the tasks now revealed to his mind—until its fulfillment be verified in due course ("Then the Lord appeared, *vayera'*, to Abram"; v. 7). The promise that is actualized through a divine appearance is marked by a ceremonial act: Abraham constructs an altar to the God "who had appeared, *ha-nir'ah*, to him" (v. 7). This consecrating act is less the sanctification of a specific place than his celebration of the completed promise. To live in expectation is therefore to live bound by an earlier decision, open to the future and in anticipation of validating clues. The inaugural moment is radical in every respect. Indeed, in the present case, even the initial imperative was not self-confirming (for the God who addressed Abraham was not the "god of his father" or his own God), and required trust in its stated possibilities. The fundamental tension is between a settled self and the challenge of the unknown. At any point, Abraham could have lapsed into lethargy or despair—no matter how far he had traveled in space and time. Steadfastness to a life-altering decision is both fragile and fateful. Abraham lives in suspension, but with inner resolve. He lives prospectively, as he goes from a known "here" (his homeland, his birthplace, and his paternal home) to an unknown "there" (the projected place of promise) in hopeful anticipation. His initial decision is carried into the future as the decisive aspect of subjective time. Profound trust in God's promise—based on no prior experience or validation—is the deep syntax of Abraham's life. His life offers a model of spiritual fortitude—of a life lived in deferment. It comprises the first textual example to bear in mind.

A second instance of spiritual resolve also occurs in the midst of life. On this occasion Abraham was sitting in Elonei Mamrei, after his circumcision and having received God's assurances of a blessed progeny. "Then the Lord appeared, *vayera'*, to him" (Genesis 18:1). The nature of the event is not further disclosed, and the reader may wonder, How does it relate to the immediate sequel, where we are told *vayar' ve-hinneh*, "he saw, and behold"—three persons passing nearby his home? The use of the term *hinneh* marks the suddenness of the occasion. We are left to speculate: Are there two events depicted here, or one? Is the appearance of God to Abraham an isolated (private) spiritual event, or does it mark the onset of a (self-transcending) consciousness that inspired Abraham to look and observe more attentively? The syntax offers some suggestions. Through its succession of verbs denoting seeing or appearance, there emerges a portrayal of increased awareness—of a capacity that opens the inner eye. The initial divine appearance sets the stage for the ensuing drama. At first glance Abraham only "saw" something happening; but then, with a jolt (signaled by the adverb *hinneh*), his perception sharpened, and he swiftly responded with direct action: *vayar' va-yaratz*, "he saw and ran" to the strangers (v. 2) and offered them hospitality (v. 4). Each statement of "seeing" occasions a new decision, as Abraham shifts from a mere onlooker to a decisive moral agent. This transformation of a social spectacle into one of singular ethical import is *not* characterized as a divine epiphany. Abraham did not know that one of the three messengers was an angel of God (Genesis 19:13, 33), or that his works of care and kindness would serve as a prelude to the divine annunciation of Isaac's birth. Nor could he know it. But just this act of social care marks his readiness to be a father and the bearer of national blessings; for although Abraham was still recuperating from his circumcision, he disregarded his subjective situation and responded to the moral tasks at hand. Just this spiritual thread unites the tableaux of this episode.

As compared with the first case, where Abraham is catalyzed by a "voice" of instruction, this one provides a different theological setting by syntactically joining the divine manifestation to Abraham's ensuing states of awareness. For after "the Lord appeared to him ... he (Abraham) raised his eyes, *and behold!—three men!*" We are left to infer that this appearance of God marks a shift of consciousness in the patriarch, and that his perception of worldly occurrences (the life conditions of an unconditional demand) *is* the full content of the hierophany. To be worthy of scripture is to allow this narrative event to address one's modern consciousness, and provide a model for one's theological life. To perceive life events as divine evocations *is* the spiritual matrix of this *peshat* theology. It is the sense that the call of worldly happening is the address of God—a divine imperative with the duty to respond. The Infinite Torah of God-given reality demands a corresponding human responsibility: to serve God in and through the conditions of everyday life, with a thoughtful heart of wisdom—to the degree possible and within the limits of human abilities. A true visibility (seeing with attentive regard) is a revelatory occasion. We are addressed.

A third episode of spiritual resolve occurs as Abraham's final test, when his long-awaited progeny was put in jeopardy by a demand for divine loyalty (Genesis 22). The challenge of religious integrity is portrayed as a life moment that must be borne, despite its incomprehensibility and uncompromising harshness. When this father was commanded to take his dear son and "go" to another place (this language notably replicates the initial command of spiritual destiny that transformed his life), the harsh instruction was unqualified, and the location of the event again not disclosed. Abraham thus carried both the dreadful commandment and the unspecified place within him in deafening silence, as he walked forward with his son. His psychic burden was twofold: to bear the weight of this specific knowledge (the sacrificial character of the demand) and the uncertain place of its realization (hence the place was, for all intents and purposes, lodged in his heart). In the course of this spiritual trial, the precise locale was eventually perceived; for in due time "he saw, *vayar'*, the place from afar" (Genesis 22:4). But in the interim Abraham affirmed his resolve with an inner prayer—spoken aloud as his halting assurance to his son's query about the absent lamb for slaughter. Abraham's response was that God would surely "show" (*yir'eh*) or provide the lamb for the sacrifice. Thus the place of the offering and the disclosure of the sacrificial lamb were fused in his mind: the first recalling the undisclosed place of his original pilgrimage (Genesis 12:1), the second embodying the hope that the promise of progeny would be fulfilled. With his firm trust in the guarantee of this commitment, Abraham attempted to complete this task, trying to hold in mind both his faith and his heartbreak. Caught in this double bind—and perhaps because of a decisive pang of compassion (perceived as an angelic voice that he withdraw his hand)—Abraham "raised his eyes" and "behold, a ram was seen" (*vayar' ve-hinneh ayil*) before him. He therefore called the site "The Lord will show" (*yir'eh*; v. 14), since this place-name revealed his absolute trust in God's directing voice, despite the awesome terror. Subsequent generations (and more pertinent for them) referred to this religious site with the saying "On the mountain the Lord will appear" (*yeira'eh*), this assertion being a proclamation of their faith in the manifestation of God's saving acts. With it, a new watchword of national resolve was inscribed into the original narrative of Abraham's trial—a hermeneutical addition of redemptive promise and hope.

Both dimensions present scriptural challenges for later generations. The first one narrates the destiny of a hero of faith, marking his concluding statement with words that highlight its integrity; the second reinterprets this terminology for later times. Perhaps individuals like Abraham perceive their lives as having some integral destiny (and that may explain his prayerful words to his son); or perhaps this final assertion of faith denotes the resolve of later readers, who revised their ancestor's life in terms of its exemplary significance for themselves. In either case, the term *ra'ah* (in its variant forms, *yir'eh* and *yeira'eh*) expresses a spiritual stance before the challenges of life. For Abraham and his heirs this is both an inner commitment (of their covenantal bond) and an outer responsiveness (to the events of the day). Theological conviction is a steadiness of resolve before the events of existence: a spiritual consciousness to be reaffirmed in the course of life, even in the shadow of the darkest mysteries.

But spiritual constancy is easier said than done. Obscurities, incoherence, or outright contradictions can cause a state of *behalah*, or "confusion." It is one thing to proclaim that God is "like a firm mountain"—providing stability and structure—when things go well or difficulties can be overcome. The statement may prove of little worth amid the terror of irresolution and inconsolable grief. It may then seem that God is hiding his face; and one feels bereft and "confused," *nivhal* (Psalm 30:9). Beset with physical or psychic suffering, some persons groan that their "soul is . . . distraught (*nivhalah*)" and plead to God to provide a healing explanation (Psalm 6:4–6). Adrift in despair, others confess: "When You (God) hide (*histarta*) Your face (all creatures) are bereft (*yibaheilun*)" (Psalm 104:29). Such a situation is spiritually precarious, and it requires a willful resolve to face existence with fortitude: to not "give birth to *behalah*" (Isaiah 65:23).

Living in time is living with perplexity. The natural risks of finitude are not resolved by decisive actions, but they do put one on a path of action. The task is to bind the conditions of one's life into a unifying deed, without clearly or decisively knowing the consequences. This is the challenge of human freedom. We cannot easily deny the life-shaping summons omnipresent in the occurrences of life. But we can ignore it. Through a firm response to the call of events, mere circumstance may become a revelatory moment; and then the anomie of *bohu* may yield a new or renewed creation.

An Exemplary Theological Event

In the extended time of "Torah-before-Sinai" there is another event of axial significance. It is a hierophany that fundamentally shapes personal and national destiny. That moment is the revelation experienced by Moses at the burning bush in the desert of Horeb (Exodus 3). It occurs within the ordinariness of life, when something exceptional fixates Moses's consciousness in a life-altering way. This episode has the character of a numinous event—not only because it overwhelms human awareness, but because the soul is transformed as well. Moses was tending his flock in the steppe land in a work-a-day stupor—and then it happened: "An angel of the Lord appeared (*vayera'*) to him in a blazing fire from the midst of a bush" (v. 2). This inaugural moment is reported in the sparest terms. Something wondrous was sensed at the edge of cognitive awareness, and had to be brought to consciousness to become epistemically "real." Just this was Moses's experience of the weird lure that unexpectedly attracted his eye: "He looked, and behold (*vayar' ve-hinneh*) there was a flaming bush; although the bush was not consumed." As the visual phenomenon begins to pervade Moses's mind, a radical shift occurs. He is no longer a mere bystander, but is drawn toward this exceptional attraction; and thus he turns to examine what was happening. "Moses said: Let me then turn aside (*asurah- na*) and see (*va-er'eh*) this awesome sight; for (he mused) why isn't the bush consumed?" (v. 3). Through the wonderment, he perceived "something there."

The narration discloses the man's thoughts while viewing this strange vision. The personal intentionality and decision involved are conveyed by a small addition to the verbal phrase "Let me then turn aside"—notably the suffix *-na*, "then." This formulation (the jussive construction plus the suffix) signals the change of Moses's focus: there is both an inner exhortation to action and a marker of the key temporal change ("then"). This rupture of his fugue state is conveyed by a sudden sense of a numinous moment cleaving the phenomenal plane of nature—a caesura effecting a change of lived destiny. Something external beckons and the will accedes. There is a sudden summons to cognitive attention, and then a spiritual shift.

This brings us to the heart of *peshat* theology.

Two Divine Disclosures

This numinous event conveys a perception of divine agency and presence. Initially, the fiery manifestation is called an "angel of the Lord" (Exodus 3:2); but subsequently, when Moses turned to examine this happening, we are informed that "God" summoned the man and disclosed his spiritual genealogy: "I am (*anokhi*) the God of your father, the God of Abraham, the God of Isaac, and the God of Jacob" (v. 6). Thus, at the outset, something was first perceived as infused with a mysterious valence (the "angel" is the "fiery" figure that evokes this sense); and then, from within this perception, a divine voice speaks and links the person to a chain of ancestors. This is a decisive turn in Moses's personal history, and it also inaugurates an axial moment in biblical religious history—for now Moses's family genealogy is less signifi- cant than the new spiritual genealogy to which he is heir. This moment of "being called" is profoundly revelatory. Natural time and the bond of gen- erations are subordinated to religious time and the destiny it demands. One does not choose one's birth or family: they are given; but one may choose to accept the rebirth that marks a turning point in one's biographical course. This moment of spiritual decision is the challenge Moses perceives in God's voice, and he trembles in terror. Expressing his doubts and confusion, he then hears God say: "I shall be (*eheyeh*) with you" (v. 12)—conveying that God's reality, the divine "I," will be "with" Moses as the spiritual guide of his own "I" as he faces the task of being a messenger. Addressed as "you," Moses is bidden to trust in the identity he must assume for the nation. To confirm their bond, God tells him that the Divine Name to be divulged to the people is *Eheyeh*—a Name that may give them a new spiritual strength, by conveying God's promise to participate in the events of their existence. This holy Name—of a God called "I shall be"—doesn't convey the exact manner of divine providence. But it does guarantee God's personal actual- ity. It is a personal voice of promise: a divine promise of futurity.

There is another way this Divine Name is expressed to Moses, and it marks a deepening of the spiritual consciousness just specified. For if the Name *Eheyeh* is a concession to the people's desire to know who calls them to freedom, it is only a shortened version of the full name-formula, *Eheyeh- asher-Eheyeh* ("I shall be as I shall be"; v. 14), a phrase that connotes a more transcendent divine dimension. If the Divine Name *Eheyeh* expresses a promise of personal presence, but without any specification of time or place, the full Name conveys a far more imponderable divine will, and requires stronger spiritual resolve (to attend to a God who shall be as he shall be exceeds all human understanding of the modes or nature of divine inter- ventions in history). And if the shorter Name (given to the people) conveys both certitude and assertion ("I shall be" is an oath-like asseveration), the longer one conveys absolute divine freedom, and thus anticipates the Tetra- gram revealed to Moses alone. For God is not then named the "God of the ancestors," called *El Shaddai*, but is now self-disclosed by the unique Name *Y-H-W-H* (Exodus 6:1–2).

A Hermeneutics of the Divine Names

What could Moses, or anyone, understand by this nomenclature? What is the world-effecting truth named here; and what is its hermeneutical import for a *peshat* theology? How can these Divine Names deepen and redirect a theological consciousness? We may ponder the following considerations.

If the Name *Eheyeh* betokens a personal divine presence, the "I shall be" of theological promise, the Name *Y-H-W-H* evokes a transcendent and impersonal divine agency, and means "It Shall Be" or "Let It Be." Such a divine agency is repeatedly evoked by the evocative verbal form *yehi* (let there be) in Genesis 1, where it repeatedly introduces events of God's creative effectuality. However, the fully "verbalized nominalization" is only conveyed by the unique Name *Y-H-W-H*—the ineffable symbol of ever-effectuating divine providence. That is possibly why the tradition about the two Divine Names conveyed to the people added, like a postscript, the supplementary formulation. For Moses was also told to inform the nation that the God named *Y-H-W-H* is the self-same "God of the ancestors" (Exodus 3:15), and that "*this*" will be the "Eternal Name" of their God "for all generations." Hence in this disclosure God is depicted both as an imponderable, transcendent mystery and as a personal actuality that will be present as the "Liberator" of the nation (thereby fulfilling his promises to the patriarchal ancestors). The disclosure of these Divine Names is a revelation of this twofold theological truth. They are verbal names without stated conditions of presence or meaning. They are Names of an ineffable divine freedom: the bounty of world-happening and its varieties, to which human creatures must bow in assent. The two Names evoke the primordial effectuality of Divinity in world-being (as intuited or abstracted from concrete experience—God as impersonal transcendence), and the diversity of the present actuality of God (as sensed or lived in the life moment—God as an effective, personal reality).

This interface between absolute transcendence and temporal immanence puts *peshat* theology on a new course. It is an insight that also compels assent to our contemporary mind. Put differently, the two Divine Names ground our theological orientation to all facets of experience, manifest and hidden. To be sure, we remain within the limits of our hermeneutic constructions; but heeding the truth of this teaching, we need no longer experience our existence in a routine manner. Through the conceptual frame of these Names, the life-world is now perceived as a bounty of vital presences: revelations of all that "shall be" given to our mortal minds. There is no place empty of God's all-infusing reality, although the tablets of its worldly meaning or value are given into our (hermeneutic) hands. According to the "hearing" of the divine voice is the "doing" of its infinite truth. This is the theological challenge.

The Divine Names and the Event at Sinai

The two Divine Names conveyed to Moses at the bush (*sneh*) reverberate in the divine proclamation of the Decalogue at Sinai (*sinai*)—addressed to the nation as whole. (And from the perspective of *peshat* theology this connotes a shift from religious experience to its social implementation.) At the first event (the bush), God is named both *Y-H-W-H* and *Eheyeh-asher-Eheyeh* (Exodus 3:14–15)—where the second name functions as a historical epithet of the first, indicating that God will be present in historical time. At the latter event (Sinai), God proclaims that "I am *Y-H-W-H*, your God, who (*asher*) took you out of the land of Egypt, from out of the house of bondage" (Exodus 20:2). This declaration joins the unique Name *Y-H-W-H* to an explication of the character of a historical event: the absolutely imponderable Divinity, *Y-H-W-H*, has become present in history as the living God "who (*asher*)" redeemed Israel. The relative pronoun *asher* in the Name *Eheyeh-asher-Eheyeh* now specifies God's act of liberation. Thus, through this combined pronouncement, all the people are informed that God's impersonal actuality (or transcendence) became manifest as a personal providence (worldly immanence). God is both a hidden, transcendent reality and a manifest, historical effectuality. As a divine self-disclosure, this serves as the central teaching of *peshat* theology. Through Moses (his personal experience and articulations) it is conveyed to public consciousness; and through public consciousness it finds expression in covenantal beliefs and social regulations. *Peshat* theology (grounded on scriptural examples) thus highlights a fundamental link between metaphysical insight and human action.

*

The two opening enunciations of the Decalogue, "I am *Y-H-W-H*, your God" and "You shall have no other gods besides Me," are theologically linked, since they are the only ones spoken by the divine voice alone, without a human intermediation (Exodus 20:2–3). On this basis, some medieval commentators deduced correlative consequences. According to Maimonides, the initial two commandments, directly from God alone, convey a philosophical truth—namely, that God's ineffable existence (or reality) and an absolute dedication to this reality are a twofold religious imperative that may be grasped directly by human cognition. That is, through natural understanding and logical deduction, the first two norms may be readily apprehended by the human mind (the gift of divine reason). They are thus distinct from the ensuing commandments, which are mediated through the voice of Moses. Reformulating this in contemporary theological terms, we may say that the experiential realization of God's world-effective presence (expressed in scripture through God's providential beneficence in nature and history) may be internalized as a life-altering truth that elicits both exclusive loyalty and devoted commitment. Or, put differently, experiencing in a direct way the effectuating presence of God, a revelation in history, one will acknowledge this reality (as an existential truth), and commit oneself to its ensuing obligations (as an act of personal affirmation). This nexus of pivotal experience and expressive deed sets forth the concrete basis for a peshat theology, lived in the factuality of the everyday. The norms promulgated in the Decalogue and Covenant Code are a foundational expression of this ideal. Hermeneutical theology keeps its concerns vital, through appropriate clarifications and creative appropriations.

Spiritual-Social Implications

The Sinaitic proclamation ("I am *Y-H-W-H* ... who") inaugurates the people as a collectivity into the theological mystery and challenge of the Divine Names—the mystery of revelation in the here and now of existence, and its daily existential challenges. For if at the bush Moses was initiated into a new personal destiny (and the narrative offers a model for the renewal of individual spiritual consciousness), now at Sinai all are called to theological responsibility and social care. There are two significant consequences for a living community: positive and negative. The positive consequence is to "affirm" and support the diverse character of the social order, whereas the negative one is to "limit" or restrain abuses of this diversity. To preserve the distinctiveness of individual differences, persons must actualize the forms and conditions of social life on their own terms—and not let self-interest or prejudice impede the ideal. Power and privilege must be harnessed for the public good; and human freedom must be protected as a fundamental right. This is not a social summons dependent on goodwill alone, but rather a call for law and justice. In response, legal rules and norms developed over centuries of communal life, and were formulated to implement the core truth of the two Divine Names (God as provident Giver of life and liberty) through the wisdom of those sanctioned to speak in God's Name. For ancient Israel and its heirs, Moses is such a figure. But since these two Names were also conveyed to the people, they are also empowered to proclaim the sovereignty of God and to take responsible care for all God's creations. These are interrelated implications of a *peshat* theology. They reflect a Joban consciousness of God-induced reverential care, formulated here for a particular community.

As noted, the two initial proclamations are theologically distinct from the other norms in the Decalogue and the ensuing legal statutes, since the latter are given through the human voice of Moses. This crucial difference marks their mediated and time-bound character. Evidence for this is attested in the biblical regulations themselves, which are formulated in the language and style of ancient Near Eastern legal codes—for example, the repeated use of the condition-result clause "if . . . then" to express hypothetical social cases that share common legal situations. The changing, temporal character of these topics is also attested in scripture, notably in the many instances that show how specific legal details were both "explicated" and reformulated in new life conditions—Moses's own didactic articulation of older statutes in the book of Deuteronomy is evidence for this pedagogical and cultural necessity. These adjustments dramatize the creative implementation of the general norms from the outset, and their use as precedents for ongoing adjudications. Over time, the words of the living oral tradition were incorporated into the authoritative "voice of Moses"; and these clarifications were similarly authorized. Altogether, the legal statutes and norms provide the culture (and its judiciary) with a matrix of binding cases—as ratified or explained by its leaders. Their public endorsement through popular acclamation ("We shall do and we shall hear"; Exodus 24:7) duly establishes the social-legal foundations for succeeding generations, and insures the ideals of *social care and restraint* in concrete terms. As the deep structures of the covenant, "life" and "limit" are its co-regulating theological principles. The Divine Names are their warrant.

The theological foundation for the successive legal instructions is the "Great Voice" (*qol gadol*) of Sinai, which "continues" to resound (Deuteronomy 5:22) across all generations. This verbal trope offers a deeper theological dimension to the creative divine words coming to expression in the world. All creatures bear traces of these divine events through the life and norms that they enact. For those who bear the covenant of Israel, Sinai is an axial moment in this universal process, for it is here that the life-empowering words of God achieved their formative social expression. As founding legal specifications, they articulate both the foundational structures and the imperatives to enact in all orders of life the living presence of God—denominated by the two Names *Y-H-W-H* and *Eheyeh*. Manifesting the essential human truths of liberty and dignity, the covenant legislation of Moses and his disciples provides the basic legal models for their implementation. These norms are not ideal juristic abstractions, but the concrete refractions of the divine principles of creative being—responsive to the conditions of life. Living in this way opens a vector toward the future and the social shape of redemption.

The Covenantal Challenge

Everywhere and always, God's creative effectuality vitalizes all beings and happenings. All creatures participate in the intersecting structures of life, and all find expression through the rules or norms that express their nature. Over time, fixed patterns and formal regulations emerge to protect individuals and groups in different situations. These statutes express settled ways of dealing with typical behaviors so that new circumstances can be dealt with in an ordered and normative manner. These rules also try to regulate actions before an event, or reassess them afterward. Overall, these norms are impersonal and formulated for the society as a whole, whereas the personal instructions (religious or civil) reflect more immediate situations of instruction. For example, the Decalogue reflects the immediacy of a direct legal address, when the nation was personally instructed, whereas the several legal codes (Exodus 21–24; Leviticus 18–25; Deuteronomy 12–26) feature more impartial formulations, for the sake of civic equity and its common social purposes.

The two types of legal formulation have their distinctive stylistics: personal imperatives, in the first case; impersonal provisions, in the other. Insofar as both biblical types mediate the speaking divine voice, they present religious legislation as a "saying" directed to one's social mind and body—instructing the polity how to think and act in general and particular. If such a presenting voice goes stale and formal, it devolves into a "said," something fixed and normative at best. Now the "word" becomes "words," and the situations of life no longer engage theological attention. We forget that Y-H-W-H is *Eheyeh-asher-Eheyeh*—and that the divine effectivity may be present in the here and now, in all the ways that it may be there.

The theological challenge is to be attentive to the manifestations of *Eheyeh* in the world, and to respond with a spiritual disposition. This involves a deliberate pause amid the flow of events so that one may receive events with a focused mind. This pause is a recollection of one's creaturely constitution. It is ritualized weekly through Sabbath rest. This is both a physical cessation of all worldly labors *and* a consciousness of one's fragile finitude. Two legal paradigms clarify these mental states. The first proclaims that on the Sabbath persons must abstain from all labor and give rest to their entire household: the immediate family, all those that serve, and one's livestock. Especially notable is the addition of the "stranger" (*ger*), the needy and homeless other—"because God created the heaven and earth, and rested on the seventh day" (Exodus 20:8–11). Hence the Sabbath day is an occasion that sanctifies existence as such, in all its variety, and may thereby refocus one's mind on its creaturely nature. This awareness has interpersonal and social consequences, since it may cultivate a disposition of care for all existence.

"Because you were slaves in the land of Egypt and the Lord, your God, took you out from there" (Deuteronomy 5:12–15) is the second motivation for Sabbath rest. This formulation shifts from the creation to a historical event of freedom—a divine benefaction that must be ritually enacted so that concern for the dignity of life (and liberation from oppression) may be uppermost in one's mind. This is more than a concern for the dignity of all existents, grounded in the distinctiveness of all life. It is rather a compassion for earthly suffering in all its forms, as a result of realizing one's commonality with other life-forms and dependence upon other creatures for one's social existence. This is a consequence of having experienced exploitation and dependence in one's life and history. Inculcating this reality ritually on the Sabbath day may extend to mindfulness of this consideration in all one's acts and relationships during the week.

The motivation for social care is built upon a recognition of the finitude of all creatures (particular expressions of the creative effectuality of *Y-H-W-H*), and a corresponding sympathy for the vulnerability of all mortal beings (earthly refractions of *Eheyeh-asher-Eheyeh*). The *ger* (stranger) is an exemplar of our fragile humanity—dependent and in need, and the value of being constantly mindful of this condition. This requires us to stress the scriptural obligation to enact creature care. The *ger* may not be oppressed, "because you know the soul of a *ger*—for you were *gerim* in the land of Egypt" (Exodus 23:9); you shall not abuse or disenfranchise the *ger*, "but shall let him live as a native . . . and love him like yourself (*kamokha*)— for you, too, were *gerim* in the land of Egypt" (Leviticus 19:33); and "you shall not subvert the rights of the *ger* . . . but shall remember that you were a slave in Egypt and the Lord redeemed you from there; therefore I enjoin you to perform this commandment. . . . You shall love the *ger*, for you were *gerim* in their land" (Deuteronomy 10:17–10). Historical experiences therefore help to condition consciousness of human vulnerability and the need for an ethical response.

But the issue goes further still since the *ger* is no mere "other," but truly "like" oneself: a co-itinerant on earth; a fellow "*ger* in the land of the living" (Psalm 119:19). This contingency is our primary existential reality. Hence one self and the other are the same: not just socially similar (each one being "like" the other), but fundamentally alike. To recognize one's creaturely needs is to be cognizant of the interdependence of all persons. This primary awareness is a "*ger*-consciousness." Within this mindset, an individual is addressed by God, *Eheyeh-asher-Eheyeh*, and summoned to be ethically attentive to what is happening in the here and now—for all persons, near and far.

The Sabbath-consciousness of care for all creatures (linked to the creation and the exodus) inculcates a pause of conscience for all beings striving to subsist. Recognition of being *'afar va-eifer* must take all creatures into account—including the mute beasts and silenced poor. A Sabbath-consciousness may thus "release" or "liberate" the normal mindset of the everyday world—one that treats others through cognitive control, emotional disregard, and brutish physical power. Interposing a pause within one's ordinary outlook may help cultivate the virtue of restraint, and limit self-centered constructs of the other. This pause is an acknowledgment of the value of other creatures and a realization of the degree to which one's mindset can condition their perceived worth. This epistemic factor cuts deeper and sponsors awareness of our fundamental hermeneutic condition (that we know the world as we interpret it)—this being yet another aspect of our fragile finitude. With this we come full circle, and return to a *peshat* theology of creation.

A Peshat *Theology of Creation*

The structure of world-being articulated at the beginning of scripture (in Genesis 1) attests to a natural stance whose orientation correlates with a human-centered standpoint. The sky is above, with rain clouds and solar bodies; the earth is below, with grasses and trees for food; and the oceans lie at the margins of the land, and descend to unfathomable depths. Throughout the existent world there is a diversity of creatures: birds in flight, animals grazing, and fish in schools; and moving between these realms are reptiles or mixed types. All these creatures mate after their kind, with food procured by hook or crook for survival. Even the seeds on earth spawn according to their type and kind, filling the earth with vegetation of sundry types. As portrayed, the different parts of this world-order serve the human species most particularly—those designated their overlord, and bidden to cultivate life for their personal necessity. Being part of this whole, humankind has a natural perspective. This is a first-order human orientation. Yet it includes a second-order conceptual structure at the same time, since the narrative reflects the hermeneutical imperative of our existence: that we must conceive and interpret the primordially given (*tohu-bohu*) of the world according to human values and thought. A human being is ever in the midst of things, with hermeneutic assessments of their myriad possibilities presenting themselves to consciousness. At first, reality was just an inchoate play of elements, but it becomes, with hermeneutical insight and probity, something evaluated and named—newly realized in human terms. Humans are thus active participants in the life-work of creation. Through their interpretative acts and creativity they are in the image of the Creator. Hence a *peshat* theology acknowledges that the lived world is from the beginning a hermeneutical event; and this renders it a new creation, each day, for human life.

Peshat: *The Cycle of Life*

We are grounded in the natural world, the humus of our existence. It is to life on the earth that we are given, in bodily fragility; and it is to the earth that we return, in physical finitude. We therefore turn on this sphere to find our orientation and perspective: for receiving and sorting, responding and initiating. Feeling the vitality of things, we are joined to them; and giving ourselves to things, they are conjoined to our life-world and destiny. The earth and sky give us the basic values of sustenance and support, and the spiritual values of humility and magnitude. Attentive to sequence and consequence, we deduce what is positive or not in our lives, and pass this on as a living tradition. The God-given world is our primary teacher: we receive its instructions insofar as we can interpret them. Called to attention and wonder, the world beckons our speech; and by responding, through language, we extend the horizons of our experience and understanding. Thus the natural is the ground for the spiritual. Through it, we are opened to transcendence.

The world is a vast interplay of forces. Only through our hermeneutical acts do we give it meaning, creating forms of consciousness and life. We look to others and their inherited wisdom to help us extend what we may see and do, and to teach us how to comport ourselves on the earth. Scripture offers just such a resource—refracting generations of responses to the natural order and its spiritual stimuli, and formulating instances of model behaviors and experiences. Because our goodwill may be blocked by misdirected desire, and our beneficent eye may be blinded by selfishness or misprision, the teachings of tradition can help us rebalance our values and focus. Thus do the written and oral collections expand our spiritual horizons and help us to realize how much we are constituted by them. New situations may stimulate a revaluation of settled laws and values, and promote a renewed spiritual consciousness. Are we alert to these moments, and do we know how to interpret them? Or do the events pass by in a routine manner, cut in the grooves of old or alien formulations? Much as new perceptions of the natural world require new articulations in a viable vernacular, so do the scriptural traditions. For even if the narratives of the *peshat* "make sense," they often require a spiritual translation to be duly appropriated for our contemporary consciousness. The ultimate goal is to recover a new theological language grounded in first-order natural experiences, but personally perceived in light of the all-effectuating and pervasive divine reality. This biblical reshaping of an engaged theological consciousness is the hermeneutical sphere of *peshat*, as it has been reconstituted here. It provides the foundation for the massive exegetical reinterpretation of its terms and principles in later rabbinic *derash*—the expressive foundation for Jewish theology over the ages. In the hands of its inheritors, scripture is the "Great Voice" (*qol gadol*)—funneling divine depositions (of law and life) from generation to generation.

Hermeneutics is the active instrument for all these developments. It arises from the seeking spirit of our mortal selves—passing between ourselves and world events, human and natural. But this yearning may correspondingly fail or falter on account of our human nature, with its vagaries of thought and impulse. Looking to the heavens above or scripture near at hand, those in search of a heart of wisdom try to attune their interpretations to God's service—to think and act wholeheartedly in the everyday. The challenge is to be faithful to the bounties of existence, which address our consciousness at all times: to respond to the voice of God, as it is and shall be. Cultivating one's personal *eheyeh* (I shall be) is therefore the spiritual task of all responsive living in the image of God. It is the pivot and fulcrum of a *peshat* theology.

Interlude Two

From Peshat *to* Derash—*Continuity and Difference*

We live on several planes of experience. First and foremost, we are *mortal creatures* of the world. We belong to it for our physical sustenance and nurture, as well as for spiritual values and projects. The earth provides the "tree of life," from whose fruit we sustain our bodies; and it produces the "tree of knowledge," from whose resources we gather information and create works of culture. Our nurture begins with familial bonds, the primary context of welfare and care, and enhanced through traditional instructions, from the chain of generations and its values. We never abandon these natural needs and endowments, but we may transform them in various ways. Food may be eaten alone, together with friends, or also shared with the needy—since tradition cultivates values that transcend self-interest. Thus, if the imperatives for personal satisfaction are grounded in our physical nature, traits of generosity are virtues cultivated for spiritual enhancement. Focused on primary concerns, one may only perceive the external nature of things, or stress the surface of experience. By contrast, a theological consciousness tries to see further, and to direct focus on the mystery of events, and their claims on our moral and religious imagination. Theology perceives physical and social phenomena, alert to the ways God may address us. It is a spiritual disposition attuned to divine transcendence. Reverence for the plenitude of life may induce awe before God and care for the creation. Similarly, religious texts may inspire new responsibilities for our fellow creatures and concern for their existence. We designated this orientation and mode of consciousness "*peshat* theology." It is grounded in our primary life reality, and constitutes our earthbound gravity from birth to death.

But we may also choose to live within *religious communities* that extend our human nature in time and space, and provide spiritual resources of generations past and present. Nothing of the primary ground of life experience is lost here, but it is now transformed by new (collective) forms of expression and understanding. For Jewish life and theology this shift means being part of an interpretative tradition that extends the values of scripture across the centuries, and being part of a millennial web of religious thought and practice. This social-spiritual genealogy transforms our natural-social being fundamentally. If the primary locus of family teachings is the home, between parent and child, and its central concern is physical and ethical domestication, under the aegis of a religious tradition this is given distinctive form: a scriptural and cultural tradition transmitted in schools from teacher to pupil. The intimacy of familial instructions is now complemented (or exceeded) by the public expression of religious values cultivated through a multigenerational hermeneutical achievement. Significant consequences follow. One's individual pedigree is not limited to an inherited or natural endowment, but achieved by learning the body of tradition and its special teachings. This latter is not a closed sum of privileged information, but an open colloquy—across the generations—concerning possible interpretations and behavior. For Jewish thought and practice the foundations of this traditional, exegetical culture comprise the "Written Torah" (or *torah she-bikhtav*) and its massive hermeneutical scaffolding, denoted as the "Oral Torah" (*torah she-be'al peh*). The latter embraces the totality of tradition, since written scripture is intellectually understood and appropriated through the prisms of rabbinic language, lore and creativity. The two constitute the authoritative streams from which the tributaries of Jewish religious life derive. Central to this hermeneutical praxis is the creativity of teachers and their disciples across the millennia. Those who aspire to accept their mantle are the agents of this ongoing process of learning and living. Tradition is the spiritual shaping of a community, and the molding of a shared religious destiny. One and all are bidden to become responsible for the continuity of the past, for the actuality of the present, and for the creative integrity of the future.

As a founding moment in early Judaism, rabbinic sages authorized a fixed anthology of "Holy Writings" (*kitvei qodesh*)—the canonical corpus of sacred scripture (the *torah she-bikhtav*) to or from which nothing could be added or subtracted. A crucial consequence of this religious event was that many of the rules and norms of scripture were insufficiently explicated, and a number of common life situations were not formalized in writing. These issues required deliberation or clarification so that the Torah could be applied to all social and spiritual conditions. Wherever the tradition explicated legal lacunae or difficult and diverse formulations, final authority was sought in the language of scripture. This result was a vast hermeneutical enterprise galvanized by intellectual ingenuity and highly technical skills.

Words and phrases (of scripture; its verbal parts) were creatively correlated to yield new hypercontexts (or thematic wholes), and subtle logical distinctions between them resulted in more precise legal language and settled practices. In the process, the voices and the terms of scripture were extended beyond their apparent contextual and semantic sense (the hermeneutical mode of *peshat*), and conjoined across the full scriptural corpus to produce the thick network of rabbinic interpretations (the hermeneutical mode of *derash*). In the process, the written "said" of scripture was revoiced by teachers and interpreters to "say" what was not explicitly enunciated; or also to "unsay" what was "said," in response to emergent legal needs or religious values. These exegetical acts (called midrash) yielded bold new valences in the written formulations of Moses, the prophets, and many other bearers of cultural wisdom. Biblical theology was also transformed in the process. New topics or values were reformulated from older phrases, and new meanings widened the scope of thought. Altogether, the range of scripture was creatively expanded (through authoritative hermeneutical forms) to yield a new corpus of interpretative cases and possibilities—creative instructions produced "for the sake of heaven." The combined result is *"derash* theology" along with ritual and other religious practices. This renewal of scriptural sense meant the continuous revitalization of theological and cultural values. Such is the soul of an interpretative culture. The corollary for a contemporary Jewish hermeneutical theology is explored in part 3.

Cultural Forms and Their Primordial Preformulations

The theological hermeneutics considered here builds on the contents of the *torah she-bikhtav*, and the revisions produced by the *torah she-be'al peh*. But it extends beyond, to include the infinite realm of world-being. Stated otherwise, this ultimate domain is the plenum of God's all-effectuating voice, enunciating *yehi* (let it be) for the regeneration of all existence. We shall designate this comprehensive reality the *torah kelulah*, meaning the primordial "Torah of All-in-All (*kelulah*)"—the all-inclusive realm of divine creativity, pulsating with all life-forms and influencing the plenitude of existence. Both the Written and Oral Torahs derive from this domain, through the inspired understanding of spiritual masters attuned to the values of life. The *torah kelulah* is thus the all-encompassing matrix of human life, the God-given source of all human meanings. It subtends all existence, and thereby sponsors our epistemic innovations and religious consciousness.

Jewish hermeneutical theology belongs to *all* the expressions of God's word, and gives them expression. This is the ontological implication of R. Ishmael's adage "The Torah speaks in the language of humankind." Emergent and revealed from the divine depths, theological hermeneutics is both ever new and ever old. It is ever new, since each moment is an occasion for reinterpreting or actualizing scripture; and ever old, since through this living process we join the chain of Jewish biblical interpretation since Sinai. Accordingly, midrash is twofold at its core. It is *loyalty* to the "said" and *longing* for a "saying" that will let its hearers again stand theologically at Sinai, attuned to the new possibilities of its words. For midrashic theology the hermeneutical dialogue with scriptural language is ongoing and dynamic. Its practitioners renew the voices of scripture as these "speak again" through viable and life-directing interpretations. Hence the exhortation *Ve-ḥay ba-hem*, "You shall live *in* them" and "*by* them" (Leviticus 18:5), is the core imperative of a vibrant Jewish hermeneutic theology—one that formulates (and reformulates) the life potential of the *torah kelulah*. The revelations of interpretation mediate the creation.

What guides the hand of Jewish hermeneutics? It is, first and foremost, a reverence for written scripture, with its linguistic forms and religious teachings; second, it is an eye devoted to a responsible elucidation of its meanings, inspired by the oral tradition and its requirements; and finally, it requires a heart attuned to the spiritual wisdom and moral valences found within rabbinic tradition, but also (when they can be assimilated or reinterpreted) the extensive realm of world culture. These and those are the words of the living God. Who then guides the hand of interpretation? Ultimately, it is God alone, though more proximately it is the human religious spirit and its sense of cultural responsibility. God's gifts of world-being thus become Torah and interpretation through an ongoing engagement. The "search" for textual meanings and significance, and the "quest" to live thoughtfully within the divine creation, are the twofold goal of *derash*. Embedded within tradition, one seeks God through God's creative word (in the world) and interpreted instructions (in scripture).

*

Part 3 ("*Derash*") will attempt to reformulate the primary grounds of experience—the natural world and its life claims—in terms of several Jewish theological categories. The topics of creation and revelation will provide the fundamental axes for our interpreted experiences of God, world, and Torah. A diversity of rabbinic sources (adduced from the Talmud and midrash) will mediate these theological components: initially by providing either the textual or ideological stimulus for hermeneutical reflection, but also by providing the template for their ongoing theological appropriation. In this way, we shall engage in a traditional way of hermeneutical thinking.

Every scriptural "said" may become a midrashic "saying" when it becomes a verbal truth that speaks to one's heart; and each "reading" of the "written" record will prove itself by its capacity to provide theological and existential instruction for our lives. Hence hermeneutics provides the means for scriptural revelation. The human voice is crucial, for it specifies God's ongoing voice and the imperative to hear and to do through the forms of religious tradition. For Jewish hermeneutical theology this is the phenomenon of rabbinic *derash*. It is age-old and ever renewed. We now join this living process and practice.

* PART THREE *

Derash

(I)

The Life-World: Reformulated

We naturally begin with the life-world; it is our physical ground. As human beings we sense this reality in personal terms. The play of light changes its effect across the sun's daily course, and the need for sustenance or rest generates different bodily states: all these radiate through corporeal experience, inducing responses of diverse kinds. At the cognitive level, they fundamentally affect our being-in-the-world and influence our scale of values. The hermeneutics of *peshat* mark out this primary framework. But Jewish theological existence—at the level of *derash*—is overlaid by another modality. Built upon the religious foundation of the *torah she-bikhtav* (written scripture) and the interpretations of the *torah she-be'al peh* (oral tradition), life is experienced through a second order of significance: Jewish liturgical existence and its ways of engaging or relating to the variety of life happenings. Nothing of the primary sphere of natural existence is lost here, but through the lens of tradition everything is transformed. Whatever is seen or noted, and whatever is experienced and recognized, is processed through a formal traditional framework. Time is experienced through a defined religious rhythm, determined by sunlight and lunar cycles; space is segmented into specific regions of private or public use; and actions are defined in terms of assorted stimuli in nature and society, or fixed practices and historical events. Through these regulations, the lived world is transfigured into a spiritual domain. What is experienced is more than "mere nature," and religious celebrants are more than "mere natural beings." Through the agency of *derash* one participates in a multimillennial tradition that shapes the total framework and content of existence, and determines the requisite behaviors or social structures for theological action. The gestures of life become sacred acts and practiced forms, through which everything has a spiritual resonance and dimension. Theological meanings annotate these actions

or perceptions. In the process, the world is reinterpreted, and the individual cultivates an inherited God-consciousness—shared by like-minded and
commonly committed members of the tradition.

At the level of *derash*, one turns from the personal occasions of life to
the public domain of a religious community. The private valence of natural
experience and its summons of Divinity are filtered through the medium
of collective behavior and thought. Theology and its cultural hermeneutics
reformulate life in a new key. Judaism is lived scripture, activated through
the prism of rabbinic interpretations over the ages. This orientation also
determines a central concern: to expand the voice of the foundational text
(the *torah she-bikhtav*) through the voices of its interpreters (the *torah she-
be'al peh*)—past and present. The mystery of scriptural language is the catalyst, and on its basis each generation constructs its own theological vision
and molds its behaviors. In the process, the realm of the "everyday" becomes
a corpus of traditional values; and experience acquires a Jewish character.
Derash generates this fundamental process, for it is both "inquiry" and
"quest" (the two meanings of the term) in tandem. Its combined result
is Midrash Aggadah (theological teachings or explications) and Midrash
Halakhah (legal regulations and theoretical derivations)—"midrash" being
both the process of scriptural inquiry *and* its literary product.

From Natural to Liturgical Living

Liturgical living is activated at the moment of awakening. During the night
we lose direct contact with events of the day, and experience a penumbral
zone of images that do not require decisions or responsibility. And then
we are awakened to sensations we knew before sleep: to a public world
still there as we left it hours before. This life-world is phenomenal in every
sense, with innumerable qualities impinging on the horizons of experience.
Can we hear the concrete appeal of God at the doors of perception? Daily
awakening is a potential spiritual event that may be liturgically affirmed
as primary sensations fill us with a thankful awareness for the renewal of
life. Gratitude is the natural prayer of the soul, and liturgical prayer joins
this spontaneous personal disposition to the fixed language of a tradition.
It resets one's spiritual focus from moment to moment. So enlivened, one
may see the world anew each day and give it expression. Jewish liturgy has
its particular forms and character. One word at a time, the language of rabbinic tradition reformulates the spirit of perception.

*

The renewal of the soul is the conscious awareness of life's gifts. In the liturgical acknowledgment of them, we are opened toward God and the bounties of existence. This is an orientation beyond self-reference, for one is now aware of a more transcendent reality and can celebrate with heartfelt gratitude. "I give thanks (*mode/ah*) to You, O living and enduring Sovereign (of all existence), for having restored my soul. How great (*rabbah*) is Your faithfulness (*emunatekha*)!" This statement, personal and specific, is subsequently reconfirmed publicly with the communal proclamation recited at the beginning of the daily liturgy: "Serve *Y-H-W-H* with joy. . . . Know that *Y-H-W-H* is God. . . . Praise (*hodu*) Him with gratitude. . . . For *Y-H-W-H* is good: His kindness (*ḥasdo*) is forever, and His faithfulness (*emunato*) is from generation to generation" (Psalm 100:2–5). By reciting these words, one joins liturgical communities of ages past. The prayer is linked to Jewish public theology. Its language raises one's individual, physical experiences to the level of objective religious expression. Private impulses or responses are transformed into liturgical practice. The individual speaks through the community; and communal language speaks through the person.

Scriptural models often provide the paradigmatic basis for rabbinic norms, and thus root the "merely natural" in the spiritual ground of tradition. Take the sequence of Jewish daily prayer, which is correlated to the diurnal rhythm of the seasons. The arc of sunlight (from morning to noon to eventide) gives the life-world its religious values and valences. The foundations for human gratitude are linked to the three ancestors who symbolize the origins of cultural generativity and religious practice within this daily orbit. Abraham, because he "arose early in the morning" to fulfill God's call with great alacrity (Genesis 22:3), is deemed the founder of the morning prayer; Isaac, because he engaged in a "contemplative" act in the afternoon (24:63), is the source for the midday supplications; and Jacob, because he sought God "at eventide" (28:12), provides the model for prayers at nightfall. Quite evidently, such rabbinic etiologies (and the proof texts) give these events an authoritative liturgical character and spiritual pedigree for subsequent generations (Babylonian Talmud, *Berakhot* 26b). But these dramatic actions of the patriarchs also echo our natural daily cycle. We arise with the morning light and soon begin our movements in the world; we then work and walk about during the day, with different perceptions as shadows cover the world; and finally we lie down at nightfall, in nocturnal repose, dreaming of past life and the days to come. Each moment is physical and spiritual: our natural course is the setting for religious actions. God-consciousness extends across the daily round. The ancestors perceived this according to rabbinic tradition—and one is bidden to follow their example, observing the statutory prayers for the *shaḥarit* (morning), *minḥah* (after-noon), and *ma'ariv* (evening) liturgical services.

The Mystery of Mixture: Limit and Bounty

The situation of embodied consciousness includes the rhythms of day and night, and the attendant sensations of confidence and anxiety: the first, because the radiations of light give the world its perceptual clarity and dis-tinction; the second, because the succession of experiences may provoke confusion and indecision. By acknowledging God's presence in both real-ities, individuals voice their creaturely dependence. Liturgical theology blends spiritual consciousness with natural states, each one informing the other. We therefore live the twofold character of existence: the thick mys-tery of worldly happenings, overwhelming in their omnipresence; and the specifics of earthly occurrences, challenging our abilities to respond to their particular evocations. The Names of God help us ponder this experiential truth and give it a theological dimension.

As noted earlier, Divine Names are fundamental expressions of theolog-ical intuitions. So has it been from time immemorial, and similarly so for the varieties of the Jewish religious imagination. Thus the vitalities of all existence are symbolized by the conjunction of God's primordial "Shall Be" (*Y-H-W-H*) with its all-effectuating presence (*Eheyeh*) in the diverse life-forms of world-being. The first Name evokes the mystery of reality, in its full-ness, whereas the second specifies the actuality of existential happenings, in all their felt particularity. Awakened to this reality, the heart acknowledges that "the world is founded upon *ḥesed*" (Psalm 89:3)—on the ever-gracious constancy of divine giving, pulsing in its munificent diversity. The *creation* is then perceived as a complex order of balances between expansion and limit: both the outward reach of possibility (the bounty of creativity) and the inner restraint of actuality (the limits of necessity). Ancient Jewish sages pondered this matter and offered a striking theological assessment. Noting that scripture first conjoins the Divine Names *Y-H-W-H* and *Elohim* only at the conclusion of the creation account—"when the Lord (*Y-H-W-H*) God (*Elohim*) completed the heavens and the earth" (Genesis 2:4)—they won-dered how this twofold divine nomenclature might best be understood, and to what it might be compared. Following an older exegetical tradition—whereby the first Name (*Y-H-W-H*) was understood to designate God's attribute of mercy and love, and the second Divine Name (*Elohim*) des-ignates the attribute of judgment and limit—the sages drew a remarkable hermeneutical conclusion. They suggested that the conjunction of Names at this point in scripture underscores their interrelationship in the creative

process: it being a blend of the two. Clearly, with these comments, the rabbinic interpreters went beyond the *peshat*, or plain sense, which portrays
creation in Genesis 1 as a series of sovereign acts by *Elohim*. But what more
did they then have in mind, and what could a parable (the comparison) add
to this instance of *derash* (rabbinic scriptural interpretation)? As their presentation makes clear, this figure provides a dramatic demonstration of the
sages' intuition about the very nature of creativity and existence.

In the parable (recorded in *Midrash Genesis Rabba* 12.15), the scriptural
account of creation, marked by the two Divine Names (*Y-H-W-H* and *Elohim*), is compared to the act of a king who, wishing to pour water into a
vessel, mused that if he only poured hot water into the vessel it would crack,
but there would be the same result if the liquid was too cold. So he decided
to mix the two and hoped that the vessel would "perhaps" (*ulay*) not break.
In the application of the parabolic event to the biblical text, we are asked
to imagine the creative process based on this scenario. Thus (we are told),
God perceived that too much *Ḥesed* (unlimited loving kindness, symbolized by the Name *Y-H-W-H*) would deprive creatures of a viable structure
and form, but also their means or drive for survival. By contrast, too much
Din (excessive limit, this symbolized by the Name *Elohim*) would set one
life-form against another without any spirit of mercy or love. Each modality, taken separately, would undo a stable world-order; hence the Creator
decided to integrate or mix the two qualities. But (the parable emphasizes)
the final outcome was uncertain; and thus, similarly, the final decision is
concluded by the divine prayer: *ulay*—"perhaps" in this way (the estimated
mixture) the creation might endure or "stand" firm (*ya'amod*). Just what is
involved or conveyed here?

The conclusion reflects a profound insight. If the bounty of *Ḥesed* sus-
tains the world in all its munificent growth and vitality, the rigor of *Din* gives
creatures the will to power and the capacity for restraint. Both elements—
Ḥesed and *Din*—are necessary; but how they might achieve an effective and
sustainable balance is never certain—neither on the formative occasion that
first established the "world" nor at any subsequent time of "worldly existence." Faced with diverse challenges or circumstances, creatures develop
creative strategies for survival or productivity. But sometimes, through the
misuse or imbalance of these means, the creations that result careen wildly
in ecological or moral disarray, leaving the balances of a well-sustained
life in crisis, with no certainty that it might withstand the new mixture of
elements. The primordial concern that attends the often unknown consequences of creativity is thus projected through the rabbinic parable into
God's primal prayer: *ulay*, "perhaps." Its sharp evocation cuts to the quick,
revealing a deep anxiety in the individual soul—aware of the fragility of

nature and existence. *Ulay* is therefore a primary *cri du coeur*, which resonates in our deepest being.

The foregoing parable is a case of midrashic "theopoesis" (portraying
God in dramatic, personal terms) at its most profound. It transforms the
creation narrative in Genesis 1 from a series of resolute divine acts into
something more nuanced or qualified. Drawing on the traditional Jewish
interpretation of the Divine Names as spiritual or moral qualities, it projects
the precarious balance of elements throughout the "world-order." Revealing
perceptive sensibilities, the account portrays an acute awareness that strife
and its resolution are fundamental components of existence—as evidenced
in the contestation of life-forms, each having the desire to flourish and
reproduce as well as the drive to survive or persevere. Hence, as an ontological perception, the parable reimagines the divine act of creation as an
act of hesitation and doubt, and renders its structural hierarchies tenuous
achievements, at best. Reflecting insight into the polar forces contending
throughout existence, the result is a hermeneutical formulation of singular
import, fundamentally revising the balanced and harmonious picture of
sovereign acts of creation presented in the book of Genesis.

The implications for a Jewish hermeneutical theology are significant.
Not only does it present created life as the repeated balance between limit
and love; the same holds for the human spirit, which tries to make conceptual sense of the world. The parable injects an empirical equivocation into
the creative process. Hence the elicitation of wonder (and seeing possibilities in *bohu*) is no guarantee that one will find the requisite hermeneutical
ability to transform the inherent "inchoate" quality of existence (indeterminate in the cognitive-cultural sense) into something certain or viable.
Indeed, on its terms, worldly reality is comprised of such a great density of
forces that the mind is both overwhelmed and humbled to the core. The
book of Job may again serve as a guide. From its concluding divine queries
we learned that all worldly creatures strive to strike their own (evolution-
ary) balance among the contending forces of existence, and that all human
assessments of the realities of life are inherently limited and fragmentary.
Hence the hermeneutical confession of *ulay*—so poignantly enunciated in
the parable—expresses the fragile finitude of the soul at all times. We necessarily live with our interpretations and assessments—but do so with invari-
able uncertainty. In the parable, theology reveals its limits.

Finding Regulative Balance

The "paramount reality" of existence that impinges on our emotional and
mental life requires constant adjustments. On some occasions this is spon-

taneous, and based on immediate intuition; at other times, it is a more deliberate affair. But since we can never be sure that matters will "stand," an "*ulay*-mentality" expresses an existential anxiety before the ever-new "Shall Be" of divine effectuality. Every moment is a balance point where we strive to regulate diverse factors, and interpret them for either purpose or pleasure. Moving from object to object, and perceiving correlations between them, we engage events as hermeneutic gestalts that serve our purposes or pleasure. Thus God's creative *Eheyeh* confronts the individual with the polymorphous nature of world reality, challenging us with new opportunities for cognitive construction. For the theological mind, reception of Divinity through the world is a revelatory truth of existence *for us*—however limited or tenuous our responses may be. Whatever we consider to be of significance (whether personal or social) derives from our hermeneutic engagement with the elements of omnipresent divine effectivity.

Through our cognitive and emotional adjustments, we continuously construe the world. Some things have an evident "measure," or *shi'ur*, and we receive them with clarity and assurance; but other perceptions are more difficult to assess, and we rely on inherited wisdom or empirically practical solutions. Even matters that seem "without measure" (*she-ein lahem shi'ur*)—whose limits are indeterminate—are not wholly so, and we strive to piece together some viable structure, based on discernible features of limit and form. For were things totally without some inherent balance between their vital bounty (content) and form (limit), they would exceed or destroy their durable expression. How and where the balance point may find its regulative valence is a matter for ongoing inquiry. We thus live within the hermeneutical and evaluative space of *ulay*—seeking stable interpretations. This is our existential condition.

But we are not alone, abandoned to only what we see and know at any moment, and forced to construe meaning from our personal experience or mental calculus. Sustainable and regulative guidance also comes from generations past and the cultural traditions—both familial and religious—which have formed over the ages. This is the hermeneutical fund of collective wisdom and legal formulations that gives social life its stability. Theology builds on this resource in its own manner. By interpreting events as a realm of divine gifts and blessings, happenstance becomes a spiritual happening, and one is able to perceive the diversity of experiences as moments of religious value. Liturgical regulations serve this theological orientation by inculcating modes of seeing and hearing, or sensing and enjoying, so that individuals may be attuned to the diversity of experiences and give them due regard or acknowledgment. But on occasion, it is hard to find their proper "measure," and one must try to evaluate which events assume cognitive or moral priority. Regularity or uniqueness may provide the best measure in these situations, based on personal experience or established tradition. Nevertheless, even when communal regulations provide a template, each individual must assess the balance of conditions at hand and try to respond with a decision fit for the occasion. Specificity is crucial. For the theological temperament, worldly events cannot be ignored or bypassed, but must be filtered through the categories of settled practices. To participate in a liturgical tradition, one must receive each moment as a distinct solicitation within God's omnipresent revelation. And that requires responding to it with the proper words of blessing or consecration—articulated with its traditional formulation, and with the proper intentions, as assessed by halakhic tradition. Gratitude to God is at the core. It binds thought, word, and deed.

Liturgical language focuses awareness on the components of existence, from morning to night. We are bodies of sensation and need, and liturgy gives a sacral dimension to this condition. It makes the adjustment between need and satisfaction a spiritual factor in our lives, and directs consciousness beyond self-reference to all the bounties one might take for granted. Thus, one typical formula first enunciates the universal character of divine beneficence, and then continues with verbs that specify the event at hand. Upon experiencing the light of day or the sense of upright dignity, or when acknowledging the vital importance of bodily functions, one will rightly proclaim: "Blessed are You, *Y-H-W-H*, our God, sovereign of the universe, who" creates the light and brings on night, (who) establishes the capacity to walk, or (who) heals all flesh and works great wonders for the body. These are all evident divine gratuities, acknowledged both for oneself and others in a public recitation. In other circumstances, a particular moment is affirmed before enjoying its goods. Then that event elicits the requisite formula, and its words focus the religious consciousness of the celebrant. Before eating bread one thanks God, "who" draws forth bread from the earth; upon seeing a long-absent friend, or a person marked by particular condition, one acknowledges God, "who" revives the dead or creates all creatures differently. Thus the eye and the heart, body and soul, unite to proclaim thankfulness to God for *Hesed* given or received. Notably, these liturgical formulas are recited in the collective plural ("we," "us"), and this underscores the fact that liturgy participates in a community of worship that celebrates the beneficence of God. *Y-H-W-H*, God of all being, is proclaimed the effective force at all times and occasions, vitalizing the omnipresent manifestations of creation throughout the world. Accordingly, the recitations mark the dual sense of divine transcendence and immanence, of bounty and particularity—everywhere and at one and the same time. Acknowledging each gift is a redemptive occasion.

Integration and Affirmation

Liturgical acknowledgment goes further. Of prime importance are moments when one affirms God's eternal "Shall Be" and centers religious consciousness on that affirmation. Exemplary in this regard is the recitation of the *Shema* prayer—in the morning and evening. Focused on the theological proclamation that *Y-H-W-H* is "One" (Deuteronomy 6:4), this theological assertion may mean that God's all-effectuating "Shall Be" is One-in-Many or Many-in-One; that is, that God's world-actuality may be experienced and acknowledged in a multitude of ways. And then the task of those who love God is to sustain this monotheistic focus and not let the jumble of experience disperse this truth from one's heart or mind. Monotheism is a spiritual value that each person must repeatedly affirm, training the self to focus—at all times and all ways—on God's omnipresent, worldly "Shall Be."

How so?

The Torah states this task in particular terms: "You shall love *Y-H-W-H*, your God, with all (*kol*) your heart (*levavkha*), with all your soul (*nafshekha*), and with all your might (*me'odekha*)" (Deuteronomy 6:5). The old midrashic commentaries go further and cultivate three forms of mindfulness. The first one is to love God (and all God's manifestations) with wholeheartedness. Noting that the word "heart" is spelled *levav* (not *lev*), the sages construed this as an allusion to the two modes of human desire or disposition—the good *yetzer* (or "instinct") and the evil one; and interpreted this instruction as a directive to serve God with both drives, integrating all one's resources in response to the multiplicities and challenges of existence. A related interpretation elicits a similar wisdom by dividing the consonants, thereby instructing each person to love God with all "the heart within you" (*lev bakh*). The second scriptural directive shifts focus, calling the worshipper to love God with all (*be-khol*) their life-force (*nafshekha*). In this way, individuals are enjoined to bind all their natural energies to spiritual desires. And finally, through their explication of the concluding phrase (*be-khol me'odekha*), the sages propose a third mode of spiritual devotion: to love God in and through "every measure" (*middah*—punning on *me'od*) that is apportioned to one's life, whether that be positive or negative.

Taken as a pedagogical ensemble, we learn that monotheistic consciousness is composed of a multifaceted spiritual attitude: a wholehearted affirmation of all life occasions as divine-human conjunctions. Cultivation of this consciousness is an ongoing task and points to the redemptive future, when God (*Y-H-W-H*) will be One and God's Name One—one, that is, in human consciousness. Centering one's heart and soul on this unitive ideal is a supreme directive of Jewish theology.

Divine Names and Religious Consciousness

At the core of the Jewish liturgical tradition are the Divine Names that mark and symbolize theological experience. As remarked, the two central designations are the biblical Names *Y-H-W-H* and *Eheyeh*, which were reinterpreted in rabbinic (*derash*) theology. Subsequent religious reflections extended this repertoire, and produced other vectors of religious intuition. Of notable significance is the sense of a numinous "otherness" often conveyed by worldly phenomena, which evoke an overwhelming sense of awe and transcendence. Such terms as "holy" and "sacred" express this spiritual sensibility; and Jewish theology characterizes them as *qadosh* (sacred), and the corresponding quality of Divinity as *Qadosh*. In a significant scriptural formulation this keyword denominates a divine epithet, when God exhorts the people to become "holy" (*qadosh*)—"because I, *Y-HW-H* your God, am *Qadosh*" (Leviticus 19:2). Such an epithet specifies absolute otherness as such. And also, because the term *qadosh* specifies and denotes distinction in the scriptural lexicon, the reference to God as *Qadosh* rings true for the experience of the God-given uniqueness and distinctiveness of forms in the panoply of creation. In response to this God-given diversity, and with reverence before Divinity as the "wholly other," the human heart (using a rabbinic parlance) dares to address God with the "Name": "The Holy One (*Ha-Qadosh*), who is Blessed (*Baruch Hu*)."

Thus, transcendent Divinity is named: *Qadosh*; and our awakened gratitude for worldly benefits evokes the liturgical formula: *Baruch*. We acknowledge both through the composite designation *Ha-Qadosh Baruch Hu*—for we know the two as one, conjoined in our hearts. God is both the imperceptible "Ultimate Beyond," whose transcendent concealment is contemplated in silent wonder, and the worldly "Infinitely Here," whose immanent presence we duly acknowledge with words of blessing. Such is the twofold consciousness of the theological mind. God is *Ha-Qadosh* (Most Holy and Other) *Baruch Hu* (the Ever [humanly] Blessed One). We live at the nexus between the unknowable "other" and the imposing "near-at-hand." The first term evokes humble awe; the other the yearning for immediacy and connection. We are creatures in between, forever outside the holy as such, but addressed by it as well. Through our words of sanctification, we may receive the mystery of existence as a sacred, transcendent moment, and render it blessed.

Effable-Ineffable

Despite their propositional character, the Divine Names are essentially evocations grounded in spiritual awareness—a summoning to consciousness of an intuited reality, grounding life experience and knowledge. The mind cannot get a hold on these named predications, so fundamentally do they exceed understanding; but their ritual evocation can direct attention to all the unsayable vocatives of daily existence—not as some "thing," but as the reality that "is" here, and "shall be": all the mixtures and qualities of God-given worldly truth. The occurrence of these Names in scripture (and their elaboration and reformulation in rabbinic culture) is itself a profound attestation of divine creativity, transmuted through the shock of spiritual sense and intuition. Suddenly the ineffable becomes something sayable—and canonized through sacred tradition. Traces of an ultimate word, they are sanctioned echoes of Divinity—markers for the mind, seeking the all-transcendent mystery.

(II)

Creation and Revelation in Tandem: Awareness and Responsibility

As the heart opens to the light of day, the dawn's radiance promises blessing and creative awareness. Daylight is not solely a natural occurrence. It is also an event of the spirit. The heart senses the primordial "Let Be" (*yehi*) of God ever pulsating throughout existence. With that perception, a sacred dimension is felt to radiate through all things. This illumination evokes cognition of an omnipresent divine effectuality that makes claims upon us. That which is naturally revealed is the world of creation. It summons us to responsibility. The word *yehi* is the God-given imperative calling to us from worldly existence.

The medieval poet Yehuda Halevi gave expression to this transformation of awareness in a liturgical prayer for the Festival of Shavuot. In it the natural "light of day" and the supernatural "illuminations of Torah" interact:

Day and night praise the Lord	who has illumined my face with His light;
Who kindled the heavenly lights	banishing darkness and sending me vision.
Who granted me of His splendor	inspiring me through His prophetic words;
Teaching me the mystery of light	as when He shined from Seir and Sinai—
When I tasted His sweet Law and	said: Come and see for my eyes are light!

In this mosaic of scriptural phrases, the singer meditates on the deepening of sight into insight. Light is both a daily radiance and a divine illumination. It is invoked here to glorify God, the Giver of light and enlightenment—shining in the heavens above and the human soul below. Thus light becomes a spiritual beacon that opens the windows of inner perception to clarify the words of Torah. Halevi thanks God for the renewal of Sinai in his heart, through his tasting the honeycomb of scripture's words and so perceiving the sacred letters anew. There is a spiritual tactility to this hermeneutical moment: a renewal of the ancient revelation through personal reception and exegetical self-transformation.

Torah Kelulah: *The All-Encompassing Splendor of Reality*

The divine light radiates throughout the cosmos, stimulating conscious-ness of the mystery and majesty of the created orders of existence. The heart receives this gift with reverence and love. Received as reverence, this is the transcendent awe (*yir'ah gedolah*) induced by the omnipresent mir-acle of existence; but when received as abundant love (*ahavah rabbah*), this is the spiritual longing to conjoin with these divine gifts and attain a spiritual connection with God. Absorbed by the mind of Moses and his disciples, with their concern for a just social life, these omnipresent reve-lations of life become particular legal formulations (both positive and neg-ative) designed to establish justice and righteousness (communal care and responsibility) for a religious polity. As balances of *din* and *raḥamim*—limit and compassion—the covenant norms and their ongoing interpretations institute these divine structures (*Din* and *Raḥamim*) within the orders of our human existence. This is done with pious intent—the *ulay* of goodwill.

The *torah kelulah* eternally generates new expressions of existence. And these are hermeneutically integrated into the norms themselves. In this way elements of the *torah kelulah* are domesticated by the human mind; and the Torah of Moses, a "crown of resplendent majesty" (*kelil tiferet*), expands its glow to wider spheres of worldly existence. Gradually our "earthly Jerusa-lem," the daily sphere or context of "encircling splendor" (*kelilat yofi*), is con-joined to a "heavenly Jerusalem"—to God's eternal, world-informing voice.

The Great Voice: "All-Embracing" (Kelulah*)*

Within the radiant divine light, the all-encompassing and all-vitalizing word of God manifests the world particulars and worldly possibilities that engage human attention. Suddenly something is seen or heard, arising from the inchoate mass of things; and then the world is perceived, phenomenally, as a silent call to consciousness. This rupture or caesura in the everyday is an opening for divine presence: one's eyes are filled with light, and one's heart with percipient insight. Only subsequently is this moment perceived as a summons. "Awake!" "*See*—I have placed before you both life and death; (so) choose life"; and—"Be silent and *hear*!" what beckons you at this moment in your life. Cognitively prethematic in their primacy, these phenomena (as impressions or imperatives) are the experiential precursor to their her-meneutical evaluation. Going about the round of life, we live among these imposing occasions; and our exegetical constructions are the verbal traces (second-order enunciations) of our sensed reality. For persons whose hearts are spiritually attuned, such appeals to attentive regard are a revelation. Suddenly the world is disclosed anew; inexplicably the heart is addressed by the living divine word, and we respond.

Scripture offers diverse accounts of the revelatory presence and word of God at Sinai, but it is only with the rabbinic reception of these accounts that a deliberate attempt to elaborate or enunciate their import emerges. Thus the biblical sources provide hermeneutical resources for the "inquiring" sages of late antiquity. Their interpretative practice of *derash* bears witness to ongoing theological deliberations and explications. In turn, this material offers the opportunity for contemporary theological reflection and the basis for a typology of revelation that resonates anew. Such a double refraction offers new possibilities of spiritual insight.

Toward a Hermeneutical Typology of Revelation

An initial scriptural exemplar of the hermeneutics of revelation occurs in Deuteronomy 32:10. It contains a poetic formulation of the divine revelation at Sinai. The language is both anthropomorphic and marked by dramatic images of the event. "He (God) found him (Israel) in the wilderness (*midbar*), a wasteland (*tohu*) of howling desolation; He surrounded him (and) instructed him, (and) protected him like the pupil of His eye." The thrust of this account portrays God's engagement with Israel in the desert in terms of protection and instruction. This divine founding and "encirclement" of the people is a pedagogical moment—an "encompassing" that transforms the inchoate *tohu* of the steppe land into a place of hermeneutical significance. The people are thoroughly reoriented in every sense: both cognitively and theologically. Though laconic, the subject-object references are reasonably clear: the third-person subject ("He") ostensibly refers to God, and the third-person object-suffix ("him") correspondingly designates the people Israel. The overall import is that God cares for this people, both physically and spiritually, and gives them instructional guidance. Stated more phenomenologically, there is initially a divine initiative (a numinous moment of divine-human encounter) that gives the people an immediate sense of their new reality (as a protected people of God). Only thereafter did the covenantal implications of the event come to mind. The two central verbs convey this double dimension: *yesovevenhu-yevonenehu*, "He (God) surrounded him (Israel) and gave him understanding." In the light of the central narrative in Exodus 20, this inculcation of knowledge undoubtedly refers to the laws and dictates revealed at Sinai.

This depiction notwithstanding, later rabbinic interpreters reconfigured this event by adducing several other biblical passages, with the result that both the subject-object pairing and the referential content assumed significantly different theological dimensions. Thus, in *Midrash Sifre Deuteronomy*, the episode in verse 10 was linked to the divine advent to Sinai recorded in Deuteronomy 33:2, where it says that God came with an "*eshdat* in His right hand for them (Israel)." Such an intertextual supplement presumes that this object (*eshdat*) was a poetic trope for God's Torah (construed as a "fiery law," or *esh dat*), and that *it* (the words of Torah, not God) circumscribed the nation. Support for this midrashic construction was further achieved through a creative rereading of Psalm 29:7: "The voice (*qol*) of the Lord hews (*hotzev*) with flames of fire." No longer depicting fiery thunderbolts (which is the plain sense of the passage), this image was now hermeneutically construed to specify the "fiery (words of) Torah," which emanated from God and circumscribed the nation—before being hewn upon the tablets at Sinai. All told, both the desert encounter and divine instruction were radically transformed, and the sequence of founding and instruction was dramatically conjoined. The result is that the formative moment of divine revelation conveyed a primary sense of significance (or meaning) that was only subsequently specified in terms of the norms and instructions on the tablets at Sinai. The inchoate sense of protective care was therefore an inaugural experience of encompassing divine presence—a numinous national event whose revelatory import and legal details were only subsequently apprehended.

A certain phenomenology of perception underscores this account of divine instruction. As with most ordinary cognition, the sense of an enveloping presence precedes interpretative understanding. We first perceive an environment of things before their particularities are hermeneutically determined (an intuition of a whole followed by the specification of individual parts). For example, we feel suffused by a sphere of sound before subjecting it to a semiotic evaluation that makes sense in terms of one's presumption of the language being spoken. Thus in our scriptural scenario, the initiating *revelatory experience* (the sense of an enveloping divine presence) is followed by its *hermeneutical explication* (the perception of a divine communication). Reformulating this, we may say that God's inaugural presence is, in a palpable sense, *kelulah*—an "all-encompassing reality" that has revelatory significance before its meaning (and content) is specified. From this perspective, the Sinai moment (of divine encounter and instruction) is a paradigm for those evocative life-moments that first reorient consciousness and only subsequently make (or are given) sense. The inaugural occasion is initially experienced as numinous and ineffable (an indeterminate silence pervades), whereas the ensuing correlate provides a hermeneutical rendition (an explication or response of some sort). Where the weight of the divine word makes a claim, spiritual consciousness is reborn.

A second exemplar of the hermeneutics of revelation occurs in an interpretation of Exodus 19:19 by R. Akiba. Immediately following the divine descent upon Mount Sinai, we read that "Moses spoke and God responded with/in a voice (*qol*)." The sage construed this phrase to mean that when Moses spoke the words of God, God enhanced or augmented them with his divine voice (that is, Moses's words reverberated with a palpable divine aura). Thus, although the precise meaning of the passage remains perplexing, it is evident that R. Akiba's hermeneutic tries to make sense of the theological mystery conveyed: that a human speaker voices (or expresses) divine words. The occurrence of the conjunction "and" ("Moses spoke *and* God responded") underscores the exegetical problem to be resolved. For human language—the ostensible language of scripture—is not the language of God, even though the conviction of a divine "voice" is an ontological presumption that informs classic rabbinic interpretations of the Sinai revelation. Hence R. Akiba cannot assert that God only echoes Moses's words, nor could he assert that God speaks like a human, and that the words of Moses are God's unmediated speech. On the horns of this theological dilemma, he interprets the passage to mean that God speaks through the language of Moses—and that this twofold conjunction accounts for the phraseology of scripture. This explanation does not weaken the event of divine revelation, but rather accords it a new theological status; for hereby the word of God is refracted through the human spirit, this nexus being a hermeneutical mystery. Where the divine impression ends and human expression begins is an ineffable conundrum: their correlation is conveyed here by the prolix formulation of a doubled or transfigured voice. Religious culture (Judaism in particular) puts its faith in that conjunction and (inevitably) in its subsequent acts of hermeneutic explication. The human *qol* of exegesis modulates the timbre of the *Qol Gadol*, for better and worse.

A third instance of hermeneutical theology occurs in a far-reaching interpretation of the subsequent passage: "God spoke all (*kol*) these words (of the Decalogue), as follows" (Exodus 20:1). In his explication, R. Eleazar ben Azaria disregards the plain sense of the passage (that "all these words" refer to the ensuing words of the Decalogue). Faced with a burgeoning plethora of rabbinic exegesis in his day, this sage explained this phrase to mean that God "spoke *all*" the potential meanings of the Torah with or through the specific "words" pronounced before the nation at Sinai. Thus, the cultural problematic evidenced by the diversity of human (rabbinic) hermeneutics is effectively removed by the assertion of the inherent comprehensiveness (for all future rabbinic civilization) of this instance of divine speech. R. Eleazar's sermon thus goes to the heart of a hermeneutical theology of revelation and the status of human interpretation. It presumes both the hypersignification of all God's words in the Torah *and* the truth of the multiple rabbinic interpretations based on them. On this foundation, it is asserted that the explications of the sages constitute ongoing hermeneutic revelations of the formative linguistic components of scripture. This example is thus a paradigmatic consideration for hermeneutical theology, and effectively reverses the preceding interpretation of R. Akiba—for it is now the interpretations of the sages that augment the divine words of scripture. Both revelation and interpretation function as co-integral realities: the entwined mysteries of Jewish hermeneutical culture. Trust in the ontological vitality of scriptural language, and the power of traditional interpretation to explicate, are fundamental. This is the bedrock of hermeneutical faith in a scripture-centered religion.

A final example takes us to another theological level. It occurs in a more radical rabbinic interpretation of the foregoing passage, preserved in *Midrash Tanḥuma*. For here, when scripture proclaims that "God spoke all (*kol*) these words," the adverb "all" specifies that God spoke about "everything (*ha-kol*) all at once (*be-vat aḥat*)." The passage is boldly explicated to embody more than the "words" of the law. The divine "words" contain everything experienced and knowable: life and death, sickness and health, growth and decay, and punishment and healing! Hence these acts of divine speech (the words of God) express the fullness of existence—not merely things as they occur temporally, in successive experience, but simultaneously, "all at once"; for God's reality and creativity are the transtemporal totality of being. Such a revelation is ultimately ineffable—it is God's Name, "Shall Be," for ever and ever. Wholly other than subject and object, or specific events, God's revelation just is. From this perspective, the key event of Sinai is a foundational vector for theological consciousness. It is the revelation of revelation as such. And therefore whatever follows is interpretation, a God-given power to make sense of the world. The deep truth of this midrash and its value for contemporary theology are that revelation reveals the creation, in all its fundamental diversity and complexity. Sinai is thus a prism of the great diversity of reality, in all its forms; and these impose an imperative of awareness beyond the specifics of covenantal law. The bounty of reality is the primary, ineffable word of God. It exceeds and precedes its explication inevitably in human terms.

The hermeneutical delimitation of the divine voice to human understanding occurs in another notable midrash, which reinterprets the revelatory event of Sinai through the language of Psalm 29 (presented earlier in terms of *peshat* theology). Now, in a striking explication found in the *Midrash Mechilta D'Rabbi Ishmael* the biblical proclamation "The Voice of the Lord is in strength (*ba-koaḥ*)" (Psalm 29:4) is understood to assert that God's "word" instructed each person "according to" their individual "ability" (*koaḥ*) to understand it (the interpretation trades on the fact that the word *koaḥ* can mean both "strength" and "ability"). That is, the revelation to the entire nation (at the public event) was appropriated differently by every individual (the personal event), given their diversity of intellectual and spiritual intelligence. In the process, this interpretation also formulates a notion of hermeneutic pluralism at the founding moment of Jewish covenantal theology. God's word is mediated through a great diversity of human interpretations. Individuals must therefore listen deeply and attentively to the voice of all those who may supplement or clarify their own understanding, limited by natural ability or cultural perspective. Paradoxically, then, realizing the finitude of cognition is the beginning of wisdom, when it may induce one person to turn to another to explain the voice of God.

(III)

Life and Death through "Yes and No"

The interrelationship between law and life is fundamental. The limits of law protect the values of life just as the spirit of life may expand the range of law. The balance oscillates. What the law imposes as rigor and reason (*din*), life (and love) disposes through compassion and care (*ḥesed*). And whereas the creative surge of life is often bounded by legal limits, the bonds of law may be humanized through social care and love.

The covenant at Sinai is central for Jewish theology—the condition of entry into its orders of life. Acceptance of it is a decisive commitment in the destiny of each individual. This crucial moment feels like a weight of legal obligation for the sake of life and sociality. But it may also provide a canopy of protective care for the nurture of self and community. Ancient interpreters expressed both aspects in two paradigmatic instances of "midrashic theopoesis." Thinking (hermeneutically) with these images will further guide our contemporary theological imagination.

The exegetical occasion begins with the biblical statement that the people "stood at the base (*be-taḥtit*) of the mountain"—Mount Sinai—prior to the divine revelation (Exodus 19:18). There is nothing particularly unusual in this depiction of the physical place of the nation if the passage is read in a straightforward manner. But early rabbinic commentators appropriated this event as a dramatic portrayal of their commitment to divine sovereignty, and projected their sensibilities onto the phrase *be-taḥtit*—not taken as referring to the people standing at the base of the mountain, but as them being (figuratively) "under" the weight of Sinai, held ominously above them. This dramatic concretization of a metaphor provides the basis for a physical figure to depict the overwhelming sense of covenantal subjectivity—of being "cast under" (or subjected to) the divine law. The divine option offered to the people (according to this rabbinic reformulation)—either to accept or reject the covenant—was stark and harsh. According to the rabbinic drama (as articulated by R. Avdimi bar Ḥama in the Babylonian Talmud, *Shabbat* 88a), God held the mountain over the heads of the Israelites, proclaiming to them: If you accept my commandments, well and good—you will live by this Law; but if not, this is the place of your death. As a putative challenge to former slaves, this episode makes certain, limited sense, for the people had just escaped the decrees of Egypt and were now asked to make a consequential decision about their spiritual identity. But as a poignant expression of the sensibilities of the ancient rabbis, another element seems more plausible. Having devoted themselves to the significance of Torah and tradition, these sages were convinced that accepting the "yoke of God's Kingdom" was the precondition for the ongoing religious existence of the people. To accept the Law meant continuity, whereas to desist meant cultural death. Under the hegemony of Rome, there was no room for equivocations. Commitment to Torah was primary; cultural survival hung in the balance. Hence the moment of Sinai marks the precarious significance of religious commitment. It is symbolized as a moment of fateful choice, required by every generation. Such a life-rendering commitment would necessarily precede a full comprehension of the obligations and implications involved: *na'aseh* (we shall do) precedes *nishma'* (we shall hear/or obey), for the very commitment opens new life paths, hardly foreseeable at the outset. Hence this midrash portrays a fundamental hermeneutical truth: choice inaugurates a pattern of existence. The balance of unknown realities depends on it.

A later rabbinic voice (R. Ya'aqov bar Aḥa, who received the foregoing Palestinian tradition in Babylonia) starkly characterized this situation as a "harsh declamation of Torah" (*moda'a rabba de-oraita*), since the divine declaration and its threat implied the total absence of personal autonomy. The choice to accept the Law was thus no choice at all, but a "severe decree" in every sense of the term. What then was the religious value of a commitment made under duress? Living the Law without any real choice was formal in the highest degree, and one's obedience was deprived of spiritual value. Hence the initial reaction to the teaching indicates a bewildered rabbinic attitude. But not for long; a later stratum of this talmudic tradition offers an unexpected solution through a bold hermeneutical act. Noting the comment in the book of Esther—that the populace "observed and accepted" (*qiyyemu ve-qibbelu*) the Festival of Purim according to the details promulgated by Mordecai (Esther 9:27)—later sages found an exegetical wedge to help resolve the earlier conundrum. In its original context, this subsequent comment merely reports the collective compliance of the people to a onetime decree. But the sages boldly introduced a deft hermeneutical turn. Against the plain sense of the passage, they took these two verbs to mean that the people freely "fulfilled" (*qiyyemu*) what they had *previously* "accepted" (or "received"; *qibbelu*) under compulsion—this being the old covenant at Sinai (initially accepted under divine duress, but now renewed in exile through an act of free volition). There is particular irony in the fact that this new decision employs a phrase indicating an autonomous act of compliance. Most likely, the generative emergence of the Oral Law at this very period elicited awareness that the exegetical innovations of the rabbis were predicated upon the authority of, and commitment to, the Written Law—especially when (as in this case) some enactments (regarding Purim) were without scriptural authority. (The theological anxiety of such exegetical freedom is also evident in yet another use of Esther 9:27 to mean that "the [Heavenly tribunal] "affirmed" [*qiyyemu*] on high what the [human] courts had "accepted" [*qibbelu*] below as law.) By means of this hermeneutical act the later rabbinic Festival of Purim was given divine authority.

To a certain extent, this literary situation parallels the phenomenology of revelation described earlier. Here as well there is at the outset an overwhelming experience—the dominion of the Law in rabbinic culture—followed by responses to this reality—a series of psychological reactions to its authoritative character (notably the apparent absence of volitional freedom), along with the hermeneutical actions that ensue. The subsequent layers of the talmudic episode thus convey a profound cultural truth: theology and its hermeneutical acts are second-order developments that transform or reformulate primary experiences. This is the recurrent core of hermeneutical theology. Textual experiences are as fundamental and revelatory (fraught with significance) as natural events; and, for the traditional hermeneutical mind, significantly more so. For R. Ya'aqov, the narrative about Sinai as learned in the midrash had the weight of Torah and tradition. Only later did others find a way to transform this moment through new insights concerning hermeneutical freedom.

Later strata of this talmudic pericope deepen its theological import. These textual sequences begin with an apparent non sequitur, for without any transition the subject turns from the events of Sinai, and their aftermath in the Persian period, to a perplexing passage in the book of Psalms. What, it is asked, is the meaning of the verse "You (God) have proclaimed a judgment from heaven; the earth feared and became still" (Psalm 76:9), since neither the subject nor the sequence is clear in any evident way? The initial answer proposes that the earth was initially afraid, but subsequently calmed down. To what may one attribute both the initial mood and its sequel? The answer hangs on a correct understanding of the opening phrase—which refers to divine judgment. To determine this, another seemingly unrelated matter is adduced—namely, the fact that the definite article *heh* (the) occurs only in connection with the sixth day of creation ("*the* sixth day"; *yom* ha-*shishi*). This philological feature is then linked to another midrashic proclamation, in which God stipulated that if Israel would accept the Torah *on the sixth day* of the third month (after the exodus; the date of the revelation at Mount Sinai), the creation would be preserved; but if they did not, God would destroy the world and revert it to *tohu* and *bohu*! At one level, this teaching explicates the passage in the Psalms by back-sourcing the divine proclamation and emotions of the earth to the final day of the creation— when God's stipulation put the creation into dreadful fear. Now, after Israel's acceptance of the Torah, it became "tranquil," since the world would not be destroyed. One may observe a rough parallel between this text and the opening teaching discussed earlier. In both cases, the nonacceptance of the Torah has dire consequences (the death of the people or the destruction of the world). But we may wonder, Could more be at stake for the sages, at a deeper theological level?

Cosmos *and* Nomos

It is arguably a profound perception of the correlation between *cosmos* and *nomos* that inspired this chain of exegetical associations: the conviction that moral and social law derives from divine realities latent within the created world-order, and that human disregard of these implications affects the structure of lived reality and renders it a cognitive and ethical chaos. The two divine conditions (regarding the fate of Israel or the world) mark an evaluation of the interrelationship between human actions and the state of creation: notably, that the establishment of a social order has fateful implications for all the intersecting ecological realms of existence. Thus revelation and creation are fundamentally connected, and the world-order is implicated by ongoing hermeneutical decisions. Any potential deconstruction of the world-order (into *tohu* and *bohu*) is conditioned by the nature of hermeneutical freedom, with decisive consequences for its misuse or abuse. Torah is not separate from earthly life: the two are decisively interdependent. The connections between ethics and existence thus have ancient biblical reverberations, but in this rabbinic ethos they assume a new and more ramified significance.

The midrashic figure of Israel under the weight of Sinai palpably correlates with a sense of the cultural weight of its *nomos*, and the imposing transcendence of divine reality. Both the Law and God overarch human experience, providing the external conditions of possible action—with consequences for their compliance or rejection. But rabbinic sensibility understood and expressed another dimension of the relationship between the Law and God—and did so with a significant variation of the mountain image. In this instance (fully formulated in the ancient *Mechilta D'Rabbi Ishmael*), this mountain was raised above the people to provide them loving protection. Using different parables, the sense of law as divine care and love is expressed.

To what was this situation compared? In one instance, the sages compared it to a bird sheltered in a mountain crevice, whose warble the fowler longs to hear. Just as the mountain gives aid to the bird, and the gamer cares for its well-being, so does God yearn for Israel's acceptance of the Law, saying, "My dove in the cranny of the rock . . . let Me hear your voice" (Song of Songs 2:14). Such bold imagery conveys the theological conviction of the relationship between divine love and the beneficences of Law: of the immanence of God through the Law in the life of the nation, and of the sense of God's providential care through the Law. The legal stipulations would correspondingly be deemed protective hedges for social life and dignity: forms of rigor necessary for communal welfare and the balance of freedom and care in the social world. This dynamic conjunction of limit and largesse is a life project for ongoing covenantal hermeneutics—grounded in a theological sense of God's demands and beneficence.

Perceiving this "metaphysical mixture," some commentators noted two types of speech in the prologue to the Decalogue: "God spoke (*va-yidabber*) all these words (*devarim*), saying (*lei'mor*)" (Exodus 20:1). The first speech-type, marked by the verb *dabber*, was taken to denote the rigors of language and law, when life issues must be conveyed distinctly and firmly; whereas the second speech-type, marked by the verb *amar*, was taken to denote a more gentle use of language, when circumstances require the voice of care to affect the content of speech. Refracted through the lens of legal formulations, two dimensions of language are highlighted. On the one hand, language requires formalities necessary to establish social justice; but it must also provide the means to benefit lives held in the balance. Considered from the perspective of normal discourse, language must also balance conventional formulations with sensitivity for the way words convey meanings in conversation and dialogue. The expressive power of speech must be regulated to join formal articulation and moral purpose—forthright communication with concern for the bonds of lived social life.

(IV)

Seeing the Voices—Entwinements of Revelation and Redemption

In the world, a multitude of voices solicit our attention. Gradually certain priorities become settled practice, easing the need to make judgments at all times. But routine tends to diminish the special character of each moment. For the heart cultivated by rabbinic tradition, every event has its unique valence. One tries to determine its liturgical character, lifting the occurrence out of its natural aspect and transforming it into a moment of consecration. In this way, the shapes of "lived experience" are evaluated in terms of their "covenantal duties."

Yet many occurrences may remain indeterminate, and the responses required must be assessed. *Qolot* and *beraqim*: just as "flashes of light" follow "thundering claps" of sound, interpretative insights follow the resonances that may summon us to attention. We weigh things, make mental balances, and hope that the action will stand the test. The intractable mixtures of life often make moral or ritual decisions a challenge. The halakhic tradition previsions certain acts or dispositions in order to prepare a template of values for unknown events. Another mode of guidance is to study the personal examples of the ancestors, as they are formulated in scripture and subsequent rabbinic commentaries. These paradigmatic depictions offer new calibrations for thoughtful examination. Thinking with scripture and tradition offers models (moral and halakhic) for theological living. Hermeneutics focuses and grounds the imagination, and provides ways to reassess the balances between freedom and restraint.

Learning from Abraham—Once Again; Balancing Events and Evaluations

Passages of scripture can help guide one's responses to complex situations. The case of God appearing to Abraham "while he (*ve-hu*) was sitting" before the entrance of his tent (Genesis 18:1) was considered earlier to involve more than a physical situation prior to the advent of wayfarers (v. 2). One of the topics noted was the relationship between that divine appearance and the subsequent acts of the patriarch. What was involved, and how did this precondition his response? For a person schooled in rabbinic legal tradition, evaluation of this event is influenced by halakhic or spiritual precedents. In this instance, the temporal clause referring to him (*ve-hu*; "while he") in a certain situation would evoke, initially, the halakhic consideration of a person (or object) deemed to be in a particular "existential state" (*be-havayato*), due to a prior designation (Mishnah, *Menaḥot* 4:4). Confronted by some unexpected event or situation, a reconsideration of the status of that person (or thing) would have to be made. Would the individual remain independent of the impacting situation, or would the latter affect their (or its) status? Stimulated by this consideration, and applying it to a reading of the episode about Abraham, one rabbinic view opined that Abraham was then engaged in prayer—involved in an act that preconditioned his relationship to external events. The conceptual issue would then be how Abraham (or anyone in a similar situation) should act. Which event should take priority, the status quo ante (the existential state of prayer) or the new or interrupting circumstance (the social event of welfare)? Clearly, Abraham is caught in a double bind, since he is already absorbed in a relationship to God (in prayer) when the guests appear (requiring an act of hospitality). Were he to choose one and defer (or dismiss) the other, on what basis should he do so? If, as one might reason, the particular situation (prayer) involves a fixed religious obligation, time-bound in character, the divine duty should prevail over the human event and its moral requirements. However, even on that premise, one might also consider whether this new event is immediately necessary and cannot be done by anyone else—in which case the present divine duties (the status quo ante) may be deferred. Such deliberations depend on there being two separate situations that are conjoined, so that one must try to determine whether to decide in terms of law and its limits (*din*), or love and its expressions (*raḥamim*). Or even more, whether it is possible to combine these obligations, so that one's religious duties might coexist with the need to perform an act of kindness (*gemilut ḥesed*) to strangers. And then one would seek a viable balance between them. Such hermeneutical perplexities affect our theological and moral lives. The contingencies of the narrative leave much to ponder.

A second consideration of the biblical episode notes that Abraham was in a certain "state" (be it a spiritual disposition or an actual practice) at home, when a certain realization transformed his religious consciousness. For example, while in the act of prayer he sensed that a new divine duty was required by a specific social situation (the appearance of the wayfarers). Since now the two factors are on the same plane (both being religious obligations), a different consideration is possible—namely, that the new event take priority, since the presence of *orḥim* (wayfarers-guests) reveals a divine obligation that must be responded to "according to its specific manner" (*le-fum orheih*). In such a case, the social demands of hospitality override the preexisting private state of prayer. According to a traditional view of this situation, a person must abandon a prior practice or "state" (*havayato*) if and when an unexpected occasion must be done there and then, and in a particular way. The duty is to respond immediately and with a gracious gratuity (*gemilut ḥesed*) to God's immediate gifts of existence (*ḥasadim*). Hereby, the theological and ethical tasks conjoin, being effectively an expression of *imitatio dei*. Reverence for God (*yir'at elohim*) is now expressed through acts of beneficent love (*ahavah rabbah*) and creature care. It reflects a theological case of integration and balance, rather than one of division or distinction.

A final use of this episode as an exemplum for action offers the opportunity for a person to conjoin the two events in one state of consciousness. According to one Hasidic discussion, our text presents a spiritual challenge: to be attentive to the life events at hand (the case here: the appearance of strangers), and pray that one's preexisting spiritual state (as here: prayer) "will not pass from" the person "when" or "while" they are responding to the new situation (Genesis 18:3). Thus the person wants to respond to the life moment while sustaining their previous mental focus. On this understanding, Abraham's request that the wayfarers "not pass from before" him constitutes his prayer that the spiritual state he has achieved will be retained when responding to the new social occurrence. For then he (and others) could worship God (have God in mind) while engaged in the particularities of life circumstances (*'avodah be-gashmiyut*). Taking this scriptural case to heart, later readers might try to appropriate it as a paradigmatic episode. Following Abraham's example, one would intend to bring contradictory events into spiritual harmony—as much as possible. In this way, the intersecting events would not create a cognitive rupture or emotional dislocation, but stimulate a quest for a balanced religious integration.

Seeing but Not Seeing

There are other modes of consciousness that defer or deny the divine reality staring one in the face. Scripture provides particular exhortations to open one's eyes. "Do not see your compatriot's ox or sheep wandering astray and disregard them; but go and return them to your compatriot"—or, if they are far off, safeguard their goods at your home until they are sought for, and then restore them to their owner without niggling or making false distinctions about what should or should not be returned: "for you are not allowed to disregard" anything lost by your brethren and found by you (Deuteronomy 21:1–3). Such moments require attentiveness and responsibility, for the covenant demands ethical trust across the social realms. Blinding one's eyes to actual circumstances is seeing without seeing—looking past the presenting reality with a closed heart and not making the immediate event the primary concern. Similarly, scripture notes other occasions where one sees one's compatriot's animals stumbling along the way, but ignores what transpires in plain sight. Such blatant disregard is also prohibited, and moral action is required: "You must help him lift them up" (v. 4). For although these cases cannot be brought to court (being exhortatory in nature), they are fundamental to one's moral and social conscience, and put one's inner worth in the balance. Closing one's eye to ethical involvement is a fatal misprision: the insidious blindness of omission and disregard. To see and know—and thus bear witness to an event—is a fundamental individual responsibility. Negative complicity has consequences. If one sees or hears something, it must be rightly attested (Leviticus 5:1), for the immediacy of reality—God's presence—calls out in every created form. We give witness to it with our lives. The singularity of each person's face requires such ongoing validations (see Mishnah, *Sanhedrin* 4:5, citing Leviticus 5:1).

Seeing but Not Knowing—Knowing but Not Seeing

Our existence in the world puts us in phenomenological jeopardy. We see, but not completely, given our situated nature; and we know, but never decisively, given our finite cognition. Assertions must be checked and corroborated, just as allegations require cross-examination. If bearing responsibility for oneself is a weighty matter, all the more is this so when we testify to happenings in the social world that implicate others. For according to scripture and tradition, the word of one is insufficient in such cases. It has no "substance." The "matter (or case) will stand" only on the valid testimony of "two" or more witnesses (Deuteronomy 19:15), who attest to an event independently, without either one of them involved or participatory in the situation being investigated (Babylonian Talmud, *Makkot* 5a). The world stands firm on the word of persons whose verbal "yes is truly a yes" and their "no truly a no." There is no mixture of intent here; no duplicity characterizes their lives.

"You are My witnesses, says Y-H-W-H; and I am God" (Isaiah 43:10)—concerning which R. Shimon bar Yochai taught: "If you are 'My witnesses,' I am God; but if you are not My witnesses then, as it were, I am not God" (*Sifre Deuteronomy* 346). Living testimonials of God's "Shall Be" in the world affirm the theological truth of God's omnipresent reality, beckoning human attestation and response to the phenomena of existence. To derogate or invalidate such theological responsibility perverts the testimony of life, and one is an *'ed zomem*, a "malicious witness," before God (Deuteronomy 19:16). For all intents and purposes, in such cases, Divinity is annulled—or rendered *sheqer* (false). By contrast, the multitudes that stood at Sinai in spiritual witness inaugurate the chain of generations that testify to God's eternal "Shall Be," through their attentive awareness and liturgical celebration. A community of faithfulness is a community of witnesses.

The Revelation of Creation in Redemptive Deeds

Jewish theology conjoins a twofold reality: the world of creation, always present and always renewed if we have the eyes to see; and revelation, the occasions of spiritual value in the world. The key paradigm for the first is the "account of creation" (Genesis 1:1–2:4), with its teaching of the transformation of inchoate *tohu* into the structures of world and social order. Its conclusion states: "These (*eleh*) are the generations (*toledot*) of the heavens and earth during their creation (*be-hibbar'am*)." In one sense, this statement refers to the sphere of reality we deem the all-environing world that precedes and conditions our human situation (the verb *be-hibbar'am* highlights the primordial factuality of worldly existence). The phrase also attests to our ongoing hermeneutical condition, as the varieties of world possibilities are constantly reconstituted through interpretation (thus the verb *be-hibbar'am* also highlights the creative nature of our existence— the ever-renewed status of heaven and earth through acts of the exegetical imagination). The pronoun *eleh* (these) points to the natural world, available for human significations in the here and now. Taken as a statement of our human situation, Genesis 2:4 acknowledges the factuality of worldhood as an existential truth; and the ongoing process of the divine creation, which includes the hermeneutic imagination.

The fundamental paradigm for the second reality of Jewish theology is the "event of Sinai" (Exodus 19–24), with its various descriptions of the revelation of norms and statutes: the creation of a "holy people" through a covenantal ordering of life. An elaboration of these matters is announced by the verse "And these (*ve-eleh*) are the regulations (*ha-mishpatim*) which you [Moses] shall set before them (*lifneihem*)" (Exodus 21:1). This passage refers to the factuality of a body of legal norms and rules that set forth regulative cases for the public domain. They propose conditions and procedures for a range of civil and cultic acts, as well as a variety of exhortations that bear on ideal attitudes and practices. To address these purposes, the legal regulations formulate hypothetical situations in an impersonal voice ("if one"), or speak to individual participants of the covenant individually in the second person ("you"). Either way, these norms all have a statutory quality—presenting their details as set cases bearing on life. Viewed from the perspective of topics placed "before" the people, these pronouncements regulate typical or complex situations that might arise. They are therefore put cognitively "before" the people, who will have to adjust their precise meanings to the ambiguities that inevitably arise from lived experience (the domain of *torah kelulah*). All these discernments are hermeneutical in nature, and produce the regulations (*mishpatim*) necessary for social stability. Moses, our master teacher, understood and lived this theological truth. Conscious of the civic complications of existence, he sought to perceive the covenantal tasks that confronted the polity in the here and now. The phrase *eleh ha-mishpatim*, "these are the regulations," is thus both a descriptive and a prescriptive formulation. The former articulates the existing legal norms; the latter broadcasts a formal pedagogy for enacting justice in new circumstances.

It behooves a living theology to ponder the co-relationship between *eleh toledot ha-shamayim veha-aretz* and *eleh ha-mishpatim*—between the generations of heaven and earth and the regulations of the covenant. The forms of interpreted life transform the natural order, rendering all our worldly habitats of prescriptive value—giving God's eternal voice embodiments in deed and deportment. '*Eleh*' (these) is a term of measure, reflecting the mixed achievements of life and law, for both the natural world and culture. The *mishpatim* serve as intermediating structures between persons and the world—norms that address individuals through tradition and its various modes of expression. They become actual (not mere legal abstractions) in the course of life, when the voice of God resounds through them in all its living directness. But because the content of experience is fluid and often ambiguous, tensions may arise between established law (the received *mishpatim*) and the commandments (the imperatives of life events; or God's living presence in the world). Both *eleh* (*toledot*) and *eleh* (*ha-mishpatim*) are the words of God, and require a co-regulation between the pulse of life and the patterns of law. It is a task of theology to perceive the divine word in both. Living theology cannot abandon its partnership with the natural world or its covenantal forms. It is a bond that must be lived with integrity.

Life and Law: Love and Limit

The revelation of Torah, and its communal stabilization in *mishpatim* and through *halakha*, are refractions of the glory of God through the forms of worldly reality. A complex symbiosis of "divine giving" and "human receiving" recurs across the spectrum of existence—both being components of God's Ḥesed. The primordial divine evocation "Let Be" (*yehi*) occurs everywhere and at all times, and results in the imponderable interconnections that constitute the totality of what is. As a primordial life-force, the imperative "Let Be" is the raw impulse for life and survival. As a social force, it is the utopian drive for liberation and human dignity. As a legislative principle (*hesed* formulated to insure social justice) it is the imperative to adjust these primordial forces to the requirements of multilateral human coexistence: the balance between excess and limit. "Let Be" is thus dual in nature. It is both the divinely engendered life-force itself and the human duty to respect the life-needs of others. The universal truth of Job's consciousness is the particular truth of Jewish covenantal theology.

The world and all therein are recipients of the gift-giving of God. Whoever would ascend this spiritual mountain, and stand for holiness on earth, must purify their heart to perceive the presence of God's glory throughout existence. Such a person must be both a devoted seeker and interpreter: searching life and language for the best instantiations of *hesed* in each situation. Like Moses, who gave legal expression and social stability to God's mysterious giving, all those who accept Moses as their teacher and guide must likewise seek to interpret this world bounty righteously. They must have teachings of *hesed* on their mouth and seek paths to establish redemptive partnerships with God in the upbuilding of creation—each person *le-fum shi'urei*, "according to their own measure" or capacity.

The ongoing balance between creation (*eleh toledot ha-shamayim vehaaretz*) and revelation (*eleh ha-mishpatim*) requires a perception of the correlation between set "limit" (*shi'ur*) and "going beyond." The regulative principle for this balance is moral *hesed*, as it seeks to adjudicate between the primary value of life (the vitalizing bounty of God—"Let Be" as lifeprinciple) and the social acts of care required in particular circumstances (the formal boundaries of law—"Let Be" as a moral principle).

A Biblical Case Explored

The formulations of a righteous law offer diverse paradigms to consider, especially where factors complicate a precise calculus of the remedies required. Consider this case in point. "When you reap the harvest of your land, you shall not reap up to the edges of your field, or gather the gleanings of your harvest; nor shall you pick your vineyard bare, or gather the fallen fruit of your vineyard: you shall leave them for the poor and the stranger: I the Lord (*Y-H-W-H*) am your God" (Leviticus 19:9–10).

These words speak to a landowner who is also an earth-sharer with the poor, upon an earth where both are beneficiaries of the gratuitous gifts of God's vitality: the *hesed* upon which the world was founded and is "renewed every day." Hence the strong force of this exhortation, since it is precisely in the context of gathering produce, when one's labor has appropriated the goods of the earth and one's focus centers around one's particular place, that persons may forget their dependence on bounties for which they have worked *but not created*. Thus landowners are called upon to be givers: to allow others to enter their private space and, for the moment, to enact a ritual of ethical beneficence—the sharing of food between an owner and the needy ownerless. Hearing this command, owners are bidden to transcend self-interest and recognize the natural duty that moral finitude demands.

The Written Torah becomes a living word of God through the Oral Torah, when the scriptural teachings inspire a perception of how they may be brought into accord with the moral imperatives of life and creature care. Scripture itself records several instances of how this dynamism was enacted by "our teacher, Moses"—in various reformulations of earlier rules for later generations. These explications are recorded in the Written Torah for future generations to both ponder and enact. They constitute a virtual prophetic voice of social counsel within the Law. So hear in this regard what was formulated as a hortatory "exposition" of the aforementioned instruction (the italicized words are the clarifications): "When you reap the harvest in your field *and forget a sheaf in the field, do not return to get it: it shall be for the stranger, orphan, and widow—in order that the Lord, your God, may bless you in all that you do.* When you beat down your olive trees, do not go back over them again: that (fruit) shall be for the stranger, orphan, and widow. When you *harvest the grapes of* your vineyard, do not *go back and* pick it over *again*: it shall be for the stranger, orphan, and widow. *And remember that you were a slave in the land of Egypt: therefore I enjoin you to do this commandment*" (Deuteronomy 24:19–22). The addressee now hears more details. The sheaves left over from the initial act of harvesting are now specified as forgotten goods, and no longer part of one's property; the fruit of olive trees are also added to the harvest of grains and grapes, and it is emphasized that only the initial act of taking is permitted; similarly, with regard to harvesting a vineyard, one is limited to the first plucking. Finally, Moses repeatedly clarifies that these poor are orphans and widows, and adds to the initial divine proclamation the duty to remember that the people had once been destitute slaves in Egypt. The "other" is "oneself" in a different social iteration. As a result, thoughtful ownership requires the recollection of one's human vulnerability.

Rabbinic Expansions and Clarifications

At the core of the biblical exhortation is the duty of creature care: both an impartial bestowal of property and a ritual act of care for the sustenance of society. Collective responsibility requires a delimited disregard of personal benefit within a structure of social support. To insure this, later rabbinic rulings sought to adjudicate or adjust normative boundaries and provide moral clarity to both the letter and spirit of these biblical injunctions. Thus we find a specification of provisions regarding the minimal measures to be left for the needy; how one should glean the crop or pick its produce, especially where sheaves may fall or stocks are left standing in the process; and how one should regard fruit that remains on the top branches during a harvest, even though these might be deemed out of reach and not normally accessible. Ownership has its rights as well as its limits, when there is a norm or exhortation to provide care for the needy. These distinctions, or catalog of provisions, help cultivate a social-moral disposition of responsible generosity, as much as possible. To help facilitate this concern, there are explicit statements that exhort the landowner to inform the aged or infirm when the harvest times will occur so that they can be prepared for the collection—and not be pushed aside by more able-bodied persons. To foster this procedure, the weak are allowed to enlist aides or children for assistance. And it was even taught that temporary migrants or foreigners should be included among the native strangers "for the sake of peace"—not merely for social peace, but for the "repair of the world" order. In this sense, the spirit of the laws expands beyond the strict letter of the scriptural regulations. Safeguarding dignity—addressing the despair of disenfranchisement or ignominy of begging—the wounds of circumstance are healed. In this way, law helps enact redemption.

Liturgical Midrash and the Redemptive Deed

Cultivating a spiritual disposition of ḥesed requires knowledge of the covenantal norms and values. One traditional setting for learning these matters was a genre of liturgy that incorporated these midrashic teachings of scripture—weekly, during the Sabbath, when the weekly lection was recited; and during the festivals, when special topics were chosen to highlight the teachings of the sacred occasions. These liturgical-poetic renditions of rabbinic teachings, recited among the statutory prayers, are known as *piyyut*. The pedagogical distinction of these liturgical compositions is that both the Written Torah and its oral explications were interfused, such that both were enunciated by the cantor as part of public worship. This effectively gave rabbinic instruction a sacred aura and character. A liturgical recitation based on Leviticus 25, with its exhortations to care for the needy, serves as a case in point.

The rabbinic concern to highlight social concerns for the indigent is evident in the decision to begin one of the weekly Torah recitations (from the old triennial cycle) with Leviticus 25:5: "If your kinsman becomes impoverished, and comes under your power (literally, "his strength fails, *matah yado*, with you"), you shall strengthen him (*heḥezaqta bo*) as a resident stranger, so that he may live with you (*ve-ḥay 'immakh*)." This opening exhortation signals the chief concern of the unit and was duly incorporated (according to established practice) by the cantor into the fixed liturgical stations of his public repetition of the Amidah (Statutory Prayer) on that particular Sabbath. Thus, echoing the weekly scriptural lection, the repetition opens with the phrase "The poor and the rich You [God] made" (a reformulation of the biblical dictum "Rich and poor met, the Lord made them both"; Proverbs 22:2). And since this theme was reworked in the midrash to emphasize both the codependence of rich and poor, and their interlocking fates (which may be reversed by the wheel of fortune), the cantor goes on to exhort the congregation to aid the needy for both reasons (codependent responsibility and their intertwined fates, for weal and woe). Another admonition to care for the indigent is adduced in this prayer by a citation from the prophetic unit publicly recited together with this pentateuchal selection: "Strengthen the hands (*ḥizqu yadayim*) that are slack, firm-up the tottering knees" (Isaiah 35:3). In context, this verse urges spiritual support of the weak-of-spirit, whereas it functions in this prayer to reinforce the emphasis in the Torah on behalf of the physically poor and needy.

The rendition of the biblical and rabbinic materials by the liturgical poet Yannai (who flourished in the sixth–seventh century CE in the land of Israel) is particularly notable for the way the prose formulations of tradition are thickened by stylistic parallelism (conjoining human actions to a divine response) and deft ambiguity (as in the second stanza). Throughout, the "hand" serves as a metaphor for concrete beneficence and a metonym for providential acts—divine and human. Through the voice of the cantor, the rabbinic homilies become sacred service: prayer as religious instruction.

> Strengthen (*haḥaziqu*) others through the force of your hand (*ḥezqat yad*)
> Thus the Mighty One (*ḥazaq*) admonished, He Who strengthens you with a mighty hand
>
> Give to the poor according to your capacity (*yadakh*)
> Then H/he will give to you according to H/his means (*yado*)
>
> His hand (*yado*) will not fail to save
> Nor (will) His (heavenly) treasuries lack in sustenance

For as a hand is to the body so shall you be for each other (*zeh la-zeh*)
To strengthen and support each another (*zeh et zeh*) through charity
  (*tzedakah*)

This concatenation of teachings alternates between exhortation, obligation, and the interlocked fates of members of society. These features, which highlight self-interest, operate at both the social level, which specifies reciprocal care, and the religious level, which promises a divine reward for acts of social beneficence. Not least striking is the presentation of the covenantal society as one body politic. In all this the voice of the synagogue poet is paramount—reformulating the many midrashic teachings in a way that condenses the divine instructions for pedagogical effect. Throughout, the cantor is the bearer of rabbinic tradition and the voice of authority. In his mouth scripturally based admonitions are directed to the people—with particular force in the conclusion that reprises and brings to a climax the entire composition. It rings with particular force:

Happy are those who help those whose strength fails (*matei yad*) to
  rejoice
For (this act) will benefit (*ta'amod*) the one (the poor) at once (*miyyad*)
And stand (*ta'amid*) surety (*yad*) for the other (in time to come).

Liturgical midrash is a form of hermeneutical theology, and it serves here to direct one's heart to the duties of communal care. The rhetorical setting is the synagogue, but it leads into the world. Just here is the place where God's worldly revelations occur, and where Torah and tradition must be enacted. *Derash* helps institute a practical theology applied to lived experience. Covenantal values are reformulated to activate social responsibility. This concern notwithstanding, a living theology must also speak to the individual, their conscience and commitments. Attention to such personal development is and has been the province of *remez*. It is to this hermeneutical realm that we now turn.

Interlude Three

Communities of Interpretation and Spiritual Development

Belonging to a community of interpretation influences one's dispositions in fundamental ways. Initially, common modes of understanding, belief, and practice are conveyed through the words of parents and teachers, and patterns of behavior are transmitted through the model of their lives. These shape one's sense of being a person and the way things are or should be. In time, these primary influences are supplemented by the content of traditional texts, through their formal instruction or explication. Learning is exemplary and character-building in every sense, since the goal is to inculcate the values and practices of the culture in a new generation. The primacy of this process reinforces the authority of the content and conveys a sense that the components of culture are embedded in the nature of things. As a result each individual is rooted in a collective wisdom that infuses their life with significance. Tradition is the matrix of shared meaning.

Religious cultures also seek to transmit their knowledge across the generations. In addition to a common core of beliefs and practices, the concern to inculcate theological values and dispositions has particular importance in the schemes of education. The latter constitute the aspirations that develop over time, and are geared to promote a distinctive personality type. In most cases, these goals are embedded in the norms of a society—both written and oral—and play out in multiple ways. When successful, traditional practices reinforce individual purposes, so that collective behaviors will provide spiritual direction for each person. Religious seekers invest these public practices with particular value, since they form the basis of their personal sense of religious integrity and development. As a result, the inherited contents and their hierarchies of significance are repeatedly weighed for their personal value, and their capacity to inspire purpose and wisdom. A robust tradition fosters this dynamic and lends an aura of authenticity to one's commitments. In this way, the hermeneutics of the individual complements those of the collective.

Judaism is a public religion of action and attention. To seek the reality of God requires one to assess how God is present in the world. This quest is guided by the terms or values of tradition (the *torah she-bikhtav* and *torah she-be'al peh*). In the process, persons may also draw on the fund of Jewish intellectual or spiritual content developed over centuries, or even the teachings of other traditions, insofar as these can be integrated into the value-structures of Judaism. Both resources are central to the hermeneutical concerns of *remez* (the exegetical mode concerned with intellectual, spiritual, and ethical self-development). Accordingly, various medieval Jewish philosophers, like Maimonides, perceived hints (*remazim*) of a universal philosophical wisdom at the surface level of scripture—concealed there for like-minded thinkers to discover, even if these truths were (allegorically) derived from such foreign philosophers as Plato and Aristotle. On this basis, both Maimonides and his disciples sought wisdom wherever it lay, and tried to recover the metaphysical and ethical truths encoded in both biblical and rabbinic literature. The hermeneutical goal was to both purify the mind and train the body through various intellectual and behavioral practices, leading to the ultimate ideal: the knowledge of God. Following another track, medieval mystics like R. Ezra of Gerona and the fellowship of the Zohar believed that sacred scripture contained a most recondite wisdom of primordial divine realities—symbolically encoded into its language. For those schooled in esoteric semantics, decoding the allusive "hints to the wise" (*remiza le-ḥakima*) was the key to attaining the ultimate spiritual ideal: consciousness of God and the supernal verities. Thus many mystics, like Abraham Abulafia, searched near and far for true theosophy and meditative disciplines, and perceived this wisdom in the philosophical works of Plotinus and Eriugena or the practices of Sufi saints. These (and other) elements were deemed universal truths, and were therefore, on this basis, reformulated and integrated into the living Jewish tradition.

For seekers both ancient and medieval, these intellectual traditions provide guidelines for the development of one's soul, and study of scripture was deemed a spiritual practice that revealed its esoteric truths to the initiated. Our present task is different, particularly for those who reject the presuppositions of an arcane wisdom encoded in scripture. Accordingly, part 4 focuses on the dynamics of concrete experience and exoteric instructions recorded in scripture. This emphasis comports with the theological concern of this book, which may be characterized as the cultivation of one's personal consciousness while attuned to God's omnipresent vitality throughout existence. This dual dimension is explicitly stated in scripture, which exhorts: "Know God in all your ways (*be-khol derakhekha*)" (Proverbs 3:6)—nothing less. Taken at face value, this means that one must be God-centered in both thought and action across the full spectrum of God-given life (in its range of experiential particularities and possibilities). As a comprehension invocation, the individual is summoned to cultivate a focused theological demeanor. As a spiritual task, this exhortation requires both intentionality and discernment, for the challenge exceeds the formal performance of the legal-ritual commandments. Not only are these to be enacted with God-consciousness, but one must respond to all life occasions with a similar God-oriented intention.

Mindful Doing: A Commentary

We meet the God-bestowed world with mind and body. The theological challenge is to cultivate an alert mindfulness that receives earthly reality as expressions of Divinity. The bounty of life reveals these manifestations in numerous ways. Some of them may be evaluated through the measures of Jewish tradition (its teachings and practices), others through personal dispositions or worldly instruction. Accordingly, divine heteronomy and human autonomy are intertwined. God's formative presence is received by seekers as expressions of the creation, and humans shape these into social forms through their creative acts. To know God in all one's "*ways*" makes the individual an active participant in God's worldly activities. One "knows God" by being cognitively attuned to the multiple "ways of the world." Developing this awareness requires discipline and determination, stimulated by the study of spiritual practices. Adepts deem this a lifelong commitment. Each moment offers spiritual opportunities.

If we shift our focus to the personal pronoun, emphasizing "all *your* ways," the emphasis falls on individual expression. This is a fundamental component of the hermeneutic practice of *remez*, for it underscores the fact that all God-minded deeds are expressed through one's personal traits and understanding. Subjectivity is therefore not a play of private enjoyments, but a cultivated deportment whose intention is to dedicate all one's limbs to the service of God. The individual thus engages the claims of existence through cultural practices (mental and physical) in uniquely personal terms. The God-mindedness of these ritual actions serves as a means of focused "knowing"—of God in (and through) all *one's* earthly "ways."

What about those moments that foster confusion (*behalah*)—when no way seems right or unambiguous? Help may be found in the conclusion to Proverbs 3:6. Following the exhortation to know God in all one's ways, we

are told: "Then He will make your paths upright," *ve-hu yeyasher orhotekha.*
If the adverb "then" indicates a result clause, consequent to the prior exhortation, the meaning would be that a God-centered life (in all one's ways)
can inculcate a spiritual disposition that may help one discern the proper
or "upright" acts to be followed during such times of ambiguity or confusion. On this view, one's *derekh* marks a straightforward "way" of engaging with the events of the world, whereas the *orah*, or "path," marks more
uncharted options that need deliberate resolve to be made straight. Beset by
perplexity, an individual may recall this teaching and hope that their earlier,
God-inspired actions may orient them in new circumstances. Religious-
theological disciplines may help sharpen spiritual alertness and reflection,
but they cannot eliminate perplexity and hermeneutical decision.

A Meditation on the Heart

How may a spiritual seeker find the right balance for each circumstance?
By using both received traditions and personal experiences for guidance.
Traditions provide the primary framework for moral principles or dispositions, whereas lived experience provides the measures of enactment and
evaluation. Norms may give us the general structure, but modifications are
required amid the complexities of life. A proper integration must be sought.
Faced with cases of need, one must wonder, Have I allowed a presenting
situation to have its moral impact? Still other cases may also give pause,
and then one will ask, Am I open to a reconsideration of the evidence, or
have I blocked proper receptivity because of self-interest? Repeatedly, the
fault-lines must be judged, and the proper balances assessed. The ideal is
to cultivate a heart of wisdom, spiritually disposed to the panoply of God's
universal "Shall Be."

Turning inward, the seeker wants a *lev nachon*, a "heart rightly attuned"
to life and its challenges. This wanting is a spiritual longing, and an awareness of fallibility. Sometimes this desire is expressed as a prayer: "O God,
create for me a pure heart (*lev tahor*), and renew in me an upright spirit
(*ruah nachon*). Cast me not from You, and do not remove Your holy spirit
from me" (Psalm 51:12–13). The pathos and sense of fracture expressed here
are poignant. Equally significant is the conviction that inner purity and an
upright spirit are the necessary components of a relationship with God.
Meditating on this issue, R. Simhah Bunim, the great Hasidic master of
Przysucha, stressed that one's spiritual quest must reach the center of one's
being (*'atzmuto*) in order to discover the core that binds it to God—whose
center is everywhere. From this core, one's spiritual disposition can radiate
outward.

And the Soul

Since antiquity, the soul has been considered a substance of sorts, with traits and capacities. Following these precedents, Jewish tradition identified an "animal soul" (called *nefesh*), which animates the spirit of existence at one's vital core; an "appetitive soul" (called *ruah*), which directs the mind to specific goals, be this for survival or intellectual ideals; and a "cognitive-spiritual soul" (called *neshamah*), which yearns for ultimate transcendence and the divine reality. For numerous thinkers, these soul-types denote a hierarchy of dimensions; and philosophers and mystics measured their place on this scale, with each element having its specific function and challenge.

What remains of this heritage when these soul qualities no longer ring true—psychologically or philosophically—since they reflect medieval ontologies of the self? In the following, I shall regard the soul as the overall structure or gestalt of a person's activities, as one strives for psychospiritual development over a lifetime. So considered, the soul is not a substantive or metaphysical entity but the dynamic psycho-social formation of one's character from birth to death—in all one's ways. In addition to one's corporeal nature, the vital questions of individual personality ("Who are you?" or "Where are you?") are addressed to the center of one's spiritual consciousness—the "soul-center" of emergent selfhood, with all the sensations and memories attendant thereto—and only the self can answer these queries. The heart seeks to find a proper balance among the God-given possibilities of existence, by assessing the evidence and directing it to different goals. Just like the individual taste of desert manna of old, so the sense and value of one's life change over a lifetime, with different sensibilities emphasized by the young or old. One cannot expect that life to have the same meaning for the youthful, still exploring life, as for the elderly, facing diminishment and death. What a person seeks, or needs, or desires will vary accordingly, and the dynamic balances between *din* (fixed structure) and *rahamim* (creative flexibility) will recalibrate in due measure. The incremental achievements of virtues produce, at each life stage, the salience of one's personality. Cultivating a *lev nachon* is crucial. It provides the ballast and orientation on one's "way." Even more fundamentally, it strives to focus spiritual intention and direct it toward deliberate decisions. The inherent correlation between intention and identity thus becomes an embodied hermeneutic practice. It occurs (Husserl once said) in the "living now"—repeatedly enacted and repeatedly reconstituted. In such ways, the mystery of God comes to life expressions—in lower or higher degrees, depending on each person and their cultivation of the conditions of existence.

Toward a Hermeneutics of the Self—in the First Instance

The self comes to awareness in stages, through the resources of culture. Touch and tone, and gesture and word, are fundamental factors in the communication of values. Each moment is laden with significance, and the parsing or apportionment of these events is occasion for development. Attachments play a part, too, with consequences both positive and negative; and the realities of rejection or insecurity are similarly consequential. We carry the implications forward into numerous unsuspecting circumstances. Boundaries appear or are erased, depending on instruction or sheer will, while social norms impose certain limits that circumscribe individual possibilities. And sometimes all these matters are overlaid with religious and psychological considerations.

For certain individuals, care of the self is an exclusionary matter, and this determines how one reads life experience and assesses its value. This is a hermeneutical activity in its own right. Others put an aesthetic gloss on self-care, and regard themselves as a project-in-process, where hedonism takes many forms. Among the latter, self-absorption can be a primary character trait; and then one reads the world with this concern in mind, ignoring those self-transcending values that put one in relationship to larger cultural and social purposes. Ego-centrism is a restrictive moral ecology, whereas more cosmopolitan concerns reach beyond these limits to include a global ecology of interests. This is a hermeneutics of the self that entails responsibilities large and small, and a realization of the permeable contours of life that require constant attention and regard. For such persons, cultural pedagogies instruct the self across the generations, and they read texts and the world for this benefit. At the core of this process are canonical resources, spiritual products that have stood the test of time, require intellectual investment, and are a counterpoint to personal interests or myopia. The hermeneutics of the self are duly tempered and cultivated thereby. Seeking these resources is therefore deemed an essential value for those involved.

*

For the Jewish seeker, primary resources for self-cultivation include the canonical narratives and moral counsels of scripture. Through their means and content, one's personhood may be influenced by literary exemplars that provide models for the structuring of values and the shaping of experience. Integrating them into one's self-development is a fundamental factor in the "hermeneutical constitution of the self." But because we are also a soul-subject in process, faced with uncertainty and ambiguity, *ulay* (perhaps) is a counterpoint to our intentions and acts of self-development. We act in the hope that a viable balance between the limits of life and our higher aspirations may "stand" the test. In the Jewish tradition, the hermeneutics of *remez* guides and supports this concern.

PART FOUR

Remez

Hermeneutics of Tradition and Self-Development

Creature consciousness is one's primary sense of being-in-the-world. It begins with bodily and emotional sensations, and remains of decisive significance even after these qualities are complemented by thought and the forms of language. We never transcend our earthbound nature or physical environment; they suffuse our sensibilities and identity in every way. Becoming an "I" involves awareness of being concretely located in space; and this reality affects our communications with every "you," "it," or "thing" we encounter in the world—positively and negatively. Positively, since it sponsors productive links to other creatures and their worldly needs; and negatively, since it affects competitive differences for self-preservation. A critical task for *remez* is to cultivate values that balance concerns for individuality and self-development with the social claims or existence of other creatures. These values are drawn from the funds of cultural tradition and personal experience. The hermeneutics of *remez* harnesses these resources for the sake of self-cultivation and self-regulation. The ideals are further intensified in the service of transcendent aspirations, moral and spiritual—especially when the self is oriented to a God-consciousness and seeks to implement this value through mental or ritual practices. The process begins with an awakening.

"Who may ascend the mountain of *Y-H-W-H* and stand in His holy place?" (Psalm 24:3). Who may hear this call of spiritual pilgrimage, so that the spaces of life become a transfigured sanctuary? This query calls the self into question. The word *miy* (who) expresses the challenge: How can I stand before this question and its spiritual demand? An answer rises in response: "One who has clean hands and a pure heart, and has not spoken falsely— O my soul (*nafshi*)!—or sworn deceitfully" (v. 4). Note the embedded exclamation. In the midst of a litany of virtues the speaker interrupts the sequence with a cry of personal pathos ("O my soul!"). If the virtues enunciate the spiritual task, this interruption evokes the psychic difficulties involved. The issue is not only the establishment of a spiritual-ethical agenda, but the willpower necessary for its realization. The exclamation reveals precisely where one's pilgrimage must take place: in the complex "ways" of the heart. And it is also here that one hopes to receive a divine blessing (v. 5). Standing in God's holy place requires resolve. But where are the points of entry? An answer follows: pay heed to the "gateways" (she'arim) of life and raise them to attentive awareness (v. 7), for these gateways are the life "measures" (shi'urim) of existence that are apportioned to us in the here and now. It is to the manifold of creation that we must attune our spirit and bodies. These "gates" are the "worldly openings" (pithei 'olam) to eternity (v. 7), the diverse occasions through which the immeasurable depths of the divine glory are contracted to our mortal minds and may "come" to consciousness (v. 9). They are the forms through which we intuit God's omnipresence on earth.

A Second Meditation on the Heart: Perplexities and Desires

But there is a palpable anxiety besetting the self while it strives for attunement or balance in the course of life: the sense "that the world ('olam)" is "God-given into the human heart (libbam)"—"without one being able to grasp the work (ma'aseh) of creation from beginning to end" (Ecclesiastes 3:11). Because our minds are partial in reach and limited in depth, we can only work with the worldly things "given" at hand, never knowing their true or ultimate meaning. We may signify things as they come to awareness, and sense: "This is right for its time" (Ecclesiastes 3:11); but in the process we merely impose our human constructions on the world. Similarly, we may turn things about or rotate ourselves in relation to them, but all our perspectives remain incomplete, and never achieve a view from above, transcendent to the play of phenomena. We are invariably embodied here below, in perplexity and frustration. This anguish arises from the "hidden depths of the heart" (ta'alumot lev; Psalm 44:22), longing for certainty and self-overcoming.

Feeling the travails of finitude, one's heart is "broken" (lev nishbar; Psalm 51:19) and "convulsed" within (libbi yahel; Psalm 55:5)—yearning to be set or "established" (nakhon) on a firm foundation (Psalm 108:2). We pray for insight and the ability to acquire a "heart of wisdom" (levav hokhmah; Psalm 90:12), and know our place in the natural order. Preparation and readiness comprise a spiritual disposition to be cultivated through ongoing consideration of one's mortality and limits. The self must heed the demands of the moment and not "contract" one's "heart" (te'ametz et levavekha) in blind self-regard. One must extend an open hand, and give without hesitation in one's "heart" (Deuteronomy 15:8–10). Such a self-transcending generosity is the mark of those who are "upright of heart" (*yishrei lev*; Psalm 32:11). Witnesses to the conditions of reality, they offer their "ready heart" (*nakhon libbo*; Psalm 112:7) to the tasks of life. Within our mortal limitations, these are the regulative ideals we desire.

To cultivate readiness is a spiritual praxis; to enact it is the living challenge. Scripture may help guide this quest. In the longing for inner development, this resource may impart time-tested and collective wisdom. To do so, its instructions must be properly studied and personalized. Appropriation is the hermeneutical goal, but the particular valence depends on one's traditional inheritance and personal proclivity. A disposition of longing is crucial; it orients the heart.

"Tell me, you whom my heart loves: Where do you shepherd (your flock), or have them rest at noonday; for why should I be like a misguided wanderer among the flocks of your friends?"—"If you do not yourself know, O loveliest of women, then go out among the tracks of the sheep, and shepherd your kids among the tents of the shepherds" (Song of Songs 1:8–9). Tradition has often pondered this dialogue, and some teachers have interpreted it as a figural request for spiritual wisdom: the "loveliest of women" understood as an allegorical trope for the seeking soul; and the addressee, the beloved of the heart, the ideal of divine-like wisdom. The heart confesses its desire and present state of confusion, wandering among the fields of knowledge, but without standards or guides for orientation. This compounds the distress. Hence the crucial reply offered the seeker of knowledge: if "you do not know" the way yourself, through your native abilities or acquired knowledge, go beyond this limited sphere and seek other deposits of wisdom. Go to the places where truth is cultivated and learn wisdom from its teachers. Resources of spiritual truth await the seeker, but they must be sought and assimilated. This is a hermeneutical task. The personal search for meaning and its formulation is a lifelong challenge. The language of scripture may offer guidance and hints (*remazim*) on the way. But these too must be recognized and hermeneutically appropriated.

Calling (or Recalling) to Mind: Being Addressed by Scripture

To belong to scripture means belonging to its narratives, memories, and teachings. This belonging is both communal and personal. The pronoun "you" brings it to the fore. Sometimes the voice of Moses speaks to the people Israel in the plural, addressing them as a collective "you"; at other times his voice addresses the group in the singular, summoning their attention as if an individual "you." It is notable that in the book of Deuteronomy Moses addresses the words of God to the people in this twofold manner. He speaks to the nation as a whole especially when their actions affect them conjointly; and also singularly, when they are commanded with personal religious duties. Thus when the worshipper is called upon to love the Lord "your" God, this exhortation is addressed to the individual person. But when the community is commanded to love the stranger, they are exhorted with a plural "you." This principle aside, scripture repeatedly oscillates its points of reference, so that readers must adjust their perspective to the duties at hand; for inasmuch as the speaking voices of scripture proclaim a call to transcendent virtues and values, they require their listeners to attend to what is said and how it affects their personal or collective being. Whether in the singular or plural, the words of scripture are a direct address: an imperative to the soul and will. They reach across the chasm of time, to be heard by later readers as well. Spiritual listening is vital.

How do textual memories function for later generations? And how may one "belong" to them? In several instances, all the people are enjoined to "remember" that they had been slaves in Egypt, and should remember the needy for that reason. Such acts of remembrance are intended to motivate people in the present; other liturgical units emphasize the dire consequences of not remembering divine acts of beneficence (Psalm 106). Overall, the pedagogical purpose of these cases is to emphasize the importance of memory and its function as a catalyst for religious consciousness and dispositions. If the negative instances specify cases of spiritual failure or ingratitude, the positive ones are designed to motivate empathic or moral awareness. By joining the historical past with the present, the texts help inculcate a veritable "hermeneutics of the self." An individual is induced to belong to this past, and to interpret their life in its light. Doing so requires constructing a psychological correlation between the historical events of national experience and the spiritual identity of the individual. The hermeneutical procedure includes both the literary appropriation of scripture and a personal assimilation of its central values. Memory keeps one attuned to the canonical events of the past. The realities of the present challenge the creative convergence of these two vectors.

Finding a Contemporary Praxis

In the past, the hermeneutical role of *remez* was focused on the purification of physical desires and training of the intellect in the service of philosophical and ethical ideals (Maimonides's *Guide for the Perplexed*, and his "Introduction to *Pirke Avot*," the adages known as *Ethics of the Fathers*, are classical cases in point). The modus operandi was an allegorical rereading of scripture to specify these concerns and cultivate the self (physically and cognitively) toward that end. The task was to restructure one's natural self (a congeries of mental and physical dispositions) by becoming aligned to the hierarchical cosmos known through the influence of Greek thought and cosmology. The modern challenge is different, and requires another approach to scripture for the sake of cultivating our mind and balancing emotions. It requires attentiveness to the mysteries of existence, and the complex ethical issues involved. Under the impact of modern physics, we no longer feel located within a hyperstructured or closed universe, and must adjust our epistemic coordinates to the vastness of an expanding pluriverse that does not guarantee certainty of judgment. In addition, we no longer evaluate emotions and virtues according to premodern Aristotelian "categories," or the "rational duties" of Kantian ethics—even though some of these were assimilated to Jewish values over the centuries. We now consider virtues in nonformal terms, as dynamic valences of the inner life, where the self is not an ideal abstraction but a concrete actor, subject to numerous intersecting realities. Hence a contemporary "hermeneutics of the self" that uses episodes in scripture must integrate these considerations. Our canonical sources constitute an archaeology of the cultural imagination. Hermeneutics is a means for "sounding" these depths.

Self-Actualization and Scripture

It is a commonplace for Hasidic masters to ask, in the course of interpreting a scriptural passage dealing with a given belief or praxis, How does this bear upon one's spiritual life? If the Torah is eternal, what, they ask, is its meaning here and now? How might this text support or guide one's personal *'avodah*, or "spiritual work"? This concern goes beyond the content involved, and points to the need to cultivate a personal path of spiritual development. This task is the formulation of a *derekh la-derekh*: a (personal) "path for the way" (of a self-responsible inner life).

For Jewish hermeneutical theology, the events and commandments of Torah can provide the means for self-examination or transformation. Their appropriation is an act of practical theology. In the process, scripture becomes a guidebook for the individual soul.

What inaugurates this process? It is often the sudden awakening of spiritual need, through a sense of lack; a realization that one's inner life is in a state of *tohu*. When settled modes of ego or habitude hold sway, there is little expressed need for a new hermeneutics of the self. But if and when these are disrupted, whether because of external events or personal decisions, change is possible. This opening is not yet a reorientation of consciousness, but rather an incipient awareness of the work to be done. Thus the onset of hermeneutical self-examination begins with the sense that "something is there" (*bo-hu*) in the soul—something inchoate that may be radically transformed.

To what may this be compared? One Hasidic teacher proposed a rereading of the ancient law regarding "one who smites (kills) a person (*nefesh*) by accident" (Numbers 35:11). Historically, this statute served to protect society against undue revenge in cases of involuntary manslaughter (by accident or inadvertence). But if seen through a theological lens (as does the nineteenth-century master R. Avraham Yehoshua Heschel, of Apt), the text is hermeneutically revised into an exhortation addressed to any person who "smites" or wounds their "soul-self" (*nefesh*) "by accident." Suddenly, this old legal regulation becomes a teaching for all those who have become aware that their soul has been debilitated through a lack of care, and provides counsel for its repair through an act of personal *'avodah*. Just as the ancient ruling offers provisions for the physical safety of the manslayer in a city of refuge—after giving testimony about the circumstances (vv. 12–24)—the new spiritual rereading focuses on finding a place of personal refuge where one may engage in a process of self-examination and rehabilitation. For the "Apter Rav" the "places" of protection are no longer sites in the external world, but qualities of one's inner consciousness, through a focused recitation of certain biblical passages occurring in the liturgical tradition. These texts include the six principal words of the Shema recitation, in Deuteronomy 6:4, which correspond to the six principal cities of refuge mentioned in scripture; and the forty-two words of the ensuing exhortation to love God, in vv. 4–6, which correspond to the forty-two "additional towns" mentioned in Numbers 35:7. Thus the personal "refuge" and "repair" (*tikkun*) of one's wounded soul can take place through a meditative recitation of the words of scripture in the course of the daily liturgy.

Such a bold appropriation of scripture is an example of the hermeneutics of the self we have in mind. It is an act of *'avodah* in thought and deed. The quest is for a sanctuary for one's injured soul—a *miqlat* or "place of ingathering" to effect spiritual healing. The words of scripture thus provide a "place of refuge" for one's soul: a textual setting for hermeneutical self-evaluation and scriptural healing. Put differently, properly enacted study of scripture may provide a therapy for the self. One "flees" inward, to recover inner psychic resources that scripture may activate.

Memory as a Hermeneutical Exercise in Self-Cultivation

With this example in mind, we turn to a listing of biblical "remembrances" (called *zekhirot*) that Jewish liturgical tradition has enjoined for daily recitation. If "remembrance" (*zekhirah*) is a specific act of consciousness—a calling to mind—its opposite, "forgetting" (*shikhehah*), refers to a loss of awareness. Many teachers have suggested ritual ways to guard against this negative situation. Scripture itself already advocates the wearing of a colored fringe (*tzitzit*) on one's garment to help prevent distraction or disregard, and to serve as a "sign" to stimulate memory with respect to one's covenantal obligations (Numbers 15:37–41). Daily recitations of this passage (morning and night) are intended to inculcate constant mindfulness of the commandments.

In its quest for an attentive accounting of one's life and days (Psalm 90:12), human wisdom must reach beyond personal perspectives and "recall (*zechor*) . . . the years of prior generations" (Deuteronomy 32:7). Parental perspectives offer narratives of previous generations and their impact on experience and destiny—extending the chain of interconnection well into the past. Canonical memories condition cultural identity through their ongoing ritual enactments, thus allowing historical events to be internalized and made personal. Scripture provides such a resource for Jewish theology. "Very deep is the well of the past. Should we not call it bottomless?" (Thomas Mann). It requires a concentrated gaze and critical retrieval. Accessing fundamental memories means the cultivation of a culturally specific mindfulness and orientation. The psychological and spiritual challenges vary, requiring each person to find their own path. The convergence of individual types constitutes the community of memories in every generation.

The ensuing list of biblical events was intended to help persons keep certain themes and topics in mind, or not forget them. Recalling past events in the present has a dual effect: ancient biblical history is ritually appropriated and becomes part of a living religious consciousness. This is achieved by hermeneutical exercises to help cultivate a heart of reflective wisdom. History is therefore not diverse strata of information to be excavated and sifted for objective facts, but rich resources for the retrieval of spiritual virtues and the generation of a new life narrative. In this sense, hermeneutics is a ritual process that realigns the public language of scripture with the inner speech of one's soul. The letters of the text provide the canonical lattice of spiritual perception.

(1)

So that you <u>remember</u> the day you departed Egypt
all the days of your life.

(DEUTERONOMY 16:5)

Memory is the recovery of an earlier occurrence at a later state of knowledge and history—thereby making the past a new present. Inevitably, one's memory is a modification of the retrieved event and influenced by the conditions bearing on its recovery. It is thus a re-presentation in the double sense of the word: a modality of mental mimesis in which the individual reformulates an earlier event that comes to mind, intentionally or otherwise. This act might even be deemed an archaeology of experience—both because it is retrieves prior strata of memory and because it sorts these deposits into a new order. What, then, is the situation when memories derive from ancient historical narratives—stylized and embedded in larger literary cycles, and mediated by later historical experiences? The challenge is how to appropriate these accounts for one's personal development and spiritual life.

The emphasis in the citation is on memory, not recitation; and it is addressed to every member of the people: "*you* shall remember" (*tizkor*). Thus to remember the exodus—not as historical fact but as a living reality—one must first attempt to recover (though empathy and the imagination) the conditions that precede a release from oppression. One must consciously work this through in one's heart and mind. This involves accessing the emotional and psychic state of being overwhelmed by circumstances: to be without breathing room or the capacity to conceive any life alternative. Just this is the state of *qotzer ruaḥ*: of "shortness of breath" because of hard labor, and the "smallness of spirit" that can result (Exodus 6:9). For radical oppression burdens both spirit and body, and narrows the horizons of thought and feeling. According to the literary testimony of Vasily Grossman, such a burden is "an invisible force . . . crushing [the individual with] . . . hypnotic power. . . . Those who have felt it . . . feel astonished that one could rebel against it even for a moment—with one sudden word of anger, one timid gesture of protest."

To remember the exodus one must also imagine the radical suddenness of an improbable or unexpected change, and the awakening of new possibilities. The voice of freedom breaks the chains of bondage, inducing a never-to-be-forgotten sense of miraculous release. When this happens, redemption is not a term but a transformative reality. The senses are reborn, suppressed feelings are revitalized, and the stupor of numbness yields a new sensibility. Where torpor had darkened vision and hope, there is an inchoate sense of a future. This is akin to a rebirth of self-awareness. And if one achieves these realizations by meditating on the exodus, there may also surface the acute sense that others suffer—and that release from oppression has moral ramifications. Look at the wasted faces that shockingly peer out from the photos of concentration camp survivors, or look at the despairing pain in the eyes of Brazilian mineworkers, so poignantly photographed by Salgado. Look and remember. They scream out: you cannot see my face (in such suffering) and live (as you do). The voice of blood and hunger calls out. Hear. Remember.

One day's memory is unlike another, even when wrought of similar themes or experiences—for one day is unlike another. Sometimes (as we may imagine, using midrashic images of the exodus), this renewal is like a bird freed from a fowler's grip, lifting lightly into the air of freedom; and sometimes it seems like the slithering forth of a newborn calf, or a brand blasted free from a blast furnace, aflame with life. Freedom is all this and more, when God's "Shall Be" shines through existence, and one feels the regeneration of life and the transformation of an enslaved will. In gratitude, the heart exclaims: I thank You, *Y-H-W-H*, "for You have released my soul from death and my eyes from tears" (Psalm 116:8). Release and personal renewal conjoin.

Newborn freedom marks the onset of new horizons, dispelling the anxieties that induce the safeties of servitude and the sureties of habit. How might a horizon shackle or liberate the mind? A horizon is a personal viewpoint: it is an epistemic frame of reference from wherever we stand in the course of life. As events address us we construct new correlations, linking our mind to the world in what we hope is a beneficial measure. These cognitive frames are usually not called to mind unless they break down, and then we feel bereft and seek cognitive cover. Like horizons in the natural world, horizons of the spirit shape what we can see and know. R. Naḥman of Bratzlav called these mental enclosures *maqqifin*, or "thought-frames" that structure or limit spiritual and intellectual potential. Reflecting on the sense of release from such constraints, some commentators appropriated the term Egypt (*mitzrayim*) to formulate a prayer of thanks: "From the straits (*meitzar*)" of existence (physical and mental) "I called upon God (*YaH*)"; and "God answered me with expansive being (*merkhavyah*)" (Psalm 118:5). Mental limits are blinders one cannot see, but are revealed when challenging situations are confronted. Then one senses limit and constraint. More insidiously, a person may be duped or self-deluded and not realize their cognitive enslavement. Czeslaw Milosz labeled such a state a "captive mind." For this and other reasons, study of the narratives of memory may jar one to a new consciousness, and then the praxis of spiritual reading will serve one's *'avodah*. The self may be spiritually reborn when natural dispositions look beyond self-centered perspectives to the conditions of life that summon a higher awareness. This is a covenantal alliance with God's "Shall Be"— a relationship we valorize and prove valid or true through moral responsibility and steadfast resolve.

(2)

Remember what Amalek did to you on the way, when you came forth
from Egypt: happening upon you on the way, when you were hungry
and weary and not fearing God—cutting down all the stragglers at the
rear. Therefore, when the Lord your God grants you respite from all
your enemies around you, in the land the Lord your God gives you as
a hereditary portion, you shall blot out the memory of Amalek
from under heaven. Do not forget.

(DEUTERONOMY 25:17–19)

This is a difficult and dire command, recited as an exhortation in Jewish
life for millennia, in order to ingrain the historical realization that, in every
generation, there were persecutions; and that all must be remembered, and
not forgotten. Our case here refers to an attack that occurred soon after
the exodus. It is presented in scripture as a raw psychic stratum from the
beginning of the nation, and lives on as an unhealed trauma. Our own
generation endures this wound through the memory of the Holocaust and
earlier persecutions. So we must ask, starkly and firmly, Can this strong
directive serve our *'avodah*? Or more providentially, what events must be
remembered and never forgotten, and what traumatic situations must be
erased and not remembered, if possible? In the face of national and personal catastrophes, we must also ask, Are there moral or emotional limits
to human memory? Or are some acts without expiation, and some wounds
so implacable as to be beyond the pale of forgiveness—especially by survivors who have endured the most heinous crimes? Such questions stop us
in our tracks. This is not a return of the repressed. For most survivors, the
raw imprint of savagery is still alive. Such memory is a relived actuality.

To engage the command to "remember" Amalek and "blot out its memory" as a hermeneutical *'avodah*, one must first determine its components
and consider them in terms of their psychological and spiritual dynamics. We begin with the reported narrative. As suggested in the foregoing
discussion, a sudden liberation may open a psychic space of release and
bewilderment, together with its emergent challenges. This was an emotional truth Moses understood long before, when he said to the pharaoh
(who wanted him to specify the details of who was to leave Egypt and how)
that the people would not know where they were going or even how they
would worship—"until we get there" (Exodus 10:26). Freedom is an initiating factor; the facts follow. This condition is also reflected in the people's
anxious query "Is the Lord with us, or not?" (Exodus 17:7). It reflects the
emotional travails of unexpected renewal. Two reactions are possible. Faced

with new realities, but not ready to assert responsibility, the self may claim (as in the case of Amalek) that another "did" (*'asah*) something to impede one's progress (physical and psychic), or that the event simply "happened" (*qarekha*). In either case the occasion is deemed external to the speakers, who feel like victims of circumstance.

It would be naive to think that evil actions do not traumatize and wound the weak or powerless. But this does not absolve them from critical self-examination, and it is just here that our text is most suggestive. It offers three dispositions for a reader to contemplate: physical need (hunger), psychological lassitude (weariness), and lack of spiritual regard (not fearing God). The first two are both corporeal and mental in nature; the third is religious in character.

Reading the episode of Amalek for one's spiritual development (*'avodah*) yields the following considerations, each to be evaluated as one contemplates the tasks of new beginnings and the challenges of freedom. The factor of physical necessity marks the primary issues for the newly liberated: mechanisms of self-care and the need to provide for one's welfare. "Hunger" is both a physical and a psychic state, newly felt because in Egypt the "enslaved" had all their needs taken care of—whether in terms of actual sustenance or the control of emotional time. Freedom imposes the sudden necessity to care for oneself in every sense—to manage resources of space and life, and adjust to the new sense of vulnerability. Having had one's body and mind ruled by others, emergent liberation may result in projecting the burdens of responsibility outward. Thus one may carry the psychic condition of captivity long after it was physically removed. To "remember Amalek" is an enactment to keep this emotional truth in mind.

The second issue is "psychic lassitude." It is related to the former, but has its own dynamics. Particularly characteristic is the way an individual, weighed down by the past, plods along under the constraints of prior events. For such persons, the phrase *neheshalim aharekha* is not merely a reference to "stragglers at the rear," who are physically disregarded. It also evokes the things left in psychic disarray and pushed to the rear of consciousness, often to return in alternate and aggressive ways. Such issues are a grave burden as one proceeds forward. The past is like a psychic pursuer; the very embodiment of those matters pushed to "arrears"—until they overpower the self at its most vulnerable points. Distracting thoughts hobble the heart and leave the will in distress. Little wonder that one is prey to whatever lies in wait. Meditating on this psychological truth is a beginning. But it must be thoughtfully appropriated by self-conscious living. The hermeneutics of selfhood must inscribe this text as a memorial upon one's heart and an instruction in one's mind's eye.

This brings us to the third reason for the catastrophe: the people lacked the "fear of God." They were without proper reverence. What can this mean for our 'avodah'?

The people's focus was not on spiritual matters. The self, burdened by the weight of the past, cannot break open to transcendence—to a principle that would give strength in adversity and the capacity to resist evil when it occurs. The decision to "turn from evil" (symbolized here by Amalek) can be an intentional act of moral courage. But it can also be an escape from evil, without dealing with the consequences. The result is that one may split off evil from the good, and produce dangerous dichotomies. Spiritual maturity demands the riskier path of integration. Reverence for God would conceivably induce reflective humility concerning one's behaviors and motivations. It would enable one to struggle against a position that deems the "other" as different from oneself, an attitude that breeds hard-heartedness against evildoers and moral blindness in one's self.

What is at stake? The text is deadly clear. The negative event is sustained in memory for a future time when revenge can be enacted, and a prior weakness is redressed by resentments awaiting the opportunity to "blot out" every trace of the culpable perpetrator. This is a psychic burden that may define one lifetime, or that of generations, until the vengeance is realized in some form or other. But it comes at great emotional and moral cost. Unleashed, this mentality sees the children of evildoers in the image of their parents—a myopia that fuels the long-smoldering heart. It must therefore be transformed by a courageous rereading of the language of scripture; but only when the time is ripe, and one has found "rest" from its pain. At that time, one will try to give the memories of evil some respite: not by denying the undeniable or expressing forgiveness through an unwarranted generosity, but by letting the memory be a real memory, and not a lens for present resentment. It is just this truth that one is bidden (on this rereading) to "not forget." Otherwise, the claims of the present are distorted, living events bent out of shape. The psychic consequences are captured in a poetic figure by Nellie Sachs:

> And night, the black tiger,
> roared, and there tossed
> and bled with sparks
> the wound called day.

Sometime . . . perhaps not yet . . . when you find "respite" from your enemies, within and without, "blot out the memory of Amalek." Let it be: heal its traumatic torment. Remember this and "do not forget"—and so find rest, for the sake of your soul.

(3)

But take great care, and give utmost attention to your self-soul, <u>lest you</u>
<u>forget</u> the things you saw with your own eyes, or that they pass from
awareness, all the days of your life—and make them known to your
children, and your children's children: the day you stood before the Lord
your God at Horeb, when the Lord said to me—: Gather the people to
Me, that I may let them hear My words, so they may revere Me all the
days they live on the earth, and so teach their children.

(DEUTERONOMY 4:9–10)

The challenge of spiritual freedom is to respond to the imperatives of life:
to cultivate one's heart and mind to heed the realities that summon responsibility and action. The revelation at Sinai gives paradigmatic expression
to how the numerous phenomena of existence provide spiritual instruction. Like the imperatives of life, this call is characterized by a transcendent immediacy—and the challenge to hear its world-effecting claims. Sinai
symbolizes the divine voice calling "Here" and "Now" at every moment:
the call of life as it is and "shall be." Revelation and the realities of existence
take place in the present: revelation is the factuality of divine presence—of
Eheyeh in the here and now. To bring Sinai to mind as a living truth is to
"take great care" and "give utmost attention" to what you see with your eyes.
Remembering Sinai serves one's theological ʻavodah by directing one's focus
to the actuality of divine immediacy in the everyday. This is a spiritual consciousness that must be awakened again and again.

The day to be remembered, the event of Sinai, models the impact of
primary experiences on the soul. But it does so only to the extent that this
textual occasion is renewed as a primary archetype—held in active awareness with "great care" and "attention." Reborn anew by God's transcendent
worldly call, the self requires ongoing adjustments, to attune new experiences to the defining truth that has given direction to one's life. Should its
memory fade or be displaced by distractions, one risks mistaking its transcendent pivot for all the congeries of feelings that beset one from moment
to moment. Hence care of the self (with one's "utmost attention") is a hermeneutic of constant self-examination. The study of scripture may help to
keep this value in mind.

To remember the great day of Sinai is also to keep in mind the voice of
all voices: the divine voice that speaks "*all* the words" to Israel at Sinai—the
infinite languages of creative existence: "Sea serpents and all watery depths,
fire and hail, snow and vapor, (and) violent storms doing God's will; moun-
tains and hills, fruit trees and cedars; wild and domestic animals; earth
crawlers and birds of flight; kings of all worldly dominions; princes and all

rules of the earth; young men and girls; and elders and adolescents: all of these give witness to the Lord's Name *Y-H-W-H*, for His Name is exalted above all" (Psalm 148:7–13). Expressing limit and love, God's creative word enlivens all life; its transcendent vitality breathes in and through our hearts and minds. We respond to this awesome manifold with finite human words and names—social terms that conceal or displace the hidden truth of reality. Utterly beyond is the Name "Shall Be," through which all "is" and "shall be"—a Name that summons the human soul to all-attentive regard.

Beyond the hearing of the everyday, and evoking God's infinite gifts of life, is the chorus of heavenly voices that enunciate the rounds of existence: day speaks to day and night speaks to night, for "there is no word or utterance other than their resounding voice" (Psalm 19:3). We strain to listen, and thus attune our spirit and shape our imagination by "what the ear can comprehend." We must remember the difference between primary moments, ever God-given, and the worldly assertions of our human desire to make sense of things. The primary and primordial are God's sanctification of worldly existence. The imperatives of Sinai help mediate this sanctity and crown each moment with the kingship of heaven. The call of revelation manifests the creation and summons our response.

The tablets of Sinai were written, we are told, "on both their sides" (*mi-shnei 'evreihem*); and then immediately thereafter, as if to clarify, we are told that they were inscribed "on one side and on the other" (*mi-zeh umi-zeh*) (Exodus 32:15). We are rightly puzzled by this statement, as were ancient sages. But this mystery of the fixing of the divine voice must guide our meditation. Facing outward into the world, the mystery of divine revelation finds linguistic forms that are adequate for the heart and lived life—at once readable and sayable in human terms. These are the tablets that address us in language. But simultaneously, facing otherwise and on the other side of this human formulation, are ciphers that face God alone—altogether unreadable and ineffable. From "our side" there is task and attention, guided by the forms of generations; but in contemplating "God's side" there is only absolute ignorance and the confession of mysteries. These comprise two separate but inseparable aspects of one theological truth—to be conjoined in living religious consciousness.

"Take great care . . . lest you forget," the teacher adjures. But we do forget, being so distracted and self-absorbed that we do not see the reality at hand or the tasks requiring attention. When our eyes wander, through the stimulus of (inner) desire or (external) images, we must hope to have cultivated practices to restore our spiritual sense, and jolt us back to the memories that instruct our soul. The claims of existence depend on one's capacity to respond. Spiritual praxis is geared to limit and correct these wayward moments, for ourselves and future generations. We have a responsibility to transform our primary theological awareness—the Sinai in our heart and world experience—into a concrete life expression for the sake of others. Covenantal living must become a spiritual pedagogy: one that serves God and the world, and centers one's life from moment to moment.

(4)

Remember, do not forget, how you provoked the Lord your God
to anger in the wilderness.

(DEUTERONOMY 9:7)

Freedom requires us to stand firm amid the mysteries and ambiguities of life, and not succumb to past enslavements. The gifts of Sinai must be engraved on the heart, spiritual markers of a living covenant with God. But the tug of personal temperaments is often insufficient for this challenge. Our hearts harden against the radical call to freedom. Insecurities and worries may weaken our spirit; and then idolatries, insidiously and silently, fill the void.

Idolatry enters the psychic hollows opened by unnerving or new experience. When known reality or expected knowledge is delayed, formulations retained from prior strata of one's life reemerge to allay anxiety. The insights that once raised our nature to higher possibilities disappear, and platitudes populate our mind. Seeing the world through their stale lens, we become idolaters in fact. When forms enslave our mind and spirit, idolatry is its name. We become their psychic prisoners—bound by the hold these representations have on our minds.

How many times can the same thing be read or said, before it is enunciated without intent—when even awe becomes callow rote and routine (Isaiah 29:13)? Sinai infuses the eternal "Shall Be" into the mouth and heart, so that speech and study may be reformed through the sounds of letters, joined anew, as for the first time. And thus Sinai may provide a spiritual font that keeps "all these things" (Exodus 20:1) vital—birth and death together, morning and night conjoined, and all the creatures of the earth. It is world-weariness or despair that works otherwise to stifle the heart; then we have eyes that do not see, ears that do not hear, and a mouth that speaks by rote. Slowly but surely, and knowingly or not knowing, the world goes stale and is sucked of spirit; and we become idolaters again and again.

What ruptures of thought or experience are required to break these idols and falsehoods? What cognitions are necessary to see things anew? Acts of idolatry pervert the living voice of God. As scripture attests, idolatry distorts our lives. It is a false 'avodah. Hence the double directive, positive and negative: "Remember" and "do not forget." In forgetting, things slide out of mind. We forget the dangers as well as the possibilities. Times of terror are especially prone to conceal the face of values. Absence may then serve as a spiritual test: the heart must fight the fear of the unknown and shatter self-fulfilling constructs. To remember and not forget primary truths is the twofold imperative directed to our Sinai-sponsored religious spirit.

(5)

<u>Remember</u> the entire way the Lord has made you travel these forty years, that He might test you with hardships, to know what was in your heart: whether you would keep His commandments or not. He subjected you to the hardship of hunger, and then gave you manna to eat, which neither you nor your ancestors had known: in order to teach you that man does not live on bread alone: but by what comes from the mouth of God does one live.

(DEUTERONOMY 8:2–3)

Spiritual impoverishment can't withstand the challenges of freedom, and holds onto figures that block vision and allay anxiety. This includes nostalgia for theological sureties whose value has waned or failed; and for religious practices whose merit is morally suspect or hollow. The already-known gives assurance, but also disenchants the spirit. Likewise, the forms of idolatry insure confidence, but leave one blind-at-heart.

Wandering in the desolations of the spirit, can one hope for wonder? Can we see things afresh, or be startled and say: "What is this" heavenly gift—*man hu*? (Exodus 16:15). What is this that spreads over the earth so wondrously, so totally unknown? It is the question itself! The phenomenon of a question is the opening of possibilities, expressing the astonishment that comes without prior expectation. Questions open the heart; and suddenly the holy spectacle of creation is revealed—before names, before distinctions, and before all grasping knowledge. It is query itself, born in the soul that may open transcendence to the stultified heart, starving for spiritual sustenance. But know: wonder is not a fixed thing. It comes and goes. When left over, it spoils; and if gathered insatiably, it is a mere commodity. One must therefore take proper measure for each occasion, and ask the right question. Then the bounty of existence may show itself in unexpected and renewed forms.

Wonder is mysterious, and satisfies each creature in a variety of ways. The young and old taste meaning according to their age, experience, and need; animals are frightened or curious, stalking about or jumping back as sound or light changes quality; sea birds flash toward the auras, shining off the waves; and humans stand in awe of the auras of heaven and the fireflies at night. All this occurs in the sacred splendor of mystery. Ears attuned, worldly sounds resound: a veritable cacophony of tones. Everything comes from the mouth of God (Deuteronomy 8:3), in a holy heaven-speak.

For humankind, the manna is "like a *zera' gad*" (Exodus 16:31), a bountiful "seed" of speech and interpretation—that nurtures expression and imagination, and allows people to formulate thoughts and feelings. Evoking questions, the manna is the bread of dialogue, enabling persons to speak to each other, eliciting their flow of conversation like a *leshed ha-shamen* (Numbers 11:8), a "rich oil" wafting from the words of one's companion. In all our speaking and saying, and the profundity of not knowing, beset by primal mysteries, God's voice informs the human heart. It is the omnipresent reality of being, spiritual sustenance for the humble and ready (Deuteronomy 8:3).

Opened to the gifts of heaven, the self becomes a channel of blessing. The reborn soul will see and speak anew to others; and they, in turn, will find renewed forms of expression. The hands that gather the beneficence of God will extend this bounty to the needy with loving care, and the heart that has been opened in marvel will receive reflections from highest heaven and refract that light selflessly to other hearts nearby. Wonder unbinds; it is a *hesed*—a source of life. *Man hu?* we ask. "What is *this*?" And suddenly, in attentive wonder, *bohu* is transfigured. *It* is *bo hu*: God's gracious presence, so vitally embodied in created existence.

(6)

> <u>Remember</u> what the Lord your God did to Miriam on the way,
> when you came forth from Egypt.

(DEUTERONOMY 24:9)

Speech can go terribly wrong, as this warning reminds us (in shorthand); and we are bidden to recall this entire episode as reported in Numbers 12:1–13. In so doing, we must reconsider the twofold travesty. The first has perpetrators initiate slander, perverting truth and resulting in another person's shame, as we learn from the wording of the act. "Then Miriam and Aaron spoke against Moses concerning (*'al odot*) the Cushite woman he married"—namely, his wife Tzipporah—"because he married a Cushite woman" (v. 1). According to rabbinic tradition, Miriam was singled out for punishment because she initiated this verbal abuse, with rumors and allegations, and Aaron was dragged into the crime. But the more apparent reason most likely concerns Tzipporah's national origin—a dark prejudice in which these parties maliciously colluded. The explanatory phrase 'al odot says it all. It marks their conspiratorial justification by a pseudo reason: it stipulates a pretext that formulates ill intent. And so the punishment fits the crime. Miriam became a leper, as white as snow; for just as slander shames a person, causing one to blanch, as if socially slain, so this culprit is made to endure this dreadful state in her own body. It is a warning to one and all, to be considered in all its particulars. If we do so, this episode may serve our 'avodah.

The second malediction goes in a different direction, and demonstrates the perversion of questions—when transformed into rhetorical accusations. After the first act, the plotters expressed jealousy, saying to one another: "'Has the Lord only spoken with Moses; has He not also spoken with us?!'—and the Lord heard" (v. 2). In this conjoint remonstration, personal jealousy and a bid for power enter the mix. The incitement is again motivated by verbal derision and the derogation of another person. The twofold query does double rhetorical duty. No social community is formed by such insidious questions. They rather destroy it, for such formulations express human resentment in a barely concealed manner. Hence the exhortation of scripture: Remember this, and keep it in mind. Misuse of presumption (the pretext of 'al odot) is a social iniquity, a virtual leprosy of the soul.

The malevolence of ill-founded speech is insidious, socially murderous in its effect. Its rabbinic name is ona'ah (verbal harm), a term that signals that all ill-tempered words are nefarious because of their negative impact. They breed deceit and libel—a language that destroys creation and unfurls bohu. Their counterpart is truth: an honest steadfastness that searches the most inward measure of events (Psalm 51:8). Truthful words are anchored in duly weighed thought and action. As scripture says, "the divine teaching" is not far off or inaccessible—but "is near at hand: in your mouth and in your heart to do it" (Deuteronomy 30:11–14). Conjoined, these features express a sequence of interrelated virtues: a ladder of ascent in spiritual practice. Torah is a resource for right-mindedness (upright thoughts in the heart), for proper speech (socially binding language), and, ultimately, for acts of goodwill: focused purpose and moral integrity.

(7)

Remember the Sabbath day to keep it holy.

(EXODUS 20:8)

The command to "remember the Sabbath day" occurs as the capstone of the sequence of exhortations to remember diverse historical events. Self-standing, this final exhortation reaches back to the creation itself, and the divine act of rest at its conclusion. The worshipper is now called upon to put this day in mind, and insure its sanctity by ceasing from labor. In precisely this way the created world and the liberated dignity of all life (the two specific motivations for Sabbath observance mentioned in Exodus 20 and Deuteronomy 5) find a maximal realization. Hence this rest is more than the cessation of physical work by oneself or any creature. As a call to personal memory, it requires a spiritual act as well: an abrogation of psychic distractions and return to a more settled awareness. This is the twofold task for the self to achieve the requisite and truly "proper rest" (*menuḥah nekhonah*). Spiritual renewal is the ultimate aim of everyone's Sabbath *'avodah*.

Under conditions of servitude, mental or physical, there is an absence of creative actions. It is hard to think or speak because of "shortness of breath and hard labor" (Exodus 6:9). Breath becomes the stale vapor of suffering, and stifles coherent language; the laborious exertions of the body weigh down the capacity for expression. Even the sudden liberation from oppression may not fully release the burden of psychic pain; the soul remains in spiritual fatigue, unable to meet the challenge of freedom. These feelings sneak up from unguarded flanks, and fuel old resentments. Such are the lingering traits of Egypt and Amalek that can cripple the liberated soul.

The redemptive summons to spiritual freedom at Sinai announces the fact of God's omnipresent "Shall Be"—and calls the hesitant spirit to resist the worship of private idols. The admonition not to have "strange god within you (*bakh*)" (Psalm 81:10) must be heard, for it symbolizes the insidious aftereffects of the golden calf, which smolders long after it was burned to ash. Treating others with malicious prattle or malediction is another misuse of freedom, as is the way the anxieties around sufficiency turn legitimate needs for survival into competitive claims over possession.

Encumbered by this psychic bondage, the Sabbath offers a release. Its quietude facilitates a spiritual stillness whereby one may nurture a God-centered consciousness. If the hubbub of ordinary life fills every mental void, the Sabbath helps recoup a true and "complete rest" (*menuḥah sheleimah*), to again hear and see the world suffused by the divine. Such life awareness is a Sabbath mind. It is a resting point of consciousness wherein the soul may know that the divine "Shall Be" most unspeakably "is." The quietude of the Sabbath is a rebirth of spiritual awareness: an infusion of soulfulness beyond the daily labors of mastery and control.

The Mystery of Sabbath

The Sabbath is a centering of the soul around its still point—an inner silence attuned to the all-encompassing world mystery. It is here that all points converge: a culmination of spiritual labor. At the onset of the Sabbath day there is a settling of one's heartbeat. The negative energies that elicit resentment or misprision are set free, so that the inner character of existence—which "is as it is"—may be seen and sanctified.

On this day the soul can praise God's Name, "Shall Be," for all that exists. The praise renews the silence of the heart—the inner sanctuary of blessing. Like a bride consecrated for love, the soul is newly empowered to experience the heavenly gifts of God in the week to come. This consciousness must be guarded and cared for. It is the spiritual breath of Sabbath observance.

Reborn, one acknowledges the primordial dimensions of God's creation, and proclaims to them, each and all: "Come in peace, you angels of peace (*shalom*)." The restoration of spiritual consciousness is newly alive to the integrality (*shalom*) of existence: not as a cognitive object, but as an intuited subjectivity that extends one's moral vision. What is now in mind is God's wondrous call: to see and hear that there is *bo-hu*—that there *is* meaning, beyond confusion and doubt.

A Final Meditation on the Heart: Integrality and Mindfulness

The weekly balance of labor and rest reenacts the primordial balance of creation since time immemorial. As noted earlier, some rabbinic sages made this "balance" the linchpin of their interpretation of the first combination of the Divine Names *Y-H-W-H* and *Elohim*, at the conclusion of the creation narrative (Genesis 2:4). This marked the conjunction of God's vitalizing "Shall Be" and stabilizing or delimiting "Power" (one meaning of the Name *Elohim*) for the sake of world-order. This lived adjustment recurs in the creative adaptation of all species to the conditions of existence, to the need to find a viable balance between love and limit. This conjunction of opposites is also a task of the human heart. The challenge of determining what may withstand the tests of life are the deliberated tasks of wisdom—cultivated through thoughtful *'avodah*.

An instructive meditation on this matter occurs in the Book of Zohar (2.26b), where R. Eleazar reinterprets a biblical verse (via later rabbinic teachings), so that the spiritual work of integrating the double impulses of the soul results in a discourse about divine unity. In effect, monotheism is revealed as an ongoing and lifelong project of the heart. The teaching reads as follows.

Rabbi Eleazar opened (his Scriptural discourse), citing: "Know today and consider it in your hearts that *Y-H-W-H* is *Elohim*" (Deuteronomy 4:29). This verse should have been written: "Know today that *Y-HWH* is *Elohim*, and consider it in your hearts." And it should also have said: "consider it

in your heart (*libbekha*)." This notwithstanding, Moses said: If you want
to understand this and know "that the Lord (*YHWH*) is God (*Elohim*)—
consider it in your hearts (*levaveykha*)" and you will know it. [Scripture
states:] "Your hearts" [to indicate] that both the good inclination and the
evil are one: each is included in the other; and the two are one. [If you contemplate this, then] you will "know that Y-H-W-H is *Elohim*", for one is
included in the other—and they are one. Therefore [it is stated:] "consider
it in your hearts" that you may know the matter. In addition, Rabbi Eleazar
said that the wicked cause a defect on high. What defect? It is that the left
is not included in the right; [that is,] the evil inclination is not included in
the good inclination because of the sins of humanity.... Hence [Scripture]
says: "And consider it in your hearts", so as to include these two as one—
namely, the [inclusion of the] left in the right.

The verse that R. Eleazar expounds is a call to theological knowledge (*ve-
yada'ta*, you shall "know") and reflection (*ve-hasheivota*, "and consider")—
that the Lord-*YHWH* is God-*Elohim*. That is to say, "knowledge" is different from "reflection"; the first proclamation is addressed to the mind, the
second to the heart. The first is deemed an act of thought; the second urges
the worshipper to internalize this knowledge as a matter for spiritual consideration. More logically, the sage states, one might have expected Moses to
have first instructed the people to "*know* that the Lord is God"—as a theological fact—and then to *reflect* upon it. But since scripture is written otherwise, the teacher utilizes this opportunity to explicate the traditional formulation. According to him, this sequence calls upon the religious seeker to
consider why scripture uses the plural "hearts" (*levaveykha*) here, and not
"heart" (*libbekha*), which should have sufficed. By doing so (and following
the midrashic exposition in *Sifre Deuteronomy* 32, discussed earlier), the
worshipper would be exhorted to dedicate both aspects of their heart—the
good and evil inclinations—to the service of God. For then one's physical
dispositions could serve spiritual ends, and positive impulses could override or redirect baser passions. The task is thus to conjoin one's two energy
fields into states of co-regulation, as an expression of the worshipper's heartfelt devotion to God.

The present teaching goes further and serves a more transcendent
theological goal—namely, that these two human impulses be "conjoined"
(*itkalil*) or integrated in order to effect divine unity. Since the two natural inclinations of "good" and "evil" are correlated with the Divine Names
Y-H-W-H and *Elohim*, their corresponding divine qualities ("beneficent
love," or *rahamim*, and "strict judgment," or *din*) are affected by their balance in the human heart and expression in life (as kindness or beneficence

and as stern judgment). As a microcosm of the divine, humans are composed of the same ontological qualities (in psychological form) that God has emanated into the cosmos and, in a mysterious and transcendental way, actually partakes of. Thus human beings are essential actors in the universe. Their own balance of the inclinations has profound consequences. It is precisely this fact that R. Eleazar instructs the people, grounding his theology on the verbal formulations of scripture. He stresses that any false splitting or separation of these two qualities (ontologically of divine origin) can have disastrous results (cosmic and earthly). The righteous understand this matter, but the wicked do not. They do not integrate the "left hand" (symbolizing evil actions) with the "right" (symbolizing good acts), with the result that human existence and Divinity are fractured and made defective. The consequences are exponential: not only for the unity of the human soul, but divine unity as well. The harmony of opposites, the structuring of the soul, is a profound spiritual 'avodah. It is theological in the most active and profound sense.

The correlation of the Divine Names Y-H-W-H and *Elohim* is therefore no theological abstraction. Its significance goes beyond their coexistence, and points to a fundamental truth about divine reality itself. Moreover, R. Eleazar reveals that this transcendental compresence comes to worldly expression through positive and negative human factors. There is a fundamental correlation (he teaches) between the diverse forces in existence—primordially grounded in the divine plenum—and the dynamics of individual self-regulation. Hence cosmic integrality is deemed (in part) in mortal hands; and a spiritual 'avodah that seeks to conjoin these opposites has profound ontological consequences. The task of monotheism is thus not mere dogma, but an ongoing, psycho-spiritual drama.

*

> *Semolo taḥat le-roshi viymino teḥabbekeini.*
> His left hand is under my head and His right hand embraces me.
>
> (SONG OF SONGS 2:6)

We exist in the depths of a divine vastness, never experiencing the whole or knowing how the parts interrelate. But we nevertheless have the sense that we are physically held in world-being, and conjoined to the polar forces that support our bodies and spirit. Both are God-given: one is a world-sustaining left hand (*Din*)—material and physical in nature; the other a life-embracing right hand (*Raḥamim*)—spiritual and inspiring our hearts and minds. We thus live in the mystery of God.

Is there a principle that may help us regulate these two primordial realities? An observation by R. Abba in the Zohar can help. He was sitting with R. Eleazar, when the latter taught the preceding exposition. Hearing his colleague speak about the "hearts," he also reflected on the biblical commandment to love God "with all your hearts" (Deuteronomy 6:5), and observed: "You should unite the Holy Name in the proper way, with a supernal love"—taking the left and right aspects of one's heart together—"embracing them on High in a place that is both boundless and without limit" (Zohar 2.27a). What might this mean? What is this embracing act, performed with supernal love and transcendental intention? At the least, it is the concern to bring the various inclinations of our heart into alignment with all the beings we encounter—through an embracing and God-oriented love. On this understanding, *love of God* is the regulative principle that may conjoin the self (and its energies) with the world (and its existents). Taking this to heart and practice is the core spiritual *'avodah*—directed to the service of God, for the sake of the harmony (or unity) of all being. Such devotion serves the mystery of God, beyond all understanding.

R. Abba's teaching brings us to the regions of *sod*.

Interlude Four

From Part to Whole—and from Oneself to Divinity

Ultimately the self belongs to God, for we are part of the cosmic plenum (or *torah kelulah*)—the world-embracing manifestation of infinite divine creativity. It surrounds and penetrates our lived reality in all respects. Caught in short-term projects or self-centered concerns, our horizons contract to these limits—blind or inured to a greater whole. Fragmentation is a consequence of our retreat to what is cognizable, or our focus on what serves our survival. But sometimes our heartbeat senses a great vibration, and evokes a more primordial longing and desire—if we dare feel it and respond to its call. We are addressed: You!

Spiritual consciousness is the focused refinement of our natural desire to live integrally within worldly reality. If our initial impulse wants to understand persons and events in order to maximize our life condition among other creatures, a higher consciousness yearns to receive these moments with an attuned responsibility for a larger whole—for something more. For the seeker, this "more" even extends to the longing for an awareness of the divine reality that inspirits all existence. Though necessarily delimited by cognitive frames and by our natural proclivities, spiritual consciousness desires to ascend to an intuition that can infuse the entirety of our life. For this reason, the level of *sod* wants "more" than cognizance of mundane particulars. It wants a transcendent perception. This is not a view from above—from "nowhere"—but a comprehending consciousness set within the fluctuations and flow of experience. The hermeneutics of *sod* is a means to cultivate this awareness, seeking to engage the mystery of God-given existence as a "personal" and "livable" truth.

Jewish mystical theology has traditionally taken a twofold approach. On the one hand, there was the belief in an esoteric tradition revealed by God in olden times to Adam or Enoch, and transmitted as a secret doctrine of

Holy Names that symbolize the intricate structure of supernal divine Being. This is a transcendental theosophy for the initiated elite. At its core are the primary elements of existence: the ineffable confluences that (in time) reveal the all-creating "voice of God." This primordial infrastructure is not a language as such, but rather the ultimate "semiotic components" or expressions of Divinity that combine in infinite patterns. All these components were deemed the esoteric nomenclature of God's ineffable Name: the core algorithms of the ultimate Name, Y-H-W-H—the absolute font of All-Being. "No thought can grasp this," mystics were wont to say, since the Illimitable is wholly unthinkable by a mortal mind. "It cannot be grasped (*itpas*) by any Name (*shem*) or hinted at (*itremiz*) by any letter (*ot*)." According to this theosophy, the entirety of Being is an effulgent expression of Divinity in structures both infinitely large and small. There is ultimately nothing "other" than this reality, despite worldly appearances. Hence this divine reality is fundamentally concealed from creaturely consciousness, and only knowable by the elite through the most esoteric allusions and recondite forms. According to some (like Nahmanides), these truths—the most concealed components of Being—cannot be inferred or estimated from the words of scripture, since the latter is an exoteric revelation imparted to Moses for the people as a whole.

In other circles, this theosophy was deemed to be encoded in scripture in various symbolic forms and configurations—initially kept secret by these groups, but eventually revealed through an explication of its exegetical hints and allusions. This disclosure (typified by the Book of Zohar) fundamentally changed the nature of scripture and its meaning. If, as these adepts held, all of "reality" ultimately emanates from God's ineffable Name, sacred "scripture" was preternaturally a matrix of divine energies that reformulated (in a series of infinite gradations) into the configurations of the created universe, *and* also into the literary formulations of the biblical text that is now manifest. So understood, scripture, in both whole and part, is nothing less than a vast matrix of holy Divine Names—embracing those normally designated as such, as well as the entire verbal thesaurus of scripture—which thereby can be symbolically decoded. In its esoteric truth, the hermeneutics of scripture carries a weighty burden: to unlock the supernal mysteries that conceal the most secret realities of divine Being—a symbolic inscription (of sacred names) that portends truths beyond all mortal comprehension. The public narratives and laws therefore comprise an external garment of esoteric features—a theosophical texture that is nothing less than the web and woof of all Being. By tracing these threads, in all their entwinements, the mystical adept may transcend the visible patterns of existential reality to higher spiritual levels. Traditionally, mystical hermeneutics is the bridge to the Beyond.

Toward a New Path

Most moderns have cut the shoots of these theosophical speculations, and cannot wholeheartedly believe their metaphysics with integrity. Honesty therefore sets limits to one's use of its symbolic imaginary. Another path is required—one that seeks the presence of the divine mystery inscribed in the flow of all existence. For mystical seekers, that quest may now lead to the inherent "languages of world-being": to all the God-given elements that inform the *torah kelulah*—to be known or discovered both through the natural sciences and the creative imagination. To imagine the *torah kelulah* as the totality of divine creative vitalities is to perceive reality as a thick inscription to be endlessly interpreted. Naturally, we see or hear only portions of existence, and do so in limited inflections, through our individual intuitions and received traditions. This cognitive task resets the frames of spiritual consciousness. Unable to transcend our mental limitations—either by negation or overcoming—a more viable task is to elevate our perceived existence through its reintegration into a more comprehensive or expanded awareness. How might we denote this process? Inspired by the terms and content of the early medieval Jewish mystical tract *Sefer Yetzirah* (Book of Formation), I would propose the following: first, to seek the "shining" (*safir*) aura of the infinite "integers" or "components" (*sefar*) of divine reality that interpenetrate worldly existence; and then, through them to become aware of all their semantic entwinements—such as put us in thrall of the wondrous "book" (*sefer*) of nature. These elements (perceived through whatever means available, scientific or intuitive) constitute an infinite semiotics—a veritable transformative grammar of existence—which is integral to (and integrates) all living things. Their "shining" is how they appear to our minds at all moments (through natural sight or an inspired insight). Human comprehension is therefore our partial attempt to give hermeneutic significance to the divine *torah kelulah*. The marvel of this infinite "inscription" fills the heart of all spiritual seekers, who sense the influx of divine creativity in their soul and the efflux of its expressions in their imagination. These spiritual dynamics pervade the God-consciousness of the mystically attuned mind. The (exoteric) "Book of Nature" thus encodes a deeper and more primary "Book of Formation": the happenings of divine creativity as such.

Jewish hermeneutical theology wishes to complement these intuitions with the "Book of Scripture" and its language. It would, thereby, rejoin the tradition of mystical hermeneutics, albeit in a new mode. And just here lies the challenge of a contemporary appropriation of *sod*. Can the older esoteric tradition be revised and reconceptualized to disclose the divine mystery for the modern mind and spirit? Can this hermeneutics ring true and remain an authentic expression of the older tradition in its new intellectual and spiritual form? We must strive to remain responsive to the hermeneutical teachings of earlier spiritual teachers, but reformulate them in the light of our contemporary mindset. This is the theological challenge.

Openings for Mystical Consciousness and Theology

The search for mystical awareness can turn to earlier hermeneutical efforts to provide terms and direction. Our spiritual predecessors realized the exegetical artifice of their interpretations, despite their belief in the ontological sacredness of scripture—a belief that inspired their interpretative quest and gave it legitimacy. The contemporary hermeneutical imagination operates in a more halting manner. Committed to scripture, one's exegetical eye is nevertheless infused with a notable self-consciousness: cognizant of the projections or intentions of its hermeneutical acts. Like our ancestors, we read scripture with a concern to discover the mystical sense and potential of its words; but as moderns, we are conscious of being without certainty in our quest for spiritual illumination. Lacking independent verification, we must lean on tradition for hermeneutical sustenance, and seek there sources and insights to guide us through the networks of scripture. It is not hubris but spiritual desire that gives us theological courage. We dare articulate the unsayable and, so doing, sustain the paradox of formulating images of the ineffable through language—always keeping the ineffable in mind.

Moderns are not the first to wrestle with these hermeneutical complexities. An instructive medieval instance occurs in the Book of Zohar 1.103a/b—inspired by another episode in Abraham's life. Through its creative exegetical prism, one may see anew.

> *He [Abraham] was sitting in the opening (petaḥ) of the tent . . .*
> *Sarah heard from the opening (petaḥ) of the tent.*
>
> (GENESIS 18:1, 10)

Rabbi Judah opened (the discourse with the passage): "Her husband is known in the gates (she'arim) when he sits among the elders of the land" (Proverbs 31:23). Come and see: The Holy One, blessed is He, has ascended in His glory, which is hidden and concealed in the exalted heights. There is no one in the world, nor even since the creation, who can understand His wisdom or endure it; for He is hidden and concealed and has ascended to the supernal realms. Neither the beings above nor the creatures below can comprehend (it), so that these beings and creatures say: "Blessed is the Glory of Y-H-W-H from His place (mi-meqomo)" (Ezekiel 3:12). Those below proclaim that He is above, saying: "His glory is above the heavens"

(Psalm 113:4); and those above proclaim that He is below, reciting: "Your Glory is over all the earth" (Psalm 57:12). In the end both say: "Blessed is the Glory of Y-H-W-H (*mi*) from [wherever be] His place (*meqomo*)"; for He is unknowable and there is no one able to assert anything about him. And yet you declare: "Her husband is known in the gates?!"

But truly "Her husband is known in the gates (*ba-she'arim*)"—her husband is the Holy One, blessed be He—for He is known and comprehended to the extent that people are able to estimate (*mesha'er*) Him in their heart, each one to the degree they can connect with the spirit of wisdom. Hence: people can know Him to the extent that they can estimate-imagine (*mesha'er*) Him in their heart. Hence: "Her husband is known (*noda'*) in the gates"—through the gates of the imagination. But that He can be known as He truly is: there has never been any one able to attain such knowledge.

The scriptural citation describes Abraham sitting before his tent, prior to the appearance of messengers who prophesy the birth of a child to Sarah—who heard this annunciation from within the same tent opening. This reference to *petaḥ ha-ohel* (the opening of the tent) ostensibly provides a domestic designation. But its deeper significance is stimulated by the way Proverbs 31:23 (the homiletic co-text adduced by R. Judah) tallies with Genesis 18:1, through its references to a husband who "sits" at the city "gates." For the mystical mind such similarities suggest scripture's deeper (esoteric) intent. The true spiritual instruction takes off from this verbal relation with its emphasis on the fact that this "husband" is "known" *in* "the gates." We are informed that this "male" is actually an allusion to the supernal "Divine Husband" ("The Holy One, Blessed is He"), who is both utterly transcendent and absolutely unknown—inestimably beyond the comprehension of humans and angels alike. With this hermeneutical turn we now realize that R. Judah's sermon is not concerned with an earthly event at all (the situation of Abraham), but rather with the recondite status of divine knowledge.

For the spiritual fellowship of the Zohar, scripture is no mere record of historical events, but a symbolically encoded distillate of mystical truths. In the present instance, the "Divine Husband" is a supernal modality that has ascended to the most secret and hidden spheres (of the divine intellect). In this supreme realm, "it" is absolutely occluded and unknowable—"concealed" and "hidden" from all beings, including angels, who can only declaim doxologies to the unknown God. This is why an interlocutor speaks up and is puzzled by R. Judah's assertion. For if God is absolutely unknowable, how can God be "known" in the gates? How is such an assertion possible? Though compelling, the query is dismissed through a bold reinterpretation of the word *she'arim* (gates). No longer simply a site in the city, it now specifies the very capacity of the heart to "imagine" or "estimate" (*she'urei de-libba*) the heavenly spirit of divine "wisdom" (*hokhmah*). Moreover, by shifting the focus from the city "gates" to the "gates" of the "imagination," this' teacher proposes a breakthrough for theological cognition. An inquirer into the mysteries *can* in fact "know" something of these transcendent matters—*but* only through the "portals" of the creative human imagination. Thus, since the "female" (of this "Husband") symbolizes the "Bride of God" (or *Shekhinah*)—the immanence of Divinity in the world—the theological imagination can only construct images of God through the figures and forms of worldly life. These creative "estimations" of Divinity are neither aesthetic acts nor mere speculations, but comprise the hermeneutical (theopoetic) components of one's spiritual *'avodah*. On their basis, one may produce a cognitively limited but nevertheless theologically authentic imagination of God.

The theological process depicted in this passage turns on a complex pivot: on the knowable and unknowable in the human quest for God, and on the sayable and unsayable in the search for a spiritual language. R. Judah's teaching explores both issues.

In the quest for God, the first gate is the realization of *limit*, the radical humbling of consciousness before the inconceivable reality of Divinity. Every thought is but a contraction of the imponderable to human proportions—to the finite constructs of the mind. The challenge is to live with the clear realization that we cannot address God as God, but as spiritual formulations of our *longing*; and that we must winnow our minds of theological hubris and let God be God. But the heart desires more. It wants forms of God to have in mind so as to direct or focus one's spiritual life. How can this be done? One way is by entering the verbal "gates" of scripture (its words and figures) with imaginative creativity. As R. Judah counsels, everything depends on the doors of perception and the uses of hermeneutic intuition. The measures of the spiritual quest begin and end within the limits of the human mind, but they also approach the immeasurable reality of God through the figures of the hermeneutical imagination. We know what we know theologically by recasting the ancient words of scripture into prisms of our spiritual longing. These images are real presences, and as such they direct our theological orientation. In that sense, the hermeneutics of the imagination are modes of prayer; its images are a means of one's theological quest—not its ultimate achievement. Through the prisms of language, heavenly light is visible.

If R. Judah emphasizes the role of imagination in the service of spiritual knowledge, a concluding voice is less sanguine. This teacher confesses a difficult truth: one is no longer certain where these gates are, or how to recognize or "enter" them. The reason for this is the "exile," which is not merely physical displacement from the homeland but an alienation of the mind from its spiritual center. We too (like the loss lamented here) have lost our ontological certitude. Many gates are shut; many others are illusory. Even more distressing is that we have lost the inner wisdom that may give guidance. Canonical sources are sealed when the interpreter does not know that these gates open to the longings of their heart. But they may speak when one seeks God in scriptural images with religious integrity and devotion. To the question, Who may ascend the mountain of the Lord? the answer is those individuals who examine their lives and seek wisdom through the God-given shapes (in scripture and in life) of hermeneutically revealed truth. This practice offers a time-tested guidance, and is our hope in the present. Without the testimonies of tradition, we would repeatedly begin from scratch and have little assurance of viable insights. With them we can measure our theological musings, and find correlates with their established forms. Loyal to the resources of these texts, we seek our own spiritual insights through faithful acts of the religious imagination.

*

The path of sod (mystical interpretation) is precarious. We can follow past masters only so far. Our minds and hearts are different. Hence the modern quest of spiritual awareness must be charted anew—through interpretations that translate the sources of scripture into a new key. We must therefore be attuned to our mental and emotional truths so they may orient us amid the labyrinths of language. Then the matrix of our soul may locate correlates in these older texts, and mediate spiritual energies we only dimly perceive—as through a glass darkly. With sod we extend our vision to the most expansive vistas of theological meaning and significance. But while doing so, we realize that we cannot abandon our concrete lives; and must engage our spiritual quest from within the particulars of our experience, language, and community. Not able to escape ourselves, we still hope to ascend to new heights. Tradition and our individual desire conjointly determine the map and its goals.

PART FIVE

Sod

Toward an Expanded Consciousness

The physical earth ever beckons and impacts our life. Our bodies respond to the elements of existence and register their qualities from one moment to the next. Simultaneously, the soul seeks these worldly gifts—and more. This is the longing that lifts us beyond limited selfhood toward the transcendent mystery of God.

We are born from the heartbeat of God; and were that heart to cease beating, so would the life-urge and creativity of all existents. This is a divine truth without limit (*shi'ur*)—for if our own heartbeat is God's creative vitality in a human formation, we (like all creatures) are ineffably embedded in our most ultimate reality. How, then, could one 'think God' as an object of intention, when God is the core of consciousness and source of life? Who is the subject, and who the object?

We ponder our place in this divine manifold, so absolutely overwhelming. Everything we imagine or know seems somehow interconnected within the cosmic chain of Being, large and small. Close analysis shows that each habitat hosts other subhabitats, and that these sustain still other zones or complexes. We strive to get a sense of the divine reality that infuses us: to conceive ourselves as beings sifted from cosmic infinities. But any viewpoint limits our understanding, and our physical experiences intersect with diverse planes of reality, beneath or beyond cognitive capacities. We are part of the mysteries that astound us. And so we must wonder, How may we put these matters in mind for the sake of theological wisdom and the cultivation of an expanded consciousness? How might we channel the unthinkable for thoughtful insight?

Within the bounty of divine creativity, human sensibility naturally contracts to the phenomenology of specific perceptions. We shall therefore begin here as well with our concrete experience. It is from this primary con-

dition that we shall formulate a contemporary interpretation of *sod*. Unable
to affirm a distinct theosophical realm, or some esoteric code to be deci-
phered (whether in the cosmos or in scripture), our consideration of *sod*
must begin with the conviction that the hidden mysteries of existence are
somehow palpable in their phenomenal complexity and diversity. These are
the initial gates that may reveal worldly existence in all its God-given vitality. On this understanding, *sod* is a mode of theological consciousness—and
not an ontological dimension as such. Hence, when reinterpreting Jewish
mystical texts, it is crucial to consider them as hermeneutical meditations
on the mysteries of existence filtered through scriptural structures—and
thereby provide exegetical prisms for new (our own) spiritual reflection.
This methodological approach rests on the assumption that although traditional explorations of *sod* were primarily intent to disclose esoteric truths
embedded in reality, this realm may still refract spiritual insights for our
contemporary theological edification. To access them involves a twofold
procedure. First, our modern hermeneutical quest will attempt to penetrate
the mystical or spiritual structures latent in these older interpretations; and
then, thereby, this disclosure may stimulate a correlative spiritual wisdom
that speaks to our modern contemporary temperament. Reformulation is
therefore a key challenge for any honest appropriation of this material. The
phenomenological potential of the older sources will therefore depend on
how they elicit new figures of thought through explications that translate
their esoteric components into new theological insights.

In search of a theology of *sod*, we turn to the mysteries of existence in
the everyday. Guided by traditional sources, we seek the portals of mystic
consciousness.

(I)

The Sway of Experience, or the Mysteries of the Particular

God breaks into our lives through all the colors, shapes, and sounds of the
world, through the manifold of the *torah kelulah*. From birth to death there
is a vibrant interplay of elements—*ba-kol mi-kol kol*, "in and from the fullness of things." The theological imperative is to become responsive to the
claims of each occasion, while simultaneously attuned to the mysterious
divine depths that pervade existence. We yearn to sense the unknown in
the known, and the hidden in the manifest. How can this dual disposition
be achieved? Where is the first gate of understanding?

Various teachers have pondered these queries. Among the passages
offering counsel is this: "You shall seek (*u-biqashtem*) the Lord, your God,

from there (*mi-sham*); and find (Him there) if you seek Him (*tidreshennu*) with all your heart and all your soul" (Deuteronomy 4:29). Originally these words were stated to anticipate a situation of communal exile and spiritual despair: a sense of distance from God. Hence the designation "there" refers to the people's exilic dislocation, the place from which the nation might return to God. Millennia later this teaching was transformed and addressed to individuals in a state of religious confusion or disorientation, and in need of inner restoration. Thus R. Israel Ba'al Shem Tov (the Besht) explained: "From there" (*mi-sham*)—precisely; from just "there (*sham*) where you are—whatever be your spiritual level (*madreigah*); from (just) there . . . one may connect (*le-hiddabeq*) with God." The starting point of religious renewal thus starts with oneself, "from" just "where" one is. One's given situation (be it high or low) is the place of new beginnings—for those who would "seek" God with all their heart and soul. Hence the verb *lidrosh*, "to seek" (in the verb *tidreshennu*), must also mark an act of self-"inquiry." For the axial point is both within and without.

How does this yearning emerge? Let us start with the Song of Songs: "I am asleep (*ani yesheinah*) but my heart (*libbi*) is awake. The voice (*qol*) of my beloved knocks (*dofeq*)," saying: "'Open (*pithi*) to me . . . for my head is filled with dew'" (Song of Songs 5:2). We may hear this text as a spiritual teaching. At first, one must cultivate a settled, quiescent ego ("*I am asleep*")—a calming of spirit, or release of prior presumptions; and then, in consequence, an alert readiness ("but *my heart* is *awake*") to respond to the voice that calls from beyond. Just this is the twofold dynamic. Initially, one's "I" is self-focused and preoccupied, perceiving things as they relate to a personal standpoint. In this cognitive state the "heart" is unable to receive experiences in the chamber of one's inmost sensibilities. Hence the inner self must be transformed, quieted, so that the world may be experienced on its own terms. Then the tempered "I"-self may record the riches of phenomena from a non-ego-dominant position—having become a self that attends to the world in order to hear its call. Now the self becomes a vessel of receptivity, able to feel things beyond personal needs or self-centered desires. The new consciousness that perceives this is the "head," portrayed here as filled with self-resurrecting dew: a mysterious substance that both rises from the ground and descends from above. Similarly, the "voice" that calls "Open" also makes a twofold appeal—from within *and* beyond the self. The two are conjoined in an integral balance. Who or what is that voice?

The "voice" is the evocative speech—the divine word—emanating from all life, declaring "I Shall Be" (*Eheyeh*) in every form and expression. The individual who perceives this call responds at different levels of consciousness, in accord with their personal "I am" and "shall be." This call *and* response reveal the reciprocity of God's infinite "Shall Be"—dynamically interfused with the finite human being. It is God's worldly immanence (the *Shekhinah*) that summons the soul. Has God's word become the inner voice of the self, a personal revelation channeled through one's devotional practices? Or is God's voice the awakened human soul? Who calls, and who responds?

The transfixing moment precedes human language: it is the very awakening of consciousness. Creation is reborn through this hearing of God's word. The self is transformed by an ineffable awareness of presence. With profound insight, R. Menaḥem Mendel of Ryminov (nineteenth-century Poland) gave voice to this silent happening when he interpreted the initial letter aleph (*a*) of God's self-declaration at Sinai, "*Anokhi* (I) am *Y-H-W-H*, your God" (Exodus 20:1), as a summons to each human "I" to hear the transcendent "Shall Be" of God just there where it opens the mind—prior to any giving or command. This evocative aleph is the imperative of presence. The self turns in response, wholly reoriented by this revelation.

Aroused, the soul receives God's gifts of life wherever both meet or are joined in the world. Scripture says: "You who cleave (*ha-deveiqim*) to the Lord, your God, are all alive (*ḥayyim kulkhem*) this day" (Deuteronomy 4:4). Noting that there are different ways of connecting with God, the Hasidic master, R. Israel of Ruzhin, taught that the "true" way is to "cleave" to the living God ("*your* God"), the veritable "life-force (*ḥiyyut*) of all existence (*kol ha-metzi'ut*)," by "focusing on the life-force that animates each thing." And where is this found? Just there, wherever one is at any time.

The core requirement of such a living faith is to proclaim (the words found in the paragraph that follows the morning recitation of the Shema): *emet ve-yatziv ve-nakhon ve-qayyam . . . ha-davar 'aleinu le-'olam va-'ed*; this divine reality is "true and firm and sturdy and enduring . . . upon us eternally." The vital force of Divinity is truly both within and upon us living creatures, as the potency animating all things. It is not necessary to go beyond oneself to partake of it, for we are ever connected to God and to all life immediately, through the soul-breath that gives us subsistence and consciousness. One is always just "there" (in the Besht's words) where one needs to be for the beginning of one's spiritual journey. The divine call beckons from without because we are also suffused by it from within. It is through this portal one is awakened to a higher consciousness.

Another, complementary proclamation is demanded; it is the confession (that follows the evening recitation of the Shema): *emet ve-emunah kol zo't ve-qayyam 'aleinu*, "True and certain is all this and we (dutifully) accept that which (all this) imposes upon us." This is an affirmation of all worldly particulars that lay claim upon us, and involves a commitment to the creation through acts of sanctification and care. The specific *mitzvah* incumbent on each occasion (fixed by tradition and emergent in the course of life) is now a spiritual "bonding," or *tzavta*, with God, the all-sustaining Giver of all life. Whatever our eyes perceive and our bodies experience provides modes of spiritual connection with existence. Each aspect of worldly life is felt in a particular theological manner because Jewish tradition has inscribed the Torah into the world by conditioning our hearts and minds to respond to these features in accord with their specific forms of halakhic enactment (or *qiyyum*). Accordingly, the pulse of life that "imposes" itself "on us" (*qayyam 'aleinu*)—that makes religious and cultural claims—*is* the voice of God speaking through the commandments (positive and negative) of existence and tradition. To accept the claims of *kol zo't* (all this) is to start just "there" where one is—in the presence of the *Shekhinah*, contracted by the limited forms of human cognition and revealed by what we see with our naked eye.

The adverb *qayyam* registers two related spiritual modalities. The first is the evident reality of God's enduring "sustenance" of all life, experienced through the ever-new reconstitution of worldly existence. The seasons come and go, for weal and woe; but the earth stands, and life is regenerated in earth and womb. This sense comes to theological expression in the modality of the Divine Name that proclaims assurance: "It *Shall* Be." The second modality is daily experience of "existence," in and through all the particulars of worldly being. It comes to theological expression through the correlated stress of the Divine Name: "It Shall *Be*." The first modality is ontological: bespeaking the durative ground of all existence; the second is ontic: referring to the actual specificity of all worldly being. Both modes elicit a sacred reverence (*yir'ah*): for the *mysterium tremendum* of God-given existence, and the awe-inspiring abundance of its worldly manifestations. A disposition of humility is born of this consciousness, and it has a unique spiritual valence under the aspect of *sod*—the sense of wonder at each moment and every breath.

How may this mystical consciousness come to daily awareness?

A Spiritual Praxis

A teaching by the Hasidic master R. Ḥayyim Ḥaike of Amdur considers the onset of this mystical consciousness in a ritual practice performed each day: "in order to purify the soul . . . so that one's thoughts shall be pure" and have God in mind at all times. It states:

> Upon arising in the morning, one should immediately become self-aware that the blessed Creator has provided beneficence (*tovah*) and loving kindness (*ḥesed*) by restoring one's life-soul, which suffuses the body; and with

this (realization) one must sanctify oneself, according to the (Scriptural) dictum *qodesh yisrael la-Shem reishit [tevu'ato]*, "Israel is holy to the Lord, the first-fruit [of His harvest]." For this (realization) is deemed the beginning (*reishit*) of thought, since it has not yet turned hither and thither (to worldly matters). Moreover: one should also sanctify the beginning (*reishit*) of all one's physical features—one's sight and hearing and speech— and by this act all one's deeds the entire day will be sanctified; as it is written (in Scripture), *ha-maggid me-reishit aharit*, "Who speaks from the beginning (about) the end"—will have a good end.

This meditation begins with the dawn of consciousness each morning, prior to any formal expression of gratitude. There is not yet (at this time) any intention upon which the mind might fix its focus for personal purposes. Rather, the person must allow this awakened feeling of selfhood to inspire a disposition of profound thankfulness to God, and with it the obligation for self-purification. This state is underscored by a quote from the book of Jeremiah (2:3). In its original context, the prophet states that "Israel is holy to the Lord, the first-fruit of His produce"—this being an assertion that allegorizes the special status of the people. R. Hayyim turns this prophetic proclamation into an exhortation directed to every person, to become "holy" beginning with their "first" acts of daily existence. The prophet's praise now speaks directly to the individual mind. Hence the teacher's precise directions for its implementation, because how one begins each morning will affect all one's behaviors during the day. Further supported by the biblical phrase about God, "Who speaks (foretells) the end (or final result) from the very beginning (or outset)" (Isaiah 46:10), R. Hayyim stresses that the "beginning" practices each day will affect all ensuing acts of speech and action. Hence the self is implored to inaugurate all daily deeds with a purified intention, to be sanctified from the outset.

Mystical Levels of Experience, or The Prisms of Perception

Mystical consciousness begins with the particular and transitions to a sense of the interpenetration of realities.

The forms of existence are expressed through their particular strain of life—the stamen of a flower and the hue of its petals, the dam of a beaver and its habitat. These elements are each constituted by their inherent nature, even when embedded in other realities—the sustaining soil, for example, or the seeds of all kinds, that draw nutrients from within and without. Nothing is self-standing. As creatures of the earth we receive them with mouth and touch, imbibing life for sustenance and pleasure, and exhaling oxygen for health and need. We are all-entwined, one way or another: our breath transforms the flower, and the works of our hand help fruit to flourish. The miracle of life is contextual, and vitalities change form in response to their intersecting environments. Our place in the spectrum of existence affects what is seen or felt, and how it interacts with all other elements. We experience life in its relation to our bodily stance and to our emotional condition. As contexts shift, our mentalities are altered. The garment of existence, threaded by the vitalities of life, is composed of infinite textures and strands, revealing and concealing all at one time, as human awareness deepens and intuition expands.

The receptive mind is never neutral. It projects a plethora of values onto this spectrum of existence. Transforming the inchoate *tohu* into cognitive constructs, human imagination joins the divine "work of creation," revealing new dimensions as it gives names and descriptions to moments of lived exegesis. As seen or felt, the bounty of existence expresses a manifold of interconnected expressions: melding and molting in profuse variety. Jewish mystics speak of these metamorphoses in terms of things repeatedly "shedding one form and embodying another" (*poshet tzurah ve-lovesh tzurah*). Bound to the interchanges of life, our hermeneutical intermediations do the same, for how we engage these oscillations lies in our hands. To stultify their interpenetration destroys the "work of creation," whereas our enhancement of reality through deeds or words can renew existence in many ways. To be mindful of this inestimable reciprocity, while intuiting depths both elusive and unknowable, is the challenge of a theology of *sod*. It requires training the inner eye to see further and go deeper. For the levels of reality are not substantive strata, ontologically preformed in existence, to be discovered as a hidden trove. They are the bounty of God's "Shall Be" as it becomes manifest through the diverse layers of human consciousness. Through these levels of perception, we may hold our narrow ground or expand our mind to higher cognitive planes—each with a different spiritual imperative and integration.

Levels of Awareness

The following text from the Zohar (2.23a/b) gives expression to God's revelation of "forms" across the spectrum of human perception. The visible world radiates these forms from primordial depths. We see what we can with our mortal vision, but our inner eye seeks a deeper, more transcendent wisdom. The passage proposes the relationship between modes of perception and spiritual consciousness through the symbolism of Divine Names. Perceiving the normal, physical domains of existence as the baseline of more penetrating spiritual realms puts the former within the ultimate framework of the latter. Explicating the hermeneutical diversity of these levels helps awaken the multiple modes of consciousness in the reader. The exegetical presentation (attesting to profound mystical experiences) reads as follows.

Rabbi Simeon was seated one day with Rabbi Eleazar his son, and Rabbi Abba. Rabbi Eleazar said: This Scriptural verse that is written: "And I appeared to Abraham, to Isaac, and to Jacob (as *El Shaddai*; but by My name *Y-H-W-H* I was not known to them)" (Exodus 6:3), should have said: 'And I spoke.' Why, then, does Scripture state: "And I appeared"? He answered: Eleazar, my son, this is a supernal mystery! Come and see. There are colors that are seen, and colors that are not seen—and both are supernal mysteries of faith which (most) people do not know and cannot contemplate. Indeed, no one was given the ability to perceive (even) the colors that can be seen—until the patriarchs came and understood them. Therefore Scripture says: "And I appeared," for (the patriarchs then) perceived the revealed colors. What are they? Those of *El Shaddai*, which are colors in a supernal prism—and they can be seen. But the colors in the higher realms, which are concealed and invisible: no one understood (or perceived) them until Moses. Hence it is written "but by My Name *Y-H-W-H* I was not known to them." (Meaning) I was not revealed to them in the most exalted colors. But should you suppose that the patriarchs had no knowledge of these (supernal) colors—(then know) they surely had some sense of them, but (solely) through the (colors) that were revealed.

It is written: "And the perceivers shall shine like the splendor (*zohar*) of the firmament, and they that turn the many to righteousness as the stars forever and ever" (Daniel 12:3). "And the perceivers will shine." Who are "the perceivers"?—The wise who, of himself, can contemplate things that cannot be expressed orally. "Shall shine like the splendor (*zohar*) of the firmament." Which "firmament"?—The firmament of Moses which stands in the center; and this "splendor" (*zohar*) is concealed and not revealed. It stands above the sky that does not shine, in which colors may be seen; and these colors, even though seen, do not shine with the (supernal) splendor of the (more) concealed ones.

Ever careful readers, mystical masters perceived profundities in the slightest nuances of scripture. In this instance, R. Simeon is asked by his son why the verb "appeared" (not "spoke") is used in a passage stating that God revealed the Divine Name *El Shaddai* to the patriarchs, but "made known" the Name *Y-H-W-H* to Moses alone. What accounts for this choice of verbs and nomenclature? It is, we are told, the concern to indicate changes in spiritual ability and consciousness. Prior to the patriarchs, no one was able to understand the true meaning of the revealed colors—these being the visual expressions of God's world-manifold (the manifest world of experience). No one yet understood that this panoply was ultimately a prismatic of unseen mysteries in the supernal realms. For earlier "sight-seers," the world was merely a multivalent phenomenal surface—not a lens for spiritual perception. But the patriarchs, with greater spiritual insight, realized that the phenomenal world was a manifestation of God through the multiplex modalities of *El Shaddai*. Building on ancient rabbinic notions, the mystics in R. Simeon's circle understood this Name to refer to all the demarcated realities in the earthly realm: the result of divine creation. According to them, the term *Shaddai* denoted the divine "might" that primordially fixed the manifest borders of the world: both land and sea. In fact, these sages even proposed that God enunciated the word *she-dai* when he decided "that" (*she*) the extensions of these physical masses were "sufficient" or "enough" (*dai*) for worldly existence. This act of delimitation was deemed a crucial event in creation, part of the separations and distinctions that characterize world-being. But (as we now learn from this passage) the patriarchs were not limited to this "worldview." They also attained apprehensions of higher, spiritual realms—albeit through their own modes of cognitive perception. Hence theirs was solely an indirect apperception of these realities, not like the direct perception of Moses, the first one to "know" God through the luminous speculum of supernal truth. Moses attained the enlightenment associated with the Divine Name *Y-H-W-H*—the source of all Being; and achieved the supreme illumination of a spiritual contemplative, perceiving all the luminous auras that refracted the radiance of supernal Divinity to religious "perceivers" below.

For the mystical circle addressed by this teaching, the full import was clear. Individuals who can attain a "Moses-consciousness" of Divinity will be illumined by their contemplation of the heavenly spheres, refracted in their mind's eye—beginning with the lowermost divine realms, through a light that "does not shine" by its own glow, but only from radiances received from above. This lower light is the divine modality named *Shekhinah*, which refracts the upper lights into a panorama of worldly forms: the diverse totality of existence denominated here as *El Shaddai*. Beyond this earthly gradation are the hidden lights and their many colors, including the higher sphere known as the "firmament," which mediates an infinitely pure light from the supernal realms. And since these refractions are bent toward finite human consciousness, they radiate all the archetypes of world-being into their earthly colors and forms—like a crystal that refracts sunlight into a spectrum of hues. Hence, for the mystics of this fellowship, the crystal symbolizes the irradiance of cosmic light throughout world-being. Livestreaming through the forms of existence, the modalities of Divinity are overwhelming, ever revealing and concealing. We mirror in our mind what our soul can envision of true reality.

Another Formulation

Later teachers reflected on the two Divine Names in our scriptural passage. According to one Hasidic master, the Maggid of Mezeritch, the Name *El Shaddai* refers to the multifaceted forms on earth, due to God's contraction (or *tzimtzum*) of God's infinite reality for the sake of human cognition. This divine delimitation is deemed an act of beneficence, since otherwise the infinity of God's creative efflux would flood the human capacity to perceive the world, and literally "blow one's mind." Hence God wisely perceived what was cognitively "sufficient" for ordinary persons and acted accordingly, that they might benefit from the ascertainable forms of life. By contrast, those who understand that these worldly forms (the ordinary epistemic phenomena) merely delimit the creative bounty of God merit something of a *Y-H-W-H*-consciousness. This deeper spiritual cognition expresses the mystic realization that the multiplicity of worldly forms (denominated here as colors) are the life vessels through which divine creativity is expressed and filtered into our hearts.

The Maggid's pedagogical appropriation of the Zoharic teaching allows its references to the patriarchs and Moses to be more precisely understood as types of spiritual awareness or consciousness. In this way, it may further instruct a contemporary theological cognition. Standing before the panoply of worldly forms, we too affirm the polychromatic spectrum of existence. Our ordinary consciousness accounts for these colors and their contours in natural terms. But a deeper spiritual vision may perceive in these configurations a veritable revelation, and focus our hearts on the wonders of divine creation. And in this state one may become conscious of God's "Shall Be" (symbolized here by the Divine Name *Y-H-W-H*). This remains a human apperception in every respect, but one that may nevertheless approximate a higher wisdom. So understood, the Divine Names of the text symbolize dimensions of consciousness: the Name *El Shaddai* referring to the perceptions and shapes of our everyday mind; and the Name *Y-H-W-H* indicating the more imperceptible realities that lie beyond—the ineffable truths of divine truth.

To what may this be compared? To a lover of God—one who seeks spiritual wisdom through the prisms of life experience, contemplating all their conjunctions, both manifest or imagined. Such seeking is an event of theological significance; it is the consciousness of God's world-manifold refracted through the constructs of human cognition—when we strive to be *meitzitz min ha-ḥarakim,* to "perceive" traces of Divinity "through the interstices" of our worldly vision (Song of Songs 2:9). This glimpse expands and contracts. It is a disclosure of awareness to our inner eye.

At the Heart of the Matter: The Mystery of Resonance

What speaks to the soul each day, from the elemental morning light to the silence of sleep, filling the world with a myriad of elements and creations? What calls one to daily consciousness and our dialogical engagements? It is the imponderable *Qol Y-H-W-H*: the divine voice of "Shall Be" eliciting existence at all times, and awareness in each soul. Ineffably expressing all that is, and all that was and "shall be," God's voice speaks through the myriad "voices" (*qolot*) of existence—each emergent according to their nature, and each resonant according to the disposition or receptivity of the hearer. The human heart absorbs these ineffable stimulations, and through speech we formulate a dialogue with God. Language lifts our minds toward truth and meaning, but primordial mystery remains: the infinite silence of the unsayable. Suddenly (we sense) the abyss of Being, *'imqa de-kola,* is revealed—and concealed. Our mute cry is a response. It expresses a primordial desire to be heard, welling up in our heart.

(II)

The Sway of Language: Its Sacred Depths

If the preceding challenge was to become conscious of the divine manifold impacting experience, the present one seeks to express these voiceless experiences in spiritual terms. How may one speak of the intersecting mysteries of life using the limited forms of human discourse? And how can we maintain a sense of these mysteries with the ordinary words of everyday life? One way is to be conscious of the transformative acts of language, and the ways they put existence into thinkable terms. The holy wonder, beyond understanding, is that our sound patterns reveal the world and bring the mystery of God to mind. The aspirations of human breath draw on primordial divine energies, and we speak words. Inestimably, these are modulations of the voice of "Shall Be."

A meditation on this theme occurs in a discourse about the patriarch Jacob at the site named Beth-El (Genesis 28:11–12), delivered by the Hasidic master R. Yehudah Aryeh Leib of Gur (known as the "Sefas Emes," the title of his written masterwork).

"Then he (Jacob) encountered (va-yifgaʿ) the place (maqom), and he lodged there since the sun had set" (Genesis 28:11); (meaning that) he established the (traditional) evening prayer. "And he took from the stones of that place" (ibid.): "the stones" are the letters which he aroused by means of (his) prayer. "And he placed them near his head (be-ra'ashotav)": (that is,) in his head (ro'sho) and heart. And then "he dreamed" (v. 12), as stated in the Midrash: "My body pines for You . . ." (Psalm 63:2); and thereby he (spiritually) actualized the verse "When you walk about, it (the Torah) will guide you; when you lie down, it will protect you; and when you arise, it will converse with you" (Proverbs 6:22); as it is written: "You shall speak of them (the words of Torah) when you lie down . . . walk abroad . . . and rise up" (Deuteronomy 6:7). For truly, there are letters of the Torah in every place—since the world was created with the "Ten Sayings" (ma'amarot) of God. Thus: by means of verbal exertion in Torah (study) and prayer, all the letters by which heaven and earth were created are aroused (raised up).

In this homily, the "Sefas Emes" transforms a biographical event in scripture into a penetrating spiritual instruction. Influenced by a paragraph from the mystical tract Sefer Yetzirah (Book of Formation), which referred to the verbal elements of creation as "stones," our teacher explains its deeper sense: when Jacob "took" the "stones" of the "place" to which he had come, he was transmuting them back to their primordial ontological essence—recombining them to form words of prayer to God, known in rabbinic parlance as Ha-Maqom, "The Place of Worldly Reality" (meqomo shel ʿolam). Going further (and reporting a tradition heard from his grandfather, R. Yitzḥak Meir), the Rabbi of Gur refers to Jacob as an exemplar of how any person may activate the words of Torah at all times in their life, and so transform all events into spiritual acts that raise them to a higher plane. Presuming the (long-established) spiritual symbiosis between the primordial "Words" used for the creation and those found in the Torah, the "Sefas Emes" teaches that when one recites the words of scripture (in both prayer, study and rabbinic interpretation), these foundational components of existence are spiritually catalyzed or aroused. In a similar manner, the physical reality that one is engaged with will also be transfigured and raised to a spiritual plane. Hence, when one speaks words of Torah, wherever one goes and whatever one does, these divine elements infuse one's actions, and existence is spiritually transformed. In truth, world-being manifests what it was and ever is: the enunciated word of God. The mystical task is thus to transmute language into new spiritual reformulations of the world: into living prayers born of God's primordial (and eternally) creative speech. The "stones" of speech will then consecrate the world as a spiritual altar, for language is the formative element of existence. It reveals the creation, and, at its limits, ineffable depths to our mortal awareness.

Jacob's actions offer a phenomenological portrayal of this process. It starts with every circumstance that we "happen" to "encounter"—at any "place," and it continues with the decision to "take" those elements and put them in mind ("at" or "in one's head")—transforming them into spiritual purposes. An awareness of one's role in the transfiguration of reality through language induces a disposition of responsibility and sense of spiritual agency. It cultivates care for the mystery of existence amid all the contexts of experience. In so doing, language vivifies being and humanizes the word of God.

The primordial vibrations of God's word vitalize the reality of all creation, and inspire the manifold expression of its life-forms and sounds of communication. Language accords with this infinite pulse of existence, binding the creation through the chemistry of breath and its tonal patterns. This bonding is dialogical at its core: worldly permutations of God's will for life—the divine "Shall Be" that so vitalizes all existence from within and without. Participation in these convolutions of sound is our share in the creation. In the saying, new contours of existence are expressed. Through human words, God's word comes to consciousness.

Sacred Longing and the Mystery of Speech

Longing for God, we confess the limits of expression. A "heart of wisdom" must ultimately fall silent before the pervasive divine ultimate. Each heartbeat is an ineffable wonder; and wonder opens consciousness to what is—in silence. This sensation is at the border of conceivable reality. Our hermeneutical awareness is *toheh* and *boheh*—stimulated into wonder; and suddenly there is an ineffable sense of *bo-hu*, of God's infinitely particularized presence. We intuit that something "is" here and everywhere, and stands out in its "this-worldly thingness." Just this sense is the wonder of God, ever beckoning.

The pulse of Being comes to us as vibrations in the ether. Its murmur is like the *ruaḥ Elohim* on the primordial deep—the ineffable "breath-spirit" of God that effectuates every life expression and enunciation in existence. When these primal sensations are not formulated, and just are, they signify "nothing" but themselves: ineffable vibrations in the void. Listen to the rustle of leaves from God's breath, or to the howl of the wind as it passes by. Behold the light in which we see. What do they connote or indicate? As such they do not speak or say anything; they are omnipresent, but their meaning is mute. The elements just are, in infinite vibrations: the *ruaḥ Elohim* upon this-worldly transports. But whenever heard hermeneutically, all existence bespeaks the "voice" of God.

We give birth to a (theological) world through our acts of signification.

How can we comprehend the mystery of human speech, born of breath and sound? Speech aspirates and modulates these tones, and in so doing manifests the miracle of language. Language is the sacred mystery of communication, evoking the pathos of one soul to another, and cultivating dialogues face-to-face (in person) and across the ages (through literature and tradition). In its world-building effects, language is the living word of God; it is the creative syntax that regulates all life but passes through (the grammatical transformations of) our mind and spirit. All language ultimately comes from God, who inspires (in every sense) its vitality. Who then would secularize speech and debase its divine ground? Poets seek to revive the spirit of language, and evoke the wonders hidden in sound.

Theology and Speech, Again

Theology does more. It hears the word of God in all speech. Opening our minds to this awareness is the hermeneutical task of a theology of *sod*.

Listen to the following teaching of the Hasidic preacher R. David Shlomoh Eibshitz in his masterwork *'Arvei Naḥal*. It is a discourse on the sacred source of speech and its God-inspirited vitality. At the end of an exegesis of Song of Songs 5:2–6, the master reflects upon the words of the seeker, who hears the call of God and says: *nafshi yatze'ah be-dabro*, "My soul left me when He spoke." According to most commentators, this is the response of a person overwhelmed by the divine presence, who dies a "mystical death." But R. David goes in a different direction.

> *nafshi yatze'ah be-dabro*—(To properly understand this passage, note) what the Ba'al Shem Tov wrote: The Spirit (*ruaḥ*) of Man within him, his life-force (*ḥiyyut*), is the power (*koaḥ*) of speech (*dibbur*). As Scripture says, "And He (God) breathed the soul of life into his nostrils, and (then) the Man became a living being (*nefesh ḥayyah*)" (Genesis 2:7). The (Aramaic) Targum explains this (phrase) to mean: "a speaking spirit" (*ruaḥ memalela*). Based on this (the Ba'al Shem said): When a person speaks words (*medabber dibburim*), these words are his *ḥiyyut*, and his *ḥiyyut* goes out (*yotzei*) when (he speaks) them. However, it is essential that a person's *ḥiyyut* be constantly joined to this Source, so that these words may constantly draw down a new *ḥiyyut*, and he will be enlivened (*ḥay*) thereby. Thus, although a person's *ḥiyyut* goes out with each word, each speech-act may bring (inspire) a new *ḥiyyut* (vitality).

Now [R. David adds], the human soul is a mixture of both good and evil—each one connected to its (heavenly) source—so that a person can have free choice. Accordingly, when one speaks good and holy words, these words arouse their source and draw down upon the speaker a new *ḥiyyut* from the realm of holiness. But in cases of improper speech, words go to the opposite realm and cause a new, negative vitality, which induces one to do evil (God forbid). The result is that whatever a person does, be it for good or evil depends on the (type of) speech-acts (involved): for one's soul and vitality are directly related to the type of speech performed. One must (therefore) be very careful not to debase their speech and suppose that only actual performance matters; for every speech-act implicates the speaker.

This teaching enunciates the mystery of speech. The relationship between one's words and soul-structure is deemed a matter of major significance. According to R. David (channeling the Ba'al Shem), the spiritual distinction of a human being is their capacity to speak. A person is more than a physical bundle of breath, for that is not what is unique about the human spirit. What *is* distinctive is that breath is the source of speech. The world is not merely a material fact. It has spiritual presence by virtue of the ability of persons to name reality and to express what they see and feel in linguistic terms. Language births our soul from muteness to life. We then become a *nefesh ḥayyah* (living being). This is a God-imbued endowment. The *ruaḥ* of God upon the primordial void takes on verbal shape in the mouth of human beings, who become a *ruaḥ memalelah* (speaking spirit). Divine speech is absolute and eternal. It is neither hearable nor effable as such. By contrast, human speech is relative and time-bound. It says things and projects them upon the face of reality. The soul of speech goes out toward existence—and transforms it spiritually. Through the conjunctions of the human soul and world reality, both are renewed.

Language is a spiritual vitality that actualizes the soul. *Nafshi yatze'ah be-dabro*: one's "soul goes forth in the saying." This is a mystery. Words emerge from one's soul-root, as it is remade every moment by intention and articulation. The self is not fixed or static in its spiritual condition, but is regenerated by the character of its verbal formulations. This is a divine freedom inscribed upon the tablets of our heart. It is breathed upon the world by the way we speak, and how we infuse it with our moral life-force. Enacted between persons, dialogue is the interanimation of spirit—infusing trust and possibilities into human relationships. Breathed upon the world, this spirit may be a world-sustaining beneficence. At the border of speech and silence we sense the great mystery of creation in the depths of God-given being.

Hearing the Silences

The timbres of sound vibrate; their limits reached, they return to silence. Silence is the font of verbal potential, before difference and diffusion. It is betwixt and between: betwixt the sounds that comprise the phonic patterns of words, and between these patterns, conjoining or separating the forms of language. Silence is a witness to divine transcendence, beyond all human expression. God's creative word emerges from this ultimate reality, and human speech elicits meanings from this divine source.

Silence recedes with every act of signification. Nevertheless, a trace of it remains. It is the testimony of transcendence, beyond our attempts to say and to know. False consciousness forgets this crucial truth of human signification, believing that words are independent realities. But a heart of wisdom may sanctify this mystery and channel at each moment the gift of God's word.

(III)

The Seeking Soul, or the Mystery of Oneself

The self receives and acts, imagines and speaks—striving to realize a higher consciousness, ever expressing the will to live and create. This primal core of one's reality brings us to the nub of a mystical theology, and to ask how we may consider the spiritual core of the "self" within the encompassing manifold of divine reality. Is consciousness merely a series of disconnected perspectives, revolving around the particular, momentary self-awareness of each individual? Or may there be a deeper awareness that connects or locates selfhood within the world-throbbing heartbeat of God? If the former, the task of consciousness is to focus awareness on the phenomena of world reality, which remain separate objects of experience, even if we are linked to them through acts of cognition. But if the latter is the ideal, the spiritual task is to attain a state of meditative awareness such that the human mind may become receptive to the supreme divine reality—both manifest and beyond all knowing—and inspire awareness that God and the self are integral to each other. In the second option, the goal is the "realization" (as a cognitive and spiritual fact) that one's axial core (one's 'soul') partakes of the omnipresent creativity of divine effectivity (the vitality that enlivens all existence). Then being in the image of God would be experienced as one's ultimate truth—an interior revelation of what one primordially is: a manifestation of the infinite mystery of God's creative truth. How might this realization be formulated through the words of tradition?

A teaching of the Hasidic master R. Ze'ev Wolf of Zhitomer brings this mystical matter to expression, and through a bold hermeneutic of scripture speaks of the spiritual center of one's self and its nexus with Divinity: the unity of unities. His exposition follows.

At the integral center (*kelalut*) of the human body is the heart, called its "Zion (*tziyon*)-point," because from this core (*tziyyun*) a person's thought streams forth. Everything depends on a person's heart. For if, through its powers of cognition, one's thought cleaves to and embraces the greatness of the Creator, knowing His lordship and greatness, so infinitely endless—suffusing and underlying all the worlds—then: "The Lord is great in Zion" (Psalm 99:2). That is: the Lord is truly great in the Zion-point of the heart, through its powers of cognition . . . [and] such a "perfected self" can "rule" over evil powers and persons through this mental capacity. [For] . . . when a person directs thought to God's exalted majesty, they become a chariot for the Divine realm of holiness to be enrooted within; and one's entire being becomes a chariot of holiness. The opposite is also true. For when a person directs thoughts to evil matters, they become in their totality (*kelalut qomato*) a chariot for the domain of impurity . . . and their body a graven image for "other gods." . . . This is the meaning of the verse "You shall not make for yourselves (*ta'asu lakhem*) graven images" (Leviticus 19:4)—that is, you, yourselves (*le-'atzmekhem*), your entire being . . . shall become a graven image and the spirit of impurity will descend upon it. Accordingly, the verse concludes: "I am the Lord, your God"—which indicates that when your inmost thoughts (or spiritual core) cleave to the exalted majesty of God, they become a chariot for the descent of Divine holiness . . . and called "the God of Israel." This is (the mystic meaning of the phrase) "I am the Lord, your God"—"I" *dayka* (as such!).

The Single Self and the Divine Manifold

How may we penetrate this passage? Following the thread of its inner logic, this teaching is a spiritual meditation on each person's most integral point—their heart. For the heart is the matrix that centers one's being; it is the spiritual pivot of one's senses and life activities. From this innermost "point" normal consciousness may expand and become mindful of God—precisely when it is directed to the divine reality that each individual partakes of at their core. On this basis, R. Zeev Wolf asserts his extraordinary teaching: that the core of the human soul realizes its ontological truth when it is wholly centered on the "exalted majesty" of the Lord—the "Zion-point" of one's heart. Indeed, when actualized, both the human self and the divine self are spiritually conjoined in consciousness—this being a realization of one's inherent God-given being. Ordinary awareness occludes this truth to different degrees, since the natural self easily falls into the epistemic traps of ego, desire, and all the assorted idolatries of the heart. These obscure or damage one's 'divine self.' Hence, only when one repairs these spiritual impediments can one know that the Lord God is "great" in Zion, and that the divine self is one's supreme truth. The spiritual challenge is therefore to cultivate a God-centered heart. Through a sustained meditative attachment to the "height" (*romemut*) of Divinity, the heart will realize its inner truth as an integral component of God's creative bounty. True sight is insight into the ultimate unicity of one's God-informed being—a revelation in the depths of consciousness. For, at the core, God is the *kelalut* of one's individual "Zion-point": one's inmost, "integral center."

What does it mean to have one's consciousness centered on Divinity and to expand from this point of mindfulness? It means that one's mind may be transfigured by focusing on God's presence in the core of the heart; and, so doing, one's heart will be conjoined to the manifold of heart-points that instantiate our worldly (divine) reality. As a component of the divine life-force that permeates all existence, the individual "I" realizes its inherent divine modality (in the words of the text, one's God, "your God," is "I, the Lord"). This realization is experienced as a mystical awareness of the truth that one truly and essentially is: *dayka* (as such)! How one may apprehend the Zion-point of one's soul is each person's silent task. It comprises the spiritual pilgrimage of one's inner consciousness: the devotion of one's soul to the divine truth that permeates all reality. Infused by this profound awareness, the seeker will enact in their life the vital structures that emanate from God's creative word in the most balanced and integral of ways. Longing and limit are mysteries hidden in the depths of Divinity, components of an eternal revelation. We channel this mystery through our heart, for good or evil.

We are not alone. Our souls are beneficiaries of generations past, gifted by their wisdom and spiritual works. Torah and tradition are among the divine gifts mediated through human consciousness—canonical expressions of cultural balance between creation and redemption. The omnipresent realities of existence pulse to each soul from the *torah kelulah*, our primary sphere of awareness. Hermeneutics begins with the affirmation *bo-hu*: the realization that God's mystery is in this and every place. This exclamation opens the soul to God and to the other, each one like oneself, a creature longing for life.

A Final Meditation—between "Where You Are" and "What Is"

The religious subject lives at the dialogical nexus of the all-imposing divine reality and human responsibility. With self-cultivation, the seeming gap between the heteronomy of God (the felt externality of revelatory claims upon our life) and the autonomy of oneself (the felt intimacy of individual will) may gradually close—and then a spiritual conjunction between them can occur. Scripture imagines this state of consciousness as a God-transformed human existence. In the words of the prophet Jeremiah, "I (*Y-H-W-H*) shall put My Torah within them (the people) and shall write it on their heart; and I shall be for them as God (*Elohim*), and they shall be for Me as a nation. No longer will any person instruct their companion and say: 'Know the Lord (*Y-H-W-H*)'; for all shall know Me, says the Lord (*Y-H-W-H*), from their smallest to their greatest ones" (Jeremiah 31:32–33).

What can this prophecy mean for contemporary theology?

For a *sod*-oriented consciousness, this singular passage anticipates a fundamental transformation of knowing, speaking, and doing. In its vision, the natural self will be spiritually transfigured: a "*Y-H-W-H*-consciousness" will suffuse each person's being. This infusion is the Torah of "Shall Be" that gives life and liberation to all creatures, and is the God-instilled *Ḥesed* that flows throughout existence, giving the capacity for ongoing life and sustenance. The human subject will be enlivened by this divine beneficence, not as a separate recipient, but as participant in the immortal "Shall Be" of God—as it impacts our sense and understanding in the lived world of persons and entities. Then the proclamation "I am *Y-H-W-H*" of the Decalogue (Exodus 20:2) will speak through the hearts and minds of all persons, each one in their own way. At that time, the objective character of the laws, the *mishpatim*, will not be external norms but internal truths of spiritual wisdom. In this mystery of *sod*, the "nomian" (human law) and the "metanomian" (transcendent truth) conjoin—for then persons shall embody the divine revelations which "in-form" their lives. Such spiritual knowing is a reconstituted consciousness—an actualization of what we always already are (before all knowing and theology): a human image of God, a creature of singular value amidst the infinite plurality of creation. The new "Torah within" is the heart of wisdom for which we yearn, with the arousal of theological desire.

Conclusion

We live in the world with our interpretations and capacity to respond, doing our best with limited insight and imperfect knowledge. Practical considerations have their place, but our longing for theological awareness takes us to another plane. It is here that our interpretations reflect the desire for expanded horizons and consciousness. A biblical proverb refers to this search for understanding and a higher purpose: "There is life (*ḥayyim*) for those who find them (*le-motze'eihem*)" (Proverbs 4:22). Boldly explicating this counsel, one rabbinic comment observed that true "life" requires us "to explicate them" (*le-motziy'eihem be-feh*); that is, to "extract" life meanings from the worldly situations that present themselves (see Babylonian Talmud, *Eruvin* 54a). Mere living is not true life, but just getting by, without thoughtfulness or spiritual intention. By contrast, we seek a disposition intent on engaging the occasions of life in a God-centered way, attuned to the divine voice that addresses us at every turn. Such a life requires a deliberated yes or no to the issues at hand. It is here that human sense and theological significance are tested.

Our hermeneutical spirit longs for meaning beyond information, and purpose beyond the need to survive. This desire is central to our attempts to transform worldly occasions into spiritual events, and mere moments into spheres of sanctity. When doing so our language transcends its role as a denotative tool, and sponsors spiritual values and concerns. Then, too, our words and their artifice may exceed normal limits and evoke ultimate mysteries. Hermeneutical theology is a guide and stay in this process, giving new meanings to experience, and recharging them with normative significance and purpose. It helps the heart remain steadfast and attentive to the divine revelations of existence. Authentic theology knows when to speak and when to be silent; when to offer interpretations and when to let God be God. At its core, theology is a prayer of the unsayable—a language of longing and limit.

'it'aruta de-libba me-'omqa de-nafsha
an arousal of the heart, from the depth of the soul

Acknowledgments

I first recall the memory of Kalman Bland, whose dear friendship was a life-long blessing. Our final conversation touched on my initial thoughts about the book of Job, now in the introduction, and his work on philosophical fables. In that exchange, many of our personal and intellectual ideals were conveyed with forthright honesty. I have no doubt that many passages in this book would have benefited from Kalman's critical wit and wisdom. His smiling face is before me as I write these lines.

Among the living, I am especially grateful to Arthur Green for decades of engaged friendship, filled with honest theological conversations. He arranged a seminar allowing me to present an early draft of the book with students at the Boston Hebrew College. Their responses helped sharpen many matters. As an external participant, Jennifer Hoffman shared in these sessions and beyond, through her enthusiastic interest and poetry. I have benefited from both.

I happily extend personal thanks to participants in a student reading group at the University of Chicago (Adrian Guiu, Maxim Levenson, Tzvi Schoenberg, and Joel Swanson, who was also of immense assistance to me in the correction of the proofs and composition of the index). Their critical and personal interventions were of much value. In addition, two former students, now friends and colleagues, Omer Michaelis and Sam Shonkoff, offered thoughtful and perceptive responses to early formulations of the book. Their intimate knowledge of my theology gave their observations special weight and significance.

Two close friends deserve special words of appreciation. Chaim Kranzler offered his ongoing comments and suggestions during our studies together, deepening our personal relations; and Elie Holzer provided a penetrating overview of structures and details of the final manuscript, inspiring new reflections and my deepest gratitude.

It is a special joy to acknowledge the thoughtful comments of my sons, Eitan and Elisha. Their personal responses and observations on initial chapters of the book were conveyed with thoughtfulness and care. Receiving their loving and honest evaluations has been a father's privilege.

When all is said and done, my words of gratitude to Mona, my life partner and soulmate, can only hint at the depth of her involvement and concern for every word in this book. She is and has been my first and best of readers—complementing my breath and soul, *ruḥa be-ruḥa*. We shared each passage innumerable times—for its ideas and tone, and for spiritual honesty and direction. She is the blessing of my life, still and always. It is to you, dearest Mona, that this book is dedicated—with a heart filled with love, and the intimacy of our shared seeing and feeling.

Michael Fishbane
March 2020 / Erev Pesaḥ 5780

Notes

Prologue

x PERSONAL KNOWLEDGE: See M. Polanyi, *Personal Knowledge: Toward a Post-Critical Philosophy* (Chicago: University of Chicago Press, 1958); and dealing from a wider range of topics, M. Polanyi and H. Prosch, *Meaning* (Chicago: University of Chicago Press, 1975).

ENTWINEMENT: Cf. M. Merleau-Ponty, *Le visible et l'invisible; suivé de notes de travail* (Paris: Gallimard, 1964).

TRUTH IS A FUNCTION ... IN ITS USE: Cf. H.-G. Gadamer, *Truth and Method* (New York: Continuum, 1975).

SYMBOLIC THINKING: See the important discussion in E. Cassirer, *The Philosophy of Symbolic Forms* (New Haven: Yale University Press, 1996).

FEELING: See S. Strasser, *Phenomenology of Feeling: An Essay on the Phenomena of the Heart* (Pittsburgh: Duquesne University Press, 1975). Cf. J. Patočka, *Body, Community, Language, World* (Peru, IL: Open Court, 1998).

"NEW THINKING" ... LIVED EXPERIENCE: See F. Rosenzweig, "Das neue Denken," in F. Rosenzweig, *Der Mensch und sein Werk: Gesammelte Schriften*, vol. 3, *Zweistromland*, edited by R. Mayer and A. Mayer (The Hague: M. Nijhoff, 1984), 139–61; and now the translation in *Franz Rosenzweig's "The New Thinking,"* edited and translated by B. Galli and A. Udoff (Syracuse: Syracuse University Press, 1999), chap. 3. Also W. James, *A Pluralistic Universe: The Works of William James*, edited by F. Burkhardt (Cambridge, MA: Harvard University Press, 1977); and see D. Lamberth, *William James and the Metaphysics of Experience* (Cambridge: Cambridge University Press, 2009).

xi "FUNDAMENTALISM": For this point, see J. Barr, *Beyond Fundamentalism* (Philadelphia: Westminster Press, 1984).

SCIENTISM: On this term, its presumption, and a critique, see A. McGrath, *The Territories of Human Reason: Science and Theology in an Age of Multiple Rationalities* (Oxford: Oxford University Press, 2019), 56–65, and seriatim.

"THE WORLD IS TOO MUCH WITH US": The poem "The World Is Too Much with Us" was composed circa 1802 and first published in *Poems, in Two Volumes* (1807).

xii HUMAN PURPOSES: According to the philosopher W. T. A. Stace, the "conception of purpose" was ignored in modern science, and that this is part of its "silent" and "greatest revolution"; see his "Man against Darkness," *Atlantic Monthly*, September 1948, 53–59. For E. A. Burtt, this constituted "the reading of man ... out of the real and primary realm;

see his *The Metaphysical Foundations of Modern Science* (Garden City, NY: Doubleday, 1954), 85.

LIKE ANCIENT IDOLS: Cf. Psalm 115:4–8.

xiii FOR SOME BASIS IN EXPERIENCE: See Cassirer, *Philosophy of Symbolic Forms*, vol. 4, *The Metaphysics of Symbolic Forms*, pt. 2 ("On Basis Phenomena").

LIKE SOME "REVOLVING SWORD": This interpretation builds on the comment of R. Mordechai of Lekhovitz, in *Torat Avot*, new ed. (Jerusalem: Yeshivat Beit Avraham Slonim, 2009), 38b–39a, dealing with a person without constancy in prayer, shifting constantly and affected by natural desires.

xvi AN EARLIER HASIDIC MASTER: Cf. R. Yeraḥmiel Yisrael Yitzḥak of Alexander, in *Yismaḥ Yisrael* (Jerusalem, 2016), II, *Be-Midbar, parshat Koraḥ*, 58 (Hebrew, 29c), who distinguishes between *mitzvot golmot* ("mute" or "fixed commandments") and the capacity of Israel "to innovate" (*le-ḥaddesh*) through the power of "interpretation."

xvii LEO BAECK: See his discussion in *This People Israel: The Meaning of Jewish Existence* (New York: Holt, Rinehart and Winston, 1964), 8–14 (book 1 was published in German in 1955, from notes compiled in Theresienstadt). For an earlier reflection on "mystery," see his essay "Mystery and Commandment," in L. Baeck, *Judaism and Christianity*, translated by W. Kaufmann (Philadelphia: Jewish Publication Society, 1958), chap. 4. This originally appeared as "Geheimnis und Gebot," in *Der Leuchter* 3 (1921/22): 137–53; and reprinted in L. Baeck, *Wege im Judentum: Aufsätze und Reden* (Berlin: Schocken Books, 1933), 33–48.

THE TREE OF LIFE AND THE TREE OF KNOWLEDGE: The dual structure of life and knowledge was subject to stimulating reflections under the headings of "Geist" and "Life" by Cassirer, *Philosophy of Symbolic Forms*, vol. 4, pts. 1 and 3.

xviii SPECIES ADAPTATION . . . HUMAN INTERPRETATION: See the comments of R. Abraham ibn Ezra and R. David Kimḥi, ad loc.

Part One

1 R. BAḤYE BEN ASHER: See his interpretation of Deuteronomy 30:14 in *Rabbeinu Baḥye 'al Ha-Torah*, edited by Ch. Chavel (Jerusalem: Mosad Ha-Rav Kook, 1982), 3:442.

MAIMONIDES: See his formulation in *Sefer pa-Mitzvot*, Root-Principle 9, in *Mishneh Torah le-Ha-Rambam*, edited by S. Fraenkel (Jerusalem-Bnei Brak: Shabbtai Fraenkel, 2006), 1:153 (Maimonides adds a fourth component: virtues or dispositions).

2 R. ELIJAH DE VIDAS: See in *Reishit Ḥokhmah Ha-Shalem*, edited by Ḥ. Valdman (Jerusalem: Or Ha-Musar, 1980), vol. 2, *Shaʿar Ha-Qedushah*, chap. 4, sec. 37 (citing Zohar, *Va-yeiʾra*, 89b), p. 63; and the elaboration in sec. 43, pp. 65–66.

SUBSEQUENT GENERATIONS OF HASIDIC MASTERS: See particularly the writings of the Maggid of Mezritch; cf. *Sefer Torat Ha-Maggid Mi-Mezritch*, edited by I. Klaphotz (Bnei Brak: Mishor, 2001), 2:421a-b (Rosh Ha-Shanah); and also R. Elimelekh of Lizensk, in his *Noʿam Elimelekh* (Krakow: D. Strum, Tarnow, 1896), 7b.

3 "MOMENT GODS": The phenomenon of "special" or "moment" gods (and their names) was studied by H. Usener, *Götternamen: Versuch einer Lehre der religiösen Begriffsbildung* (Berlin: F. Cohen, 1896).

4 A SCIENTIFIC HERMENEUTIC: Modern religious thought cannot bypass or ignore Spinoza's *Theological-Political Tractatus*, but must go through it with care. Cf. L. Strauss, *Spinoza's Critique of Religion* (Chicago: University of Chicago Press, 1967).

5 "LANGUAGE GAME": The reference both here, and with respect to language as a "form of life" (*Lebensform*), is, of course, to L. Wittgenstein's *Philosophical Investigations*; and see, for the points noted here, the formulations in I.23 and 499.

6 SPINOZA SAID THAT . . . WHOLES CONTAIN PARTS: See Spinoza's letter to Henry Oldenburg (November 1665); published as Letter 32 in *The Collected Works of Spinoza*, edited and translated by E. Curley (Princeton, : Princeton University Press, 2016), 2:18–22; and cf. the penetrating analysis of W. Sacksteder, "Spinoza on Part and Whole: The Worm's Eye View," *Southwestern Journal of Philosophy* 8.3 (1977): 139–59.

"VIEW FROM ABOVE": For this formulation and issue, see P. Hadot, *Philosophy as a Way of Life* (Oxford: Blackwell, 1995), chap. 9.

10 OTHER READERS: Martin Buber, *The Prophetic Faith* (New York: Harper, 1942), suggested that the book takes up questions raised during the Babylonian exile; Margarette Susman, *Das Buch Hiob und das Schicksal des jüdischen Volkes* (Zurich: Steinberg-Verlag, 1946), takes up certain cultural-political considerations after World War II, but offers a problematic explanation of Jewish suffering.

THE TALMUD SPECULATED: See Babylonian Talmud, *Baba Batra* 15a.

11 "DUST OF THE EARTH": See Genesis 2:4, which depicts Adam as a creature formed from the '*afar* (dust) of the ground.

12 FILLED WITH "SYMPATHY" (*NIḤAMTI*): Cf. the related reading by R. Isaiah de Trani, published in *Tikwath Enosch*, edited by Israel Schwarz (Berlin: Louis Geschel Verlagsbuchhandlung, 1868), 66.

14 RUDOLF OTTO: See his classic work, *Das Heilige* (Breslau: Trewendt und Granier, 1917), widely known in its English translation as *The Idea of the Holy* (Oxford: Oxford University Press, 1958). Other aspects of the phenomenon were treated by Otto in *Das Gefühl des Überweltlichen (Sensus Numinous)* (Munich: C. H. Beck, 1935); and "The Sensus Numinus as the Historical Basis of Religion," *Hibbert Journal* 29 (1930): 1–8.

17 "EVERYTHING IS A VOICE": An excerpt from the poem "What the Mouth of Shadow Says," by Victor Hugo, from his collection *Contemplations*, as translated by Anne Davenport, referenced in Jean-Louis Chrétien, *The Call and the Response* (New York: Fordham University Press, 2004), 43.

NOMOS AND NARRATIVE: I adapt these terms to this setting from the classic essay by R. Cover, "The Supreme Court 1982 Term—Forward: Nomos and Narrative," *Harvard Law Review* 97 (1983): 4–25. For a congruent consideration, see below in part 3, *Derash*, pp. 80–81.

Interlude One

21 WE BELONG TO THE WORLD: As a way of characterizing the human ontological condition of finitude, see P. Ricoeur, "Phenomenology and Hermeneutics," *Noûs* 9 (1975): 88–89. The related concept of *Zugehörigkeit* (belongingness) is famously found in Gadamer, *Truth and Method*, 416 and 419, similarly with regard to finitude, the linguistic constitution of the world, and hermeneutical experience.

PRIMARY "REALITY": A similar notion, called the "real," occurs in the work of H. Bergson. Cf. *Matter and Memory*, translated by N. M. Paul and W. S. Palmer (New York: Zone, 1990), 175, 183–85; originally published in 1911 by George Allen and Unwin.

22 "ACTUALITY": See the related reflections of G. Simmel, *The View of Life: Four Metaphysical Essays and Journal Aphorisms* (Chicago: University of Chicago Press, 2010), 99–103.

23 PROBLEMS TO BE SOLVED: P. Häberlin, *Das Wunderbare* (1930; repr., Zurich: Schweizer Spiegel Verlag, 1975), 7–8, cautions against the reduction of the mystery and wonder of existence to "riddles" to be solved.

WALLACE STEVENS: Cf. "Collect of Philosophy," in his *Opus Postumous* (New York: Vintage Books, 1990), 267–80, and frequently elsewhere.

25 WE BELONG TO SCRIPTURE: For Franz Rosenzweig, the idea that we belong to scripture is a fundamental feature of Jewish consciousness, and constitutes the readiness to be instructed. See his essay "Die Schrift und Luther," in M. Buber and F. Rosenzweig, *Die Schrift und ihre Verdeutschung* (Berlin: Schocken Verlag, 1936), 110 (where he uses the verb *zugehört*).

26 THE AIM IS NOT TO APPROPRIATE: For theoretical reflections, see P. Ricoeur, "The Hermeneutical Function of Distantiation," in *Hermeneutics and the Human Sciences*, edited and translated by J. Thompson (Cambridge: Cambridge University Press, 1981), 142–44.

Part Two

27 QUALITIES AND QUANTITIES: Cf. A. Lingis, *The Imperative* (Bloomington: Indiana University Press, 1998), 14–15, where he also emphasizes the adjectival and adverbial aspects of these dimensions.

28 SIGNALS THAT WILL HELP REGULATE BEHAVIOR: See C. S. Pierce, "Issues of Pragmatism," *The Monist* 15 (1905): 448n1: "The entire . . . universe of existents . . . is perfused with signs, if it is not composed exclusively of signs." For Pierce, this is a metaphysical truth. On the issue of signs and signals as the basis of semiotics, see the discussion below.

29 CAESURAS: Caesura is a key concept in my theological thinking; it was first discussed in *Sacred Attunement: A Jewish Theology* (Chicago: University of Chicago Press, 2008).

"ANIMAL FAITH": This phrase and the primacy of feelings allude to the work of G. Santayana, *Scepticism and Animal Faith: Introduction to a System of Philosophy* (New York: C. Scribner's Sons, 1929).

30 "BE SILENT AND LISTEN": Deuteronomy 27:9. Traditionally, "obey and hear.".

APPORTIONS THE SPIRIT OF LIFE: I adapt the terms "apportions" and "proportions" from R. Gogel, *Quest of the Measure: The Phenomenological Problem of Truth* (New York: Peter Lang Publishing, 1987); this study focuses on the problem of measure in the works of Husserl and Heidegger.

A "SPEAKING" THAT DOES NOT REFER TO ANY SIGNIFIED THING: This formulation occurs in a letter from I. Calvino to the Italian author G. Manganelli, subsequently included in the latter's *Nuovo commento* (Milan: Adelphi, 1993), 149–50, and translated in G. Agamben, *The Fire and the Tale* (Stanford: Stanford University Press, 2017), 96.

31 CAPACITY FOR RESPONSIVENESS: See the rich discussion in J. Hoffmeyer, *Biosemiotics: An Examination into the Signs of Life and the Life of Signs* (Scranton: University of Scranton Press, 2008).

GILLUI VE-KHISUI BA-LASHON: An allusion to H. N. Bialik's classic essay "*Gillui . . . ba-Lashon*" (Revealment and Concealment in Language), where he demonstrates how words oscillate over time. My concern is the profound dialectics of language—simultaneously revealing by concealing, and vice versa.

33 *TOHE AND BOHE*: For this striking interpretation of Genesis 1:2, see *Midrash Bereshit Rabba*, critical edition by J. Theodor and Ch. Albeck (Jerusalem: Wahrmann Books,

1965), 1:15; and, in a different vein, cf. Babylonian Talmud, *Kiddushin* 40b. See also in *Sefer Ha-Bahir*, para. 2; cf. *The Book Bahir, an Edition Based on the Earliest Manuscripts*, by D. Abrams (Los Angeles: Cherub Press, 1994), 119.

33 BO-HU: See already *Sefer Ha-Bahir*, para. 2. It also appears in *Rabbeinu Behaye: Be'ur 'al Ha-Torah*, edited by Ch. Chavel, 6th ed. (Jerusalem: Mosad Ha-Rav Kook, 1982), 1:16; and in R. Moses Nachmanides, *Kitvei Ha-Ramban*, "Torat H' Temimah," edited by Ch. Chavel (Jerusalem: Mosad Ha-Rav Kook, 1962), 1:157.

TO PERCEIVE . . . "AS THIS" OR "AS THAT": Cf. the fundamental observations of G. N. A. Vesey, "Seeing and Seeing As," *Proceedings of the Aristotelian Society* 56 (1955–56): 109–24.

34 "OUR INTERPRETED WORLD": From the first elegy of the "Duino Elegies" ("in der gedeuteten Welt"); following *The Selected Poetry of Rainer Maria Rilke*, edited and translated by S. Mitchell (New York: Vintage Books, 1984), 150–51.

CÉZANNE: Cited in J. Gasquet, *Cézanne* (1921; repr., Paris: Éditions des Belles Lettres, 2012), 170.

35 KLEE: See the reflections in *Das bildnerische Denken: Schriften zur Form- und Gestaltungslehre*, edited by J. Spiller (Basel: Schwabe & Co. Verlag, 1956), esp. chaps. 6–9.

37 "TOUCHES BUT DOES NOT TOUCH": A medieval kabbalistic locution marking such incomprehensible perceptions. Cf. Zohar 1.15.

R. YITZHAK MEIR OF GUR: This teaching is reported by his grandson, R. Yehudah Leib of Gur (the Gerer Rebbe), in his collections of homilies on the Torah lections for Sabbaths and festivals; see *Sefas Emes 'al Ha-Torah veha-Mo'adim* (Jerusalem, 1971), 5:27b and 28a (1871 and 1873, respectively). This teaching is also collected in *Hiddushei Ha-RI"M* (New York: Mosad Ha-RI"M Levin, 2007), 241.

39 THEME-WORD: In a related vein, see the essay by Martin Buber, "Shelihuto shel Avraham," in *Darko shel Miqra: 'Iyyunim bi-Defusei Signon Ba-Tana"kh* (Jerusalem: Mosad Bialik, 1964), 65–81; originally entitled "*Shelihut Avraham*," in *Ha-Aretz* (Tel Aviv, 1939).

40 "AND BEHOLD!—THREE MEN!": This reading and emphasis is based on the report of a sermon given by R. Nehemiah Nobel of Frankfurt (d. 1922), by Franz Rosenzweig in a letter to friends. See Franz Rosenzweig, *On Jewish Learning*, edited by N. N. Glatzer (New York: Schocken Books, 1955), 124; original in F. Rosenzweig's *Briefe*, edited by E. Rosenzweig (Berlin: Schocken Verlag, 1935), 521.

42 BIND . . . INTO A UNIFYING DEED: Cf. the powerful remarks of M. Buber, addressed to his oppressed compatriots, "Ein Spruch des Maimuni," *Israelitisches Familienblatt* [Beilage] 37/15, April 11, 1935, p. 9.

43 ORDINARINESS . . . EXCEPTIONAL: Insightful reflections on such experiences of order and disorder have been offered by B. Waldenfels, in such works as *Order in the Twilight* (Athens: Ohio University Press, 1996) and *Phenomenology of the Alien* (Evanston: Northwestern University Press, 2011).

45 YEHI: This verbal command ("let be"/"let there be") recurs throughout Genesis 1 (cf. vv. 3, 6, 14), and is implied in the other jussive forms of creation.

NO PLACE EMPTY: Referring to God; cf. *Pesikta de Rav Kahana*, edited by B. Mandelbaum (New York: Jewish Theological Seminary of America, 1962), 1:4 (*piska* 1), *'eino panui min ha-Shekhinah*; and the classic kabbalistic and Hasidic formula: *lit atar panui minei*, "There is no place empty of God."

46 GRASPED DIRECTLY BY HUMAN COGNITION: For this cognitive-philosophical presentation, see Moses Maimonides, *The Guide of the Perplexed*, II.33, translated by S. Pines (Chicago: University of Chicago Press, 1963), p. 364.

47 THE DISTINCTIVENESS OF INDIVIDUAL DIFFERENCES: This phrase alludes to the book by J. Sacks, *The Dignity of Difference* (New York: Continuum, 2002).
"DETAILS WERE . . . 'EXPLICATED'": For this term, see Deuteronomy 1:5. On the phenomenon as a whole, with examples, see my full exposition in *Biblical Interpretation in Ancient Israel* (Oxford: Clarendon Press, 1985), pt. 2 ("Legal Exegesis"). The medieval commentator Nachmanides frequently remarks on Moses's various explications and expansions in the book of Deuteronomy.

52 THE WORLD BECKONS OUR SPEECH: This is what K. Löwith referred to as the *Fürsprache* of objects, which evoke questions and response; cf. his *Das Individuum in der Rolle des Mitmenschen* (1928; repr., Darmstadt: Wissenschaftliche Buchgesellschaft, 1969), 69–70. Regarding "for-structure" of language as its primary intentionality, cf. W. Hamacher, *Minima Philologica* (New York: Fordham University Press, 2015), 146–52.
THROUGH LANGUAGE, WE EXTEND THE HORIZONS: See the comments of A. de Waehlens, *Une philosophie de l'ambiguïté: Existentialisme de Maurice Merleau-Ponty* (Louvain: Publications Universitaires de Louvain, 1951), 114.

Interlude Two

56 ACHIEVED BY: For this issue of pedigree based on knowledge, and the various topics noted, cf. Maimonides, *Mishneh Torah*, *Sefer Ha-Mada'*, Hilkhot Talmud Torah, chaps. 5–6.
"HOLY WRITINGS": See Mishnah, *Yadaim* 3:6.
NOTHING COULD BE ADDED OR SUBTRACTED: Cf. Deuteronomy 4:2.

57 WORDS AND PHRASES: The beginning of this creative process is evident in the Hebrew Bible, with many examples of inner-canonical interpretations. See the materials presented in my *Biblical Interpretation in Ancient Israel*.
"FOR THE SAKE OF HEAVEN": For the notion of controversies "for the sake of heaven" (*le-shem shamayim*), see Mishnah, *Seder Nezikin*, *Massekhet Avot* 5.17.
GOD'S ALL-EFFECTUATING VOICE: See R. Meir ibn Gabbai, *'Avodat ha-Qodesh, ḥeleq ha-takhlit*, chap. 23 (see further below in part 5, "*Sod*").
TORAH KELULAH: For an earlier formulation, see my *Sacred Attunement*, 61–64. This topic will be further discussed in part 2, "*Peshat*," below.

58 EACH MOMENT: See the comment on Exodus 19:1 ("that day") in *Pesikta de Rav Kahana*, 1:219 (*piska* 12.21, *Ba-Ḥodesh Ha-Shelishi*): the renewal of Torah and revelation through interpretation is "every day."
VE-ḤAY BA-HEM: Leviticus 18:5.
WHAT GUIDES THE HAND OF JEWISH HERMENEUTICS?: Alluding to Babylonian Talmud, *Menaḥot* 29b.
THESE AND THOSE ARE THE WORDS: Alluding to Babylonian Talmud, *Eruvin* 13b.

Part Three

62 THE CONCRETE APPEAL OF GOD: Alluding to the call of the beloved at the door in Song of Songs 5:2.

63 "I GIVE THANKS": The opening prayer in the traditional Jewish liturgy; the final words are derived from Lamentations 3:23.
PHYSICAL EXPERIENCES: The primacy of "experienced meaning" for our subsequent "formulations" and symbolic "schemes" is adeptly articulated by E. Gendlin, in *Experi-*

encing and the Creation of Meaning: A Philosophical and Psychological Approach to the Subjective (1962; Evanston: Northwestern University Press, 1997).

64 ANCIENT JEWISH SAGES PONDERED: See *Midrash Bereshit Rabba*, 1:112–13 (Bereshit 12.15).

AN OLDER EXEGETICAL TRADITION: See the early formulation in *Sifre Deuteronomy* 26: "Everywhere (in scripture) that *Y-H-W-H* is mentioned this indicates the (Divine) Quality of Mercy (*Raḥamim*) . . . ; (and) everywhere that *Elohim* is mentioned this indicates the Quality of Judgment (*Din*)." See *Sifre Devarim*, edited by L. Finkelstein (New York: Jewish Theological Seminary of America, 1969), 41.

66 PRIMARY *CRI DU COEUR*: On such a phenomenon, see L. Biernaert, SJ, "Prayer and Petition to the Other," in *From Cry to Word: Contribution towards a Psychology of Prayer*, edited by A. Godin, SJ, Studies in the Psychology of Religion 4 (Brussels: Lumen Vitae Press, 1968), 27–36.

"THEOPOESIS": For the terms and a wide-ranging discussion, see A. Wilder, *Theopoetic: Theology and the Religious Imagination* (Philadelphia: Fortress Press, 1976). He is aware of the overlap with mythopoesis; and both aspects conjoin in this midrash.

"PARAMOUNT REALITY": On these notions, see William James, *The Principles of Psychology* (New York: Henry, 1890), vol. 2, chap. 21.

67 *SHI'UR/SHE-EIN LAHEM SHI'UR*: Alluding to Mishnah, *Peah* 1:1, recited at the onset of the daily liturgy (matters that have no fixed [upper] limit include harvest donations for the needy and care for strangers; the ensuing discussions will make direct and indirect reference to these matters).

69 THE TORAH STATES THIS TASK: The text is from Deuteronomy 6:5 (v. 4 is the proclamation of God's unity). The midrashic discussion follows *Sifre Deuteronomy* 32, edited by L. Finkelstein (New York: Jewish Theological Seminary of America, 1969), 55.

70 WE ACKNOWLEDGE BOTH: For a related interpretation of the Divine Name *Ha-Qadosh Baruch Hu* as a combination of attributes, see *Sefer Nefesh Ha-Hayyim*, by R. Ḥayyim of Volozhin (Vilna: Y. L. Lippman, 1874), *Sha'ar* III, *Pereq* 5.

71 YEHUDA HALEVI: The poem is a *yotzer*-composition for Shavu'ot; in the edition of D. Yarden, *Shirei Ha-Qodesh le-Rabbi Yehuda Halevi . . . 'im Peirush . . . me'et Dov Yarden* (Jerusalem, 1978), 2:428.

RESPONSIBILITY: For a fundamental consideration of this term in relation to one's obligations to the created world, see H. Jonas, *The Imperative of Responsibility: In Search of an Ethics for the Technological Age* (Chicago: University of Chicago Press, 1984).

LIGHT IS BOTH: For a related poem by Yehudah Halevi, see F. Rosenzweig, *Jehuda Halevi: Zweiundneunzig Hymnen und Gedichte* (Berlin: Lambert Schneider, 1926), 91 ("Licht"), and discussion on 220.

72 "CROWN OF RESPLENDENT MAJESTY": This phrase alludes to the depiction of the Torah by which Moses was ennobled, formulated in the Sabbath morning prayer (*Amidah*).

"ENCIRCLING SPLENDOR": This alludes to the splendor of Jerusalem, as formulated in Lamentations 2:15.

"I HAVE PLACED . . . CHOOSE LIFE": Alluding to Deuteronomy 11:26.

"BE SILENT AND *HEAR*!": Alluding to Deuteronomy 27:9.

73 *YEVONENEHU*: For different formulations, see *Mechilta D'Rabbi Ismael*, edited by H. S. Horovitz and I. A. Rabin (Jerusalem: Bamberger & Wahrmann), 235 (*Yitro*, 9), in the name of Rabbi; and see also in *Midrash Ha-Gadol Devarim*, edited by S. Fisch (Jerusalem: Mossad Ha-Rav Kook, 1972), 705 (*Ha'azinu*, lines 19–22).

74 RABBINIC INTERPRETERS: See the commentary on Deuteronomy 32:10 in *Sifre Deuteronomy* (Finkelstein), 399 (*Ve-Zo't, piska* 343).

PHENOMENOLOGY OF PERCEPTION: On the issue of sound, see the rich analysis of D. Ihde, *Listening and Voice: Phenomenologies of Sound*, 2nd ed. (New York: State University of New York Press, 2007), 116–17, 147–51.

75 R. AKIBA: Cf. the specific formulation in *Mechilta D'Rabbi Ismael*, 216 (*Yitro*, 4), upon which the ensuing adaptation is based (R. Eliezer adds that God spoke after Moses—following the people's acceptance of his words).

R. ELEAZAR'S SERMON: See Babylonian Talmud, *Ḥagiga* 3a/b.

76 RADICAL RABBINIC INTERPRETATION: See in *Midrash Tanḥuma (Ha-Qadum)*, *Yitro* 12.

77 "IN STRENGTH": See *Mechilta*, 235 (*Yitro*, 9), and the later formulations in *Pesikta de Rav Kahana*, 1:224 (*piska* 12.25, *Ba-Ḥodesh Ha-Shelishi*).

EARLY RABBINIC COMMENTATORS: See in *Mechilta*, 214 (*Yitro*, 3).

81 DIFFERENT PARABLES: See *Mechilta*, 214–15 (*Yitro*, 3).

TWO TYPES OF SPEECH: Cf. the formulation of this exegetical topos by R. Ephraim Lunshitz, *Keli Yaqar* (Jerusalem: Ḥorev, 1999), 1:253 (ad loc., Exodus 20:1).

82 EVALUATION OF THIS EVENT: R. Naftali Tzvi Yehuda Berlin applied this legal model to Abraham while in a (presumed) state of contemplative prayer. Cf. his *Ha-'Ameq Davar* (Jerusalem: Volozhin Yeshiva Press, 1999), 154–55 (ad loc.). Other considerations apply if the legal model is when and how care for wayfarers or guests may defer or overrides certain (preexisting) Sabbath rulings (Babylonian Talmud, *Shabbat* 127a).

83 VE-HU/BE-HAVAYATO: See in Mishnah, *Seder Qedoshim, Menaḥot* 4:4.

84 ONE HASIDIC DISCUSSION: See the considerations presented in R. Menaḥem Mendel of Chernobyl's *Ma'or 'Einayim* (Jerusalem: Machon Ma'or Torah, 2006), 1:53a–54a (ad loc.; s.v. *Ba-Sha's*).

85 SEEING BUT NOT KNOWING: On this clause and "knowing but not seeing" as halakhic issues based on Leviticus 5:1, see Ramban, ad loc.: *Peirush Ha-Ramban 'al Ha-Torah*, edited and annotated by Ḥ. Chavel (Jerusalem: Mossad Ha-Rav Kook, 1960), 2:23–24.

NO "SUBSTANCE": Literally, *mamash*. See the commentary of Baḥye ben Asher on Deuteronomy 19:15, in *Rabbeinu Baḥye 'al Ha-Torah*, edited and annotated by Ḥ. Chavel (Jerusalem: Mossad ha-Rav Kook, 1982), 3:366.

"NO TRULY A NO": See at *Seder Eliyahu Rabba*, edited by M. Ish Shalom (repr., Jerusalem: Wahrmann Books, 1969), chap. 23, p. 128—*mitokh lav lav; mitokh hen hen*.

R. SHIMON BAR YOCHAI TAUGHT: See in *Sifre Deuteronomy* (Finkelstein), 403–4; and the variant in *Pesikta de Rav Kahana*, 1:208 (*piska* 12.6, *Ba-Ḥodesh Ha-Shelishi*).

89 THESE EXPLICATIONS: Cf. Deuteronomy 1:5 (*ho'il Moshe be'er et ha-Torah*, "Then Moses began to exposit the Torah").

90 LATER RABBINIC RULINGS: See variously in the Mishnah and *Tosefta Seder Zera'im*, *Peah*, passim; and the Jerusalem Talmud, *Peah*. A poignant digest of concerns for the elderly and indigent appears in Babylonian Talmud, *Shabbat* 23b.

91 BY THE CANTOR . . . REPETITION: The ensuing liturgical poem (*piyyut*) is taken from the prayers of the great *ḥazzan*, R. Yannai. See in *Maḥzor Piyyutei Rabbai Yannai La-Torah Vela-Mo'adim*, edited with notes by Z. M. Rabinovitz (Jerusalem: Mosad Bialik, 1965), 1:474–78 (citations taken from pp. 473 and 476, respectively).

IN THE MIDRASH: *Leviticus Rabba* 34.4; see *Midrash Vayiqra Rabba*, edited by M. Margulies (Jerusalem: Wahrmann Books, 1975), 3:778–80.

92 "STAND . . . SURETY": Literally, "the principal" (of the merits earned) will "remain" or "hold firm" for the world-to-come. This alludes to Mishnah, *Peah* 1:1, taking *gemilut ḥasadim* there as acts of charity and *yad* here as a memorial pillar (56:5).

Interlude Three

93 ASPIRATIONS: These are conveyed in various forms, especially through the moral and legal corpora of a culture. Of particular interest are the reflections of Lon Fuller, *The Morality of Law*, rev. ed. (New Haven: Yale University Press, 1969), overall and regarding the topic of "the inner morality of law," where issues of aspiration are considered.

96 *DEREKH/ORAḤ*: Cf. the teaching of R. Dov Ber of Mezeritch, in *Or Torah* (Brooklyn: Kehot, 1972), p. 75 a/b.

THE CENTER OF ONE'S BEING: See R. Simḥah Bunem, in *Qol Simḥah* (Ra'ananah, Israel: Machon Torat Simḥah, n.d.), *parshat Toledot*, 34–35.

97 THE SOUL AS THE . . . GESTALT: This particular formulation is inspired by E. Rosenstock-Huessy, *Practical Knowledge of the Soul* (Eugene, OR: Wipf & Stock, 2015), 8 ("The soul is a unique, all-embracing process to which all individual processes should be related"; including one's "whole heritage of belief and tradition" [p. 3]). For compelling and inspiring meditations on the soul and life, see F. Cheng, *De l'âme: Sept lettres à une amie* (Paris: Éditions Albin Michel, 2016).

DESERT MANNA: Building on *Pesikta de Rav Kahana*, 1:224 (*piska* 12.25, Ba-Ḥodesh Ha-Shelishi).

IT OCCURS . . . IN THE "LIVING NOW": See E. Husserl, *The Phenomenology of Living Time Consciousness*, translated by J. S. Churchill (Bloomington: Indiana University Press, 1984), 107, 115.

98 HERMENEUTICS OF THE SELF: With this phrase, I allude to the important work of M. Foucault, *The Hermeneutics of the Subject: Lectures at the Collège de France, 1981–1982* (New York: Palgrave Macmillan, 2005). His work is focused primarily on the ancient Greek and early Christian traditions of self-care and self-examination. For Jewish examples, see the extended discussion in part 4, "*Remez*," below.

Part Four

101 FORMS OF LANGUAGE: On language, sedimentation, and truth, see the reflections of M. Merleau-Ponty, *Signs*, translated by R. C. McCleary (Evanston: Northwestern University Press, 1964), 96. The sedimentation of language marks its "institutional" or deeply "deposited" character.

BECOMING AN "I" . . . LOCATED: See the striking discussion of W. James, "The Experience of Activity," in *The Writings of William James*, edited by J. J. McDermott (New York: Random House, 1964), 284; and also the remarks of E. Benveniste, *Problems in General Linguistics*, translated by M. E. Meek (Coral Gables, FL: University of Miami Press, 1971), 226–27.

"WHO MAY ASCEND": The ensuing paragraph is built on Psalm 24, a text focused on personal spiritual worthiness.

104 A VERITABLE "HERMENEUTICS OF THE SELF": Alluding to the work of Foucault discussed above in "Interlude 3."

105 WE NO LONGER EVALUATE: For an instance of revision that turns away from certain medieval and modern considerations and reconsiders the issue from a contemporary

Christian perspective, see M. Scheler, "On the Rehabilitation of Virtue," *American Catholic Philosophical Quarterly* 79 (Winter 2005): 21–37.

105 DEREKH LA-DEREKH: I found this phrase in *Ḥokhmat Ha-Matzpun*, arranged and edited by M. Ibgui (Nice; printed in Bnai Brak, Israel: Lippa Friedman Press, 1975), vol. 2 (*Shemot-Veyiqra*), *parshat Yitro*, 252b; see also for the explanation of this path as a personal path (*derekh le-'atzmo*).

106 THE NINETEENTH CENTURY MASTER: The ensuing interpretation of "smiting a soul by accident" (Numbers 35:11) was inspired by the homily of R. Avraham Yehoshua Heschel of Apt, in his *Ohev Yisrael* (Jerusalem: Siftei Tzaddikim Institute, 1996), 1:240b–241b (*Mas'ei*). The language of the homily and its spiritual terminology draw on the discussion in the Babylonian Talmud, *Makkot* 10a.

LISTING OF BIBLICAL "REMEMBRANCES": I focus below on several passages that invoke the commandment to "remember" a scriptural event. Traditions vary from four to six in traditional prayer books. Reference to the desert manna is included among the recitations discussed by R. Levi Yitzḥak of Berditchev; see *Kedushat Levi Ha-Shalem* (Brooklyn: Mechon Kedushat Levi, 1998), 2:627–34). I shall include it in my list of seven. The order of presentation is my own.

107 CANONICAL MEMORIES CONDITION CULTURAL IDENTITY: See the wide-ranging considerations in J. Assmann, *Das kulterelle Gedächtniss: Schrift, Erinnerung und Identität in frühen Hochkulturen* (Munich: Beck, 1992); and also the several studies in his *Religion and Cultural Memory* (Stanford: Stanford University Press, 2006). Note also D. Hervieu-Léger, *Religion as a Chain of Memory* (Cambridge: Polity Press, 2000).

THOMAS MANN: *Joseph and His Brothers*, translated by H. T. Lowe-Porter (New York: Alfred Knopf, 1948), 3.

108 "AN INVISIBLE FORCE": See Vasily Grossman, *Life and Fate*, translated by R. Chandler (New York: New York Review Books, 1985), 672.

SALGADO: See S. Salgado, *Workers* (New York: Aperture Books, 1993), 300–319.

109 THIS RENEWAL IS LIKE A BIRD: The ensuing images echo the similes found in *Midrash Mekhilta de-Rabbi Ishmael*, 113, dealing with the deliverance from Egypt.

"FOR YOU HAVE RELEASED": Psalm 116:8.

HORIZONS: For a phenomenological analysis, see C. A. van Peursen, "L'horizon," *Situation* 1 (1954): 204–34. For the striking notion that the world is the "horizon of all horizons," see M. Merleau-Ponty, *Phénoménologie de la perception* (Paris: Gallimard, 1945), 381.

R. NAḤMAN . . . MAQQIFIN: See in *Liqqutei Moharan*, *tinyana*, 7.6 (winter 1803; *parshat Miqqetz*), and passim. For a penetrating discussion of this epistemological-theological structure, see J. Weiss, *Meḥqarim Be-Ḥasidut Bratzlav* (Jerusalem: Bialik Institute, 1974), chap. 8 ("Ha-'Qushia' be-Torat R. Naḥman").

"FROM THE STRAITS": Psalm 118:5.

"CAPTIVE MIND": Alluding to C. Milosz, *The Captive Mind* (New York: Knopf, 1953).

PROVE . . . STEADFAST RESOLVE: I have in mind here the important notion of *Bewährung* developed by Martin Buber, in the sense that one proves the truth of one's life commitment by steadfast resolve. I have discussed this at length in "Justification through Living: Martin Buber's Third Alternative," in *Martin Buber: A Contemporary Perspective*, edited by P. Mendes-Flohr (Syracuse and Jerusalem: Syracuse University Press and the Israel Academy of Sciences and the Humanities, 2002), 120–32; and in "Religious Authenticity and Spiritual Resistance: Martin Buber and Biblical Hermeneutics," in *Martin Buber: His Intellectual and Scholarly Legacy*, edited by S. Berrin Shonkoff (Leiden: Brill, 2018), 219–32.

110 WITHOUT EXPIATION: See the searing argument regarding Holocaust perpetrators by V. Jankélevitch, "Should We Pardon Them?" *Critical Inquiry* 22.3 (1996): 552–72.

112 "AND NIGHT": The concluding lines of the poem, "Then wrote the scribe of the Sohar," by Nellie Sachs, *O the Chimneys* (New York: Farrar, Straus & Giroux, 1969), 122–23 (this verse was translated by M. Roloff).

113 TO CULTIVATE ONE'S HEART AND MIND: According to rabbinic tradition, the time between the exodus and Sinai was for the purification of one's traits, including aspects of the face. Cf. the Hasidic expression of this by R. Shalom Barzofsky, *Netivot Shalom* (Jerusalem: Mechon Emunah va-Da'at, n.d.), pt. 1, 99a–101a (vol. 5; *Devarim; parshat Shofetim*) and pt. 2, 317a–322b (vol. 2; *Sefirat Ha-'Omer*).

114 "WHAT THE EAR CAN COMPREHEND": See *Mechilta D'Rabbi Ismael*, 215. The earthly and anthropomorphic images are explained as figures that serve "to accommodate the ear" (*le-shadekh ha-ozen*) to what it can "comprehend" (*lishmo'a*); and cf. *Midrash Tanḥuma, Yitro* 12.

WE ARE RIGHTLY PUZZLED . . . AS WERE THE ANCIENT SAGES: For some speculations, see Babylonian Talmud, *Shabbat*, 104a.

WHEN OUR EYES WANDER: Cf. Numbers 15:39–40.

115 WE HAVE EYES THAT DO NOT SEE: The ensuing phrase is based on Psalm 115:4–8.

116 SPIRITUAL IMPOVERISHMENT: The biblical text speaks of God causing "distress" or "suffering" (*ve-ya'anka*) through hunger; subsequent spiritual masters reinterpreted the verb in terms of the people being "poor" ('*aniyyim*) in spirit and wisdom. Cf. R. Uri Feivel of Krisnapole, *Or Ha-Hochmah* (Jerusalem: Mechon Bnai Moshe, 2017), 2:347b–48b.

117 "ZERA' GAD": The characterization of the manna in Exodus 16:31. The differing "taste" (*ta'am*) of the manna (Numbers 11:8) led to interpretations that said that it differed according to one's age; cf. *Pesikta de Rav Kahana*, 1:224. Others said that it was called *gad* because it was able to "tell" or "speak of" (*maggid*) hidden mysteries. See *Midrash Ha-Gadol Shemot*, edited by M. Margulies (Jerusalem: Mosad Ha-Rav Kook, 1967), 334.

"WHAT IS THIS": The question in Aramaic is followed by a Hebrew formulation. The ensuing discussion is based on Exodus 16.

SHE INITIATED: This formulation first appears in *Sifre Numbers* 89; see *Sifre de-Bei Rav. Sifre 'al Sefer Bemidbar ve-Sifre Zutta*, edited by H. Horovitz (Jerusalem: Wahrmann Books, 1966), 98. It is followed by commentators like Rashi and Ibn Ezra. The other reason, Miriam's allegation that Moses had "separated" from Tzipporah, is also give in the foregoing midrash, ad loc.

118 AS SLANDER SHAMES . . . BLANCH: See Babylonian Talmud, *Bava Metzi'a* 58b (with types of verbal abuse noted, in business and social relations).

ONA'AH: Cf. Babylonian Talmud, *Bava Metzi'a* 58b. The biblical passage upon which this behavior is based is Leviticus 25:17; and see Rashi, ad loc.

A LADDER OF ASCENT: Deuteronomy 30:14 is so linked to the ladder of Jacob reaching heaven (Genesis 28:12) by R. Elijah de Vidas, *Reishit Ḥokhmah*, edited by H. Y. Valdman (Jerusalem: Or Ha-Musar, 1984), 2:65–66 (*Sha'ar Ha-Qedushah*, chap. 4, sec. 43).

119 "PROPER REST": The phrase occurs in the Sabbath afternoon *Minḥah Amidah*; several other synonymous formulations fill out this notion of a "true" and "complete rest" (see below).

THE ADMONITION: This reinterpretation derives from the teaching of R. Abin in Babylonian Talmud, *Shabbat* 105b. Annotating *bakh*, Rashi says: *mashma' be-qirbekha*, "meaning: 'in you yourself.'"

119 THE MYSTERY OF SABBATH: The ensuing paragraphs meditate on a series of passages traditionally recited during the course of the Sabbath day, from early evening through afternoon and dusk (Zohar 2.135a/b; Psalm 92; prayer for peace, Sabbath eve liturgy; Exodus 31:16–17; and Psalm 23, respectively).

Interlude Four

126 "IT CANNOT BE GRASPED": For this formulation, see R. Shneur Zalman of Liadi's remarks in *Liqqutei Torah, parshat Pinhas*, 80b.

A MATRIX OF DIVINE NAMES: For a classic exposition, see J. Gikatilla, *Sha'arei Orah* (Warsaw, 1883).

127 BOOK OF FORMATION: Alluding to the ancient Jewish composition *Sefer Yetzirah*, but now reinterpreting it as expressing a cosmic dynamic, a type of "Book of Existence," containing the formative divine signatures of world-being. For the ancient work, see P. Hayman, ed., *Sefer Yesira: Edition, Translation, and Text-Critical Commentary* (Tübingen: Mohr Siebeck, 2004).

THESE ELEMENTS: The three elements noted (*sefir, sefar,* and *sefer*) are my adaptation of the three primordial s-f-r-m (s-f-r three times) noted in the ancient *Sefer Yetzirah* 1.1—possibly also indicating *sefer* (book), *sefar* (number), and *sippur* (narrative-saying). I thus accept the threefold consonantal reading of s-f-r noted by Dunash (found in Oxford 2250). See M. Grossberg, *Sefer Yezirah Ascribed to the Patriarch Abraham with Commentary by Dunash ben Tamim* (London: R. W. Rabbinowicz, 1902); and also see R. Moshe Cordovero, *Pardes Rimonim*, Sha'ar 12, pereq 1.

130 "ESTIMATE" . . . THE HEAVENLY SPIRIT: Thus *she'arim* is glossed and clarified by the verb *mesha'er* in the commentary on the Zohar by R. Shim'on Lavi, *Ketem Paz* (repr. of Djerba ed., J. Haddad, 1940; Jerusalem: Ahavat Shalom, 1981), pt. 1, p. 240c.

Part Five

133 AND WERE THAT HEART: This formulation is inspired by a related topos in (the third speech of) the "Tale of the Seven Beggars" by R. Nahman of Bratzlav; see his *Sippurei Ma'asiyyot* (1811; repr., Brooklyn: Moriah Offset; Hasidei Breslov, 1976), 211–12.

134 BA-KOL: Literally, "in/with all," "of/from all," and "all"—these refer to the blessings of the three patriarchs, the phrases associated with Abraham, Isaac, and Jacob (Genesis 24:1, 27:33, and 33:11, respectively). The cluster is recited liturgically in the traditional Jewish "Blessing after Meals."

135 R. ISRAEL BA'AL SHEM TOV: As reported by R. Menahem Mendel of Chernobyl, in his *Ma'or 'Einayim*, vol. 2, *Liqqutim*, pp. 487b and 385b.

136 R. MENAHEM MENDEL OF RYMINOV: This profound teaching was said and transmitted in various forms, and the issues of authenticity are complicated. The 'Ryminover's teaching was transcribed by his student R. Yehezkel Ponet, in the collection *Menahem Tziyon* (Chernovitz: Meshullem Heller, 1851), *parshat Beshalah*, 13b; and also attested by another student, R. Naftali Tzvi of Ropshitz. For an evaluation of the evidence and its meaning, see the valuable study of Z. Harvey, "What Did the Ryminover Really Say about the Aleph of Anokhi?," *Kabbalah: A Journal for the Study of Jewish Mysticism* 34 (2015): 297–314 (in Hebrew). My interpretation is not the only one; and I have given it my formulation.

R. ISRAEL OF RUZHIN: As reported by R. Hayyim of Tzantz (in his *Divrei Hayyim*), and adduced in the teachings of the "Ruzhiner," in *'Irin Qadishin Ha-Shalem* (Jerusalem: Machon Siftei Tzaddiqim, 2009), 1:271a/b.

136 EMET VE-YATZIV: This is the beginning of the liturgical paragraph that follows the third paragraph of the *Shema* cycle in the weekday morning prayer service.

EMET VE-EMUNAH: This is the beginning of the liturgical paragraph that follows the third paragraph of the Shema cycle in the weekday evening prayer service.

137 TZAVTA: A common term in Hasidic literature that plays on the word *mitzvah*, expressing the bond that the command establishes with God.

MODES OF SPIRITUAL CONNECTION: This alludes to the frequent teaching in the Zohar that correlates aspects of God, Torah, and Israel. See especially at 1.134b, which speaks of multiple and correlated "limbs" (*shaifin*) of the three, as well as their composite levels (*dargin*).

R. ḤAYYIM ḤAIKE OF AMDUR: The ensuing topic line precedes a series of practices at the beginning of his book *Ḥayyim va-Ḥesed* (repr., Jerusalem: Machon Or Ha-Sefer, 1975), 8; the practice cited below is no. 1 in the collection.

139 THE GARMENT OF EXISTENCE: On the changing appearances (garments) of existence, see the remarkable teaching of R. Menaḥem Mendel of Vitebsk, in *Peri Ha-Aretz* (Jerusalem: Ha-Mesorah, 1989), *parshat Va-Yeishev*, pp. 32–34.

POSHET TZURAH VE-LOVESH: The idiom is already found in early kabbalistic sources. Cf. the commentary on *Sefer Yetzirah* attributed to R. Abraham ben David (the Rabad), chap. 2, mishneh 1 (identified by G. Scholem as R. Yosef ben Shlomo Ashkenazi).

ZOHAR: This rendition largely follows D. Goldstein, translator of I. Tishby, *The Wisdom of the Zohar*, The Littman Library (repr., Oxford: Oxford University Press, 1991), 1:322; the terms and nuances reflect the rabbinic and mystical allusions.

140 SHADDAI: God is first manifest with this Divine Name to Abraham in Genesis 17:1 ("I am *El Shaddai*"). The rabbinic midrash on the name appears in *Bereishit Rabba* 46.3 (see the Theodor-Albeck edition, 1:460–61).

142 MAGGID OF MEZERITCH: See in *Torat Ha-Maggid*, 110b–117b, *parshat Va-era*; and see further the comments of his disciple R. Levi Yitzhak of Berditchev, *Kedushat Levi Ha-Shalem* (Brooklyn: Machon Kedushat Levi, 1996), I, Va'era, 149a–150a.

POLYCHROMATIC: See the stimulating essay by W. Benjamin, "The Rainbow: A Conversation about Imagination," in *Walter Benjamin: Early Writings, 1910–1917* (Cambridge, MA: Harvard University Press, 2011), chap. 33, especially 219.

ORDINARY CONSCIOUSNESS: These aspects of color are discussed by V. Kandinsky, *Concerning the Spiritual in Art* (Boston: MFA Publications, 2006), chap. 5 ("The Psychological Working of Colour").

THE DIVINE NAMES . . . DIMENSIONS OF CONSCIOUSNESS: See the comments on our passage by R. Jacob Leiner of Izbica-Radzyn, the author of *Beit Ya'aqov* (Lublin, 1904; repr., Jerusalem, 2005), *Sefer Shemot, Va'era*, 66a–67a.

143 'IMQA DE-KOLA: For a profound usage, cf. Zohar 2.63b.

SOUND PATTERNS REVEAL THE WORLD: On the intersecting planes of semiotics and semantics (the way single words combine to create metasense), see the (1969) essay by E. Benveniste, "Sémiologie de la langue," reprinted in *Problèmes de la linguistique générale* (Paris: Gallimard, 1974), 2:64 (also 65–66).

R. YEHUDAH ARYEH LEIB OF GUR: See his *Sefas Emes 'al Ha-Torah U-Mo'adim* (Jerusalem, 1971), 1:65a (*parshat Va-Yetzei*, 1883; s.v. *va-yifga'*).

144 VA-YIFGA': This verb (here "to encounter" or "arrive at") also means "to pray" in biblical and rabbinic Hebrew. The prayer here is the main statutory prayer (*Shemoneh 'Esreih*)

recited three times daily, and each attributed to one of the three patriarchs, based on verbal associations in scripture (cf. *Bereshit Rabba* 68.9; pp. 778–80).

144   IN THE MIDRASH: See *Midrash Bereshit Rabba* 69.1; 1:791. After the citation from Genesis 28:12 there is a proem from Psalm 63:2. Following the opening phrase "My soul thirsts for You" our passage regarding the body is cited, "and the sages interpret it as just as "my soul thirsts for You," so do the 248 limbs of "my body pine for You"; meaning, all the actions of his body enact a longing for God.

DEUTERONOMY 6:7: The homily cites these phrases to align them with those in the book of Proverbs. The sequence follows Jacob's own sequence: walking, lying down, and arising.

"TEN SAYINGS": See Mishnah Nezikin, *Massekhet Avot* 5.1.

"STONES": The spiritual interpretation of "stones" as primordial "letters" ultimately derives from the medieval commentaries on the *Sefer Yetzirah* 4.12 attributed to the Rabad of Posquières and R. Eleazar of Worms (as found in the traditional editions of the work). The teaching of the Sefas Emes's grandfather is cited in *Sefas Emes*, 7a/b (*parshat Bereishit*, 1888; s.v. *ba-midrash, va-yakhulu*). A closely related interpretation also appears in *Sefer Torat Ha-Maggid Mi-Mezretch*, edited by Y. Klapholtz (1969; repr., Bnei Brak: Mishor, 2001), 1:73a/b (s.v. *va-yiqqah*), citing from *Or Torah* no. 262, *Imrei Tzaddiqim* no. 29, and *Liqqutei Amarim* no. 13.

The commentary "attributed" to Rabad has been philologically identified as the work of R. Yosef ben Shalom Ashkenazi by G. Scholem, in *Kitvei Yad Ba-Kabbalah* (Jerusalem, 1930), 80. For additional comments, see M. Hallamish, *Peirush le-Parshat Bereisheit le R. Yosef ben Shalom Ashkenazi* (Jerusalem: Magnes Press, 1985), 14–15n24.

PRIMORDIAL: On the issue of primordial letters or signs as stones, see the striking parallel in a text on creation by the Syriac theologian Narsai, head and founder of the school of Nisibis; N. Séd, "Le Memar samaritain, le *Sefer Yesira* et les 32 sentiers de la sagesse," *Revue de l'histoire des religions* 170 (1966): 159–84; and specifically the discussion and evaluation of T. Weiss, *Sefer Yesirah and Its Contexts* (Philadelphia: University of Pennsylvania Press, 2018), 64–65.

MEQOMO SHEL 'OLAM: Cf. *Midrash Bereshit Rabba* 68.9.

146   R. DAVID SHLOMOH EIBSHITZ: '*Arvei Nahal Ha-Shalem* (repr., Jerusalem: Machon 'Arvei Nahal, 1991), pt. 1, 247b–249a (the citation begins at 248b; *parshat Va-Yishlah, Derush* 2).

148   R. ZE'EV WOLF OF ZHITOMER: The teaching cited is found in his book *Or ha-Me'ir Ha-Shalem 'al Ha-Torah* (repr., Jerusalem: Even Israel, 1995), 1:311b–312b (*rimzei Qedoshim*).

150   ONE'S HEART WILL BE CONJOINED: For a related, though differently formulated understanding of this spiritual (nondual) teaching (which speaks of "One Spiritual Unity"), see S. Brody, "'Open to Me the Gates of Righteousness': The Pursuit of Holiness and Non-Duality in Early Hasidic Teaching," *Jewish Quarterly Review* 89 (1998): 33–35.

Conclusion

153   LE-MOTZIY'EIHEM BE-FEH: See also the reuse of it by R. Nahman of Bratzlav, *Liqqutei Moharan* (Jerusalem, 1968), I.11 (p. 14a).

YES OR NO: Cf. *Seder Eliahu Rabba*, edited by M. Freidman, 3rd ed. (Jerusalem: Wahrmann Books, 1969), 128.

153 ATTENTIVE TO THE DIVINE REVELATIONS OF EXISTENCE: A sense of attentive "awareness" of Divinity perceived with "utter amazement" is the striking phraseology used by Plotinus in *Enneads* 6.7.31. See the Loeb edition of Plotinus, translated by A. H. Armstrong (Cambridge, MA: Harvard University Press, 1988), 7:180–81. Notably, Maimonides also speaks of the soul as "dazzled" by God's overwhelming beauty, about which one dare not speak; see *The Guide of the Perplexed* 1.59, pp. 139–40.

Index